Religion and the Rise of Labour

*Current and forthcoming titles of related interest
from Ryburn Publishing include:*

The Centennial History of the Independent Labour Party
Essays edited by David James, Tony Jowitt and Keith Laybourn

Class and Politics in a Northern Town
A Study of Keighley 1884 to 1914
by David James. Introduced by Lord Briggs

The History of the Social-Democratic Federation
by Martin Crick

Religion and the Rise of Labour

Nonconformity and the Independent Labour Movement in Lancashire and the West Riding 1880–1914

Leonard Smith

(Leonard) Smith
took his place at
Manchester university in
1999.

Ryburn Publishing
KEELE UNIVERSITY PRESS

First published in 1993
by Ryburn Publishing
an imprint of
Keele University Press
Keele, Staffordshire

ISBN 1 85331 043 3 *pbk*
ISBN 1 85331 073 5 *cased*

Composed and printed by
Ryburn Book Production
Keele University Press
Staffordshire, England

Contents

For Joan, Susan and Gillian

Acknowledgements

Apart from all that I owe to scholars who have previously worked where the margins of Nonconformist and Labour history overlap, whose work I hope I have critically but fairly reviewed in my introduction, I am chiefly indebted to Professor Keith Laybourn of The University of Huddersfield and Dr. David Wright, who, in the course of the doctoral programme on which this book is based, generously shared with me their knowledge of British Labour movements and Victorian politics and society, respectively. Professor John O'Connell also made valuable suggestions.

I also acknowledge, with gratitude, the assistance given me by the staffs of many public and private libraries and archive collections, including Bradford City Library; Cheshire County Record Office, Chester; Colne Public Library; Halifax Public Library; Huddersfield Polytechnic Library; Liverpool Central Library; Liverpool University Library; Dr. Williams's Library, 14 Gordon Square, London; Manchester Central Library and Archive Department; John Rylands University Library of Manchester; Northern Federation for Training in Ministry, Luther King House, Brighton Grove, Manchester; Nelson Public Library; Manchester College, Oxford; Regent's Park College, Oxford; Lancashire County Record Office, Preston; New Church College, Radcliffe; City of Salford Library and Archive Department; Metropolitan Borough of Tameside Archive Department; West Yorkshire Archive Departments at Bradford, Halifax and Huddersfield; and the Metropolitan Borough of Wigan Archive Department.

Numerous individuals have favoured me by taking the trouble to reply to postal enquiries and grant interviews, giving me the benefit of their academic or local knowledge, and I would particularly like to mention Mrs. Isobel Armitage, Dr. Clyde Binfield, Mr. Stan Iveson, Mr. G. F. Kay, the Rev. Dr. John McLachlan, the late Rev. Aubrey Martin, the Rev. Dr. Stephen Mayor, Mrs. Doris Price, the Rev. Dr. Ian Sellers, Mrs. E. M. Smith, the Rev. K. Wadsworth, the Rev. Ian Wallace, and Mr. J. E. M. Gilbey and the Rev. R. Parker, respectively the secretaries of the Yorkshire and Lancashire Congregational Unions.

To the trustees of Dr. Williams's Library and Trust, 14 Gordon Square, London, I give my thanks for their financial assistance and for putting the facilities of the pre-eminent library for the study of English Nonconformity at my disposal.

My wife, Joan, has given considerable help with the compilation of the index and in countless other practical ways, not to mention her patience with me throughout the whole project. Ian Harris, my brother-in-law, has been a ready source of advice for word processing problems. Finally, these acknowledgements would be incomplete without a brief reference to my father, the late Rev. J. Harry Smith (1893–1981), Pioneer Preacher and Unitarian Minister, from whose recollections of meeting Labour pioneers my interest in the subject developed.

Abbreviations

ILP   Independent Labour Party

LP   Labour Party

LRC   Labour Representation Committee

PSA   Pleasant Sunday Afternoon

SDF   Social Democratic Federation

Preface

The sources available for a study of Religion and the Labour movement between 1880 and 1914 fall broadly into the two categories of political party records and church, chapel and connexional records. In the former group, only a few archives provide the relevant material, but fortunately for the researcher these are readily available on microfilm or microfiche. The Minutes of the ILP and its National Administrative Council, 1893–1909, the Labour Representation Committee records, 1900–1907, and the Francis Johnson Collection of correspondence, 1890–1950, provide the main body of manuscript evidence for Labour's attitude to religion. Supplementary printed material can be found in the ILP and Labour Party pamphlet collections, and in the Labour press, also conveniently available on microfilm. The G. H. Wood Collection deposited at The University of Huddersfield Library is another valuable source of printed material and ephemera, particularly because of its regional emphasis. Useful information can sometimes be gleaned from the autobiographies of Labour leaders, although these do have the weakness that by the time such men came to write their memoirs, they were apparently reluctant to acknowledge earlier associations with chapels and churches, even where these are known to have been particularly close.

On the Churches' side, the evidence of attitudes towards Labour is diffuse and more difficult to find. This may seem surprising since, in the late nineteenth century, Nonconformist congregations, which provided the closest links with the Labour movement, were numerous, and many have survived to the present day. There are, however, several possible explanations. Firstly, in the few instances of chapels where a section of the membership supported the Labour movement, it was often in opposition to the staunchly Liberal leadership, who must have been reluctant to afford recognition to Labour's advance by minuting the details. Secondly, the class structure of Nonconformity tended to mean that support for Labour was most likely to occur in the congregations that were of more recent origin, the products of mid to late nineteenth century missionary activity, and for social and economic reasons such congregations and their records are less likely to have survived. Thirdly, the preservation of chapel records and their safe deposit in archive departments has only recently been encouraged by the denominational historical societies, and much has already been lost. Nonetheless, Nonconformist chapels and denominations are rich repositories of oral traditions (few survive more strongly than those concerning political conflicts) and these provide pointers to congregations suitable for investigation. Certainly, more examples than those identified for the purpose of this study must await discovery. But, at this distance of time, barely more than one generation from the eye witnesses of the independent Labour movement's emergence, it is unlikely that there are any instances where disharmony caused by the emergence of Labour has been entirely forgotten in surviving congregations.

Yet this paucity of sources for Nonconformist attitudes to Labour at the level of the local chapel, which sometimes amounts to little more than scattered and cryptic references in minute books, can often be satisfactorily augmented by reports in local newspapers and by reference to oral history. Moreover, in contrast with the local situation, the discussions which the Labour campaign prompted in the national and regional assemblies of the various Nonconformist denominations or connexions are very fully chronicled in their year books, calendars and periodicals, and it is especially helpful for the regional emphasis of the study that Lancashire and Yorkshire both had large, efficiently administered county Congregational unions, which published impressive accounts of their proceedings, giving full reports of speeches.

Overall, therefore, there are sufficient sources to make a study which attempts to explain and evaluate the nature of relations between Nonconformity and the emergent independent Labour movement, in the period 1880 to 1914, a viable project. Its development, however, has largely depended upon the discovery of sources which throw further light on the nature of the relationship at the most basic level of rank and file ministers and members of local congregations.

Chapter 1

Introduction

The relationship between religion and the Labour movement has occupied historians at least since Elie Halévy suggested that Methodism was the reason why England did not have a revolution like those which accompanied the advance of socialism on the Continent.[1] Halévy's theory, propounded in 1906, at a time when R. J. Campbell's 'New Theology' movement envisaged a closer relationship between the churches and the Labour Party, was concerned with an earlier period of Labour history than the subject of this book, but his work nonetheless suggests the central question for any study of religion and the Labour movement, namely to what extent did the independent Labour movement take the form it did because of the participation of socialists with religious backgrounds, and Nonconformity in particular?

Both Nonconformist and Labour historians have found the relations between the churches and the early Labour movement a fascinating field for study. Unfortunately, however, some of the usefulness of their work is impaired by what appears to be sectarian bias. The work of the Church historians often borders on hagiography in their apparent desire to show that many of the early Labour leaders were really engaged in propaganda work as an extension of their religious convictions, which in earlier years had been fostered in chapels, Sundays schools and their auxiliary societies. Labour historians, on the other hand, perhaps sometimes biased by a desire to trace Labour antecedents in scientific socialism, frequently appear to dismiss too lightly what evidence there is of the churches' involvement in the development of independent Labour representation, by suggesting that it was somehow only an aberration, or a transitional process in the transfer of social energy from religion to politics.

It is generally agreed, however, that 'the Churches contributed very substantially to the growth of the Labour movement, even when full recognition is accorded to the influence of non-religious factors.'[2] With the exception of Pelling,[3] who gives rather more weight to the part played by Anglican Christian Socialists, it is also suggested by most historians of the subject, that 'the kind of religion that counted most in the history of the Labour movement was that which found its formal expression in the several denominations of Nonconformity.'[4] Indeed it is sometimes suggested that there is 'more of Methodism than Marx' in British Socialism. But, unless Methodism is here being used as a synonym for Nonconformity, the assertion is one that will need to be tested, for while Methodists were certainly numerous in the early Labour Party, their

11

support may have come relatively late, via trades unionism, mainly as a result of the conversion of the Miners' Federation in 1909. They certainly do not seem to have been as prominent as members of other branches of Nonconformity in the foundation of the Labour Church in 1891 or the ILP in 1893. Nor is it easy to trace how the religious impulses of Methodism led to support for Labour. Methodists who abandoned their traditional support for the Liberal Party seem to have done so as a result of secular ethical impulses common to many of the early socialists, whereas the more advanced elements in other denominations espoused a progressive theology, the so-called 'New Theology', which led in the direction of socialism.

Wearmouth has provided the evidence for the Methodist contribution to the emergence of Labour in his historical trilogy[5] and argues that 'Labour's ascent to political influence and authority was due more to Methodism than Marxian theories, more to the prophets and the New Testament than to the Communist Manifesto'.[6] Whilst he suggests that this was true of the beginning and remained true for a considerable period, he nonetheless does admit that Methodism eventually lost place and persuasion in politics. However, the antithesis is not a very useful one, since neither Methodism nor Marxism had more than minimal roles in the development of the British Labour movement. Wearmouth's thesis is that there was an affinity between Methodism and the reforming spirit of nineteenth-century Liberalism, and as the new Labour movement began to serve better the desired social reform, so Methodists transferred their allegiance to Labour. There is no doubt that he provided the data for Methodist support of the Labour movement, but his third volume, which deals with the late nineteenth and early- twentieth centuries, is less convincing than his work on the earlier period. He lists those with Methodist connections who were active chapel attenders, and the more numerous Labour leaders who in their speeches made references to the influence of religion in their childhood and youth, but who may, perhaps as a consequence of their socialism, have lost touch with the life of the chapels.

The weakness of Wearmouth's work lies in his failure to trace the links between Methodist beliefs and Socialism. It may be that these were implicit in the simple evangelical interpretation of the gospel, and particularly in the Sermon on the Mount, which they heard from Methodist pulpits, but, unlike Congregationalists and Unitarians, the Methodist movement was barely touched by the emerging 'New Theology', which gave theological foundations to the support of those Labour leaders who came from the denominations of the Old Dissent. Unless such links can be established, we are left with one of two conclusions – that Methodists supported Labour because the Social Conscience that had developed amongst them in the later years of the nineteenth century was best satisfied by Labour's programme of reform, or that they simply shared the general trend away from the Liberal Party to Labour. Another puzzling aspect of Wearmouth's study is that whilst using it to illustrate how the early Labour movement was allied to religious idealism, he appears to appropriate to Methodism a study of the Labour Church. It is indeed true that D. B. Foster, an ex-Methodist local preacher who in 1902 became President of the Labour Church Union, was active in the Labour churches, as were one or two others, but generally, Methodists were not very involved in John Trevor's organization, and the Labour Church cannot with any usefulness be associated with an evaluation of the contribution of Methodism to the development of the independent Labour movement. Wearmouth, however, shares the general conclusion of all commentators on Methodism and the working-class movement: they are agreed that life in the chapels provided a training ground for many of those who were to become trade union and Labour leaders. Whether this is more true of Methodism than, say, Congregationalism, is open to question. The class meetings did provide a measure of democratic participation for their members, but they were strongly controlled by the circuit, as the circuits were controlled by the Conference.

The largest body of Methodists, the Wesleyans, was organized by the direction of Conference, whereas in the chapels of the Old Dissent decisions were taken independently by a congregational meeting, and were thus more democratic. Other sections of the Methodist movement, particularly the Primitive Methodists, had a more working-class membership, and here the early associations with Labour may have been through their work in the trades unions, whereas Congregationalists, Unitarians, Swedenborgians and members of the other, more democratic expressions of Nonconformity, may have been attracted more directly to the social justice which was to be inaugurated by an independent Labour movement. For this reason it tends to be members of the chapels of Old Dissent who are found to play a more prominent part in the early socialist revival and particularly in the formation of the ILP.

Stephen Mayor's work on the relationship of the churches to Labour began in the 1950s with a study of Congregational relations with the Labour movement.[7] In this he provided the kind of biographical data which Wearmouth had done for Methodism, but linked it more satisfactorily with theological developments, perhaps because Congregationalism underwent them, while Methodism did not. It led on to a doctoral thesis[8] and, eventually, a book.[9] The latter dealt with the churches generally and principally took the form of an examination of the attitudes of the religious press to the emergence of Labour. The sources for Nonconformity were the *Nonconformist* and *The British Weekly*.

Although Mayor's work is impressive, it is rather limited in its emphasis on the press, and it pays too little attention to what Nonconformists were actually doing to support or oppose the advance of Labour at local level. The historic alliance of Nonconformity, first with the Whigs and then with the Liberal Party, prevented Nonconformity, and particularly the churches of the Old Dissent, from playing a larger part in the rise of the Labour movement. These are his conclusions about the alliance for the removal of the Nonconformist disabilities – the Corporation Act, the Test Act, Church Rates, the restriction of marriages to parish churches, the requirement to use the Common Prayer Book burial service in parish churchyards and, finally, in the campaign for Disestablishment. He suggests also that the main reason for the failure of the older Nonconformity to gain control of the Labour movement was its middle-class character. Methodism, on the other hand, although it originally had a tradition of ministerial support for the Tories and a closer association with the Established Church, was not so involved in the struggle for the removal of the disabilities; it was less tied to the Liberal Party and, therefore, in Mayor's opinion, able to play a larger role. Wesleyan Methodism shared the middle-class character of the Old Dissent, but the churches which had seceded from the Wesleyans in the early nineteenth century – the Primitive, New Connexion, Bible Christian and Independent Methodists – had a more working-class membership. However, the class divisions are not so straightforward as Mayor suggests. It is true that trustees, deacons and the formally enrolled members tended to be middle class, but even the most middle class of all the churches, the Unitarians, had congregations which were exceptional.

In north-east Lancashire, the Methodist Unitarians were essentially working-class congregations, led by working-class ministers. In the second quarter of the nineteenth century they had been involved in Chartism and were both religious and political radicals. The older established dissenting congregations were certainly middle class, but nearly all denominations had opened new churches as part of the missionary activity that attempted to attract the working classes after the depressing revelations of the 1851 Religious Census. Many Nonconformist ministers who were trained in the new Home Missionary Colleges which had been established as part of this missionary activity were drawn from the artisan classes and had experience of working-class life. When Keir Hardie suggested to R. J. Campbell that ministers had no knowledge of the condition of the working classes, Campbell informed him that many Nonconformist ministers were drawn from that class.[10] Moreover, Nonconformist chapels in this period had a broad following of those who belonged to their auxiliary groups, the Mutual Improvement Societies, Adult Classes and the PSAs. The largely working-class membership of such groups was likely to find an independent Labour party increasingly attractive.

It cannot be denied that large numbers of the working class were outside the churches, and had been so at least from the early years of the nineteenth century; or that the formal control of the chapels at denominational level was in the hands of those most likely to support a continuance of the long-established alliance with the Liberal Party. But the middle-class character of Nonconformity seems to have been too readily assumed in discussions of its relationship to the emergence of independent Labour. Even if it is true as a generalization, there is considerable evidence of exceptions, particularly in Lancashire and the West Riding of Yorkshire, where statistics of chapel and Sunday School attendances do not adequately explain the relationships which chapels had with the working-class communities.[11] There were working-class denominations and working-class congregations within middle-class denominations. Middle-class congregations often had many working-class people associated with their Sunday Schools and auxiliary activities. This was particularly true of the so-called 'Institutional Church', the model for which was provided by C. Sylvester Horne. Also, overall, too much may have been made of the class difference between Methodism and the churches of Old Dissent – Congregationalists, Unitarians, Baptists, Quakers – in trying to explain Nonconformist responses to Labour.

Mayor's work is not without its contradictions in explaining the responses of different denominations. For example, in his early work he says 'the Methodists ... were able to play a larger part than the older Dissent',[12] whereas in the later work he says 'Socialism tended to win the support of unorthodox Christians, even though they might belong to orthodox denominations'.[13] Amongst Methodist radicals there were almost no unorthodox Christians; Methodism remained untouched by the 'New Theology', which even S. E. Keeble, its most outspoken socialist, rejected.[14] The relative contributions of different branches of Nonconformity to the emergence of Labour therefore appear to be in doubt and one aspect of this study will be a re-evaluation of the part played by churches of the older and newer Dissent.

A different approach to the subject is offered by Peter d'A. Jones, who, in his broad study of the Christian Socialist revival, reviewed the role of both the Established and Nonconformist Churches.[15] In respect of Nonconformity, he not only deals with those individuals in all denominations who were known nationally for the support they gave to Labour's advance, but also provides valuable information about the denominational Socialist groups, the Socialist Quaker Society, the New Church Socialist Society, the inter-denominational Christian Socialist Society (1886–1892), John Clifford's Christian Socialist League (1894–1898) and the Free Church Socialist League (founded 1909). He concludes that much of the energy of Christian socialists was wasted in inter-denominational rivalries, particularly over the control of public education, and that the denominational socialist societies were inward looking and only concerned to convert members of their own denominations to Socialism. For an understanding of the development of Nonconformist responses to

Labour, perhaps Jones' most important argument is his suggestion about support for Socialism within the churches and how this seems to have been subverted by the 'social-unionism' which became a characteristic of most Nonconformist denominations from 1905 onwards. This was the time of the formation of the Wesleyan Methodist Union for Social Service, modelled on the Christian Social Union, which had been founded by the Anglicans in 1889, and which was quickly followed by similar bodies in other churches. Social-unionism developed from the meetings of the 'Holy Party', a group of Anglican clergymen, including Charles Gore and Henry Scott Holland, who first met for discussions in 1875, and between 1890 and 1915 for their 'parties' at J. R. Illingworth's Longworth rectory in Berkshire. All were Oxford men, High churchmen and sacramentalists. They argued against the evangelical emphasis on individual sin, and suggested the real purpose of the Christian Church was not to save individuals for an after-life, but to save the world itself. In practice, the social unions were organized to study and publicize social and economic problems. They never declared for any political platform.

Jones suggests they took the wind out of the sails of the socialist bodies, and stole members and potential members who might have been attracted to them. The historic pattern was that, within a sect, a small radical group would emerge preaching a social gospel – sometimes outright socialism, as in the case of the Socialist Quaker Society – and demanding support for social reform and labour groups. Then a few years later a milder, more generally accepted and better-supported group would appear, a social-union group rather than a Christian socialist group. The earlier, smaller group would then decline and social-unionism infect the entire church as leading members gave it their support. By this method Socialism was effectually by-passed in the churches, much in the same way that the Liberal welfare legislation attempted to steal the socialists' clothes in the political arena after 1906.

Jones' work is impressive for the overall view it provides of the support the early Labour movement received from all sections of the Church. No student of the relationship between the Churches and Labour between 1880 and 1914 can fail to be deeply indebted to him for having mapped out the subject so clearly. He has provided so many suggestions for areas requiring further, more detailed study. If there is any weakness in the work, it lies only in the fact that, having concentrated on those in the Churches who supported Labour's advance, he fails to explain the extent of the reaction against it.

Recent studies have provided information about the concern of Nonconformists at the rise of an independent Labour movement, as it emerged on the national political scene in the press and in the denominational and the inter-denominational socialist societies. They focus on Free Church leaders, famous preachers and organizations of socialist-inclined ministers. The ground has been fairly thoroughly tilled,

16

although at times there is an irritating amount of name dropping with insufficient biographical detail. For example, E. J. B. Kirtlan, a rarity in being a Methodist member of the SDF, has been mentioned by several writers, but with little other information.[16] No doubt there are still many interesting details to be added to the general picture provided by Wearmouth, Mayor and Jones, and perhaps there is a possibility for some reinterpretation of their data. But it seems unlikely that further research of the kind they undertook in the 1950s and 1960s will yield much fresh understanding of the relationship between Nonconformity and labour. It has been aptly said that 'there has been more debate than research findings can sustain on the problem of religion'.[17]

To meet the criticism, Robert Moore's study has examined three mining villages in the Deerness Valley, a few miles south-west of Durham city, and the politics of those who either attended or were associated with the Methodist chapels there. The objects of his enquiry were to find out what effect, if any, religion had on the political views and activities of the miners; whether Methodism encouraged or inhibited the development of class politics; what kind of men emerged as leaders among the miners, their *modus operandi* and how they responded to crises; as well as to what extent they developed new political attitudes and broke with traditional ways, either within Methodism or in the act of breaking with it. His main thesis is that the effect of Methodism on a working-class community was to inhibit the development of class consciousness and to reduce class conflict. He argues that while Methodism did produce political leaders amongst the working class it did not produce leaders who would articulate and pursue class interests *per se*. For the most part Moore identifies the Methodists of the district as Liberals who moved over to Labour without any fundamental change of political attitude.

However, one group meeting in the Primitive Methodist Chapel in the village of Quebec was different. Its membership formed the nucleus of the Quebec ILP branch. But Moore argues the socialism of this group owed nothing intellectually to Methodism. They discussed their ideas in the Bible class, communicated in part in the language of the Bible, preached the gospel of socialism from their pulpit, but the core of their ideas came from outside Methodism, from their reading of Maurice, Carpenter, Tolstoy and others who represented a specifically ethical type of socialism. Overall, the development of the early Labour Party in the area covered by this local study appears to have been little more than an extension of Liberal social policy, with trade union leaders assuming office in the the new party machinery, as men whose Methodism had instilled them with a desire for class conciliation rather than class conflict. As this happened the Quebec radicals began to lose influence. Methodism may not have provided any religious or intellectual influences towards independent Labour representation in the Deerness Valley, but it prepared the ground for the acceptance of one kind of socialism rather than another, a kind in which there was little place for a radical and violent class consciousness.

Moore has provided a model of the kind of local study which is necessary if the scholarly generalizations of the historians of the national scene are to be thoroughly tested and corrected. Any further advance in our understanding about the way in which the churches responded to Labour's emergence as an independent political force will most probably now come from attention to the regions where Nonconformity was particularly strong. There are a number of areas which might prove fruitful, including industrial South Wales, a mining area and thus late in the support given to Labour, where the geography of Nonconformity was more varied than in Durham and included sects which felt the influence of a social theology, to which Methodism was immune.

But Lancashire and the West Riding of Yorkshire are the most obvious regions for attention. This was where the major campaign for independent Labour representation took place, first through the Labour Church, founded in Manchester in 1891, then by the formation of the Independent Labour Party in Bradford in 1893. The kind of socialism that appealed here was of a particularly ethical kind and more likely to be expressed in the terms of the Sermon on the Mount than *Das Kapital*. Historically, both districts had strong Puritan and Nonconformist traditions, which is partly explained by the large size of parishes, in which late seventeenth century conventicles either escaped the attention of the authorities, or were impossible to control. Lancashire was the only county outside London to establish a Provincial Assembly in the Commonwealth period. At the end of the seventeenth century, Oliver Heywood, the eminent Nonconformist divine, was settled at Northowram, near Halifax, and during the eighteenth century Bolton was known as 'the Geneva of Lancashire'. Old Dissent was particularly strong in these areas; Independents had become Congregationalists, and the Presbyterians had absorbed the influences of the Enlightenment and become Unitarians. But the newer Dissent was also well represented, in the form of Wesleyan, Primitive and Independent Methodism. Here, too, was the heartland of the New Church (Swedenborgian) founded by two Manchester clergymen in the late eighteenth century, which, like the Quakers, was one of the few denominations to have its own Socialist society, the New Church Socialist Society. Unlike mining areas, where there was enough political muscle, or the lack of a resident middle-class, to return working-class MPs as Liberals, here Trade Unionism was weak and the industrial problems caused by the McKinley Tariff and the lowering of wages resulted in strikes, like that at Manningham Mills, Bradford in 1891.[18] The failure of such strikes did much to highlight the need to seek independent Labour representation in order to remedy the social ills of unemployment and low wages.

There were, however, differences in the political geography of the Lancashire cotton and West Riding woollen districts. In Yorkshire the

18

Liberal Party was entrenched, whereas in Lancashire there was a great deal of popular Conservatism,[19] the cause of which has been attributed partly to the immigration of Irish Catholics, which was perceived as a threat to the traditional way of life of the indigenous English protestant population, and partly to the paternalism which was a feature of the factory system, which was adopted earlier and on a larger scale than in Yorkshire. In Lancashire, too, there were also differences between the spinning districts to the south and the north-eastern weaving districts, which had more of the character of West Riding towns, and where, because of strong Nonconformity, a smaller Irish immigrant population and fewer sectarian schools, the Liberal Party had few problems in securing seats. But here the ILP did not make the same kind of headway as in the West Riding, because of the establishment of strong branches of the Social Democratic Federation.

In considering the response of Nonconformists to Labour's emergence in Lancashire and West Yorkshire, one should not overlook what was happening on the national scene of the Labour movement and in the different branches of Nonconformity. Local movements were part of national ones, they shared influences that came from outside and touched all regions, even though local responses were coloured by the immediate industrial and social conditions. As Jeffrey Hill has stated, 'The interesting feature in discussing a movement like the Labour Party lies in the interaction between national themes and local responses'.[20] There were differing speeds of political change from region to region and denomination to denomination, and a variety of balance in local and national forces. In the case of Labour leaders, and Nonconformist ministers too, although perhaps to a lesser extent, many were travelling and speaking on a national network, which requires a broad examination of their work. Nonetheless, the focus of this study will be upon how the Nonconformist churches of the textile regions responded to the new party, and, conversely, how the Labour movement responded when socialists in the Nonconformist churches did lend it their support.

It is widely recognized that intellectual forces played a part in the transformation of Liberals into Socialists, although it is doubtful whether these were sufficient in themselves to motivate commitment to socialist societies, which remained relatively small until the ILP adopted social policies which included the Eight-Hour Day to reduce unemployment by legally limiting the working day. It is an object of this study to establish that the churches played a considerable part in the dissemination of influences which led to the adoption of socialism. An important way that this took place was through the Brotherhood Movement with its Pleasant Sunday Afternoon meetings, for which there was a Book Prize Scheme for attendance. This not only widened the limited education of working men, but it put them in touch with authors who suggested Socialism as an alternative system to competition, which they believed produced society's social ills. In this way the churches helped to spread the general, secular influences towards the new politics. Yet, did the churches have any specifically theological insights that led some of their members to support the advance of an independent Labour party, and, if so, how influential were these?

From the early 'eighties, there had been a movement away from individualistic theology, which saw evil in terms of individual sin, towards a recognition that some evil was the product of social conditions. Bebbington has suggested that one aspect of the Nonconformist Conscience was the readiness of hitherto individualistic Liberals to seek remedies for social evils by recourse to greater participation by government.[21] Spreading from the Continent, the new historical theology, which was replacing biblical theology, was bringing insights that seemed to suggest that greater attention should be paid to this life as a place for the establishment of God's kingdom. In 1900, Harnack gave his celebrated lectures at the University of Berlin,[22] which, when translated into English as *What is Christianity?*, popularized his contention that the Kingdom of God was the central theme of Jesus' teaching, and was to be realized here. This added weight to the Pelagianism – the belief that man can be saved by his own efforts – which was always present in English theological thought and to a greater degree than on the Continent. In England the new thinking found greatest expression in R. J. Campbell's 'New Theology', which stressed the immanence of God, an emphasis, like that of the sacramentalism of the Anglo-Catholics, which made this world a sacred object of Christian concern and the place for the establishment of God's kingdom, as opposed to the view of the Evangelicals who saw this world as only a preparation for the after-life.

The New Theology led its adherents naturally towards a Social Gospel as much concerned with the conditions of this life as with the ultimate destiny of the soul, and it allied easily with Socialism. Campbell, in fact, argued that the New Theology was essentially a more spiritual Socialism. Although as Minister of the prestigious City Temple he was based in London, several other ministers who made significant contributions to its literature were settled in pastorates in Yorkshire and Lancashire during the infancy of the ILP. T. Rhondda Williams, Campbell's closest friend and disciple, was minister of Greenfield Congregational Church, Bradford, from 1888 to 1908, and K. C. Anderson was at Horton Lane Congregational Church, from 1885 to 1893, before moving to Dundee. And although Methodism was barely touched by the New Theology, its most thorough-going socialist, the Rev. Samuel E. Keeble, was also in Lancashire and Cheshire circuits during these significant years, and the vehicle for his ideas, *The Methodist Weekly*, was published in Manchester. The extent to which preaching and theology influenced Nonconformists towards giving their support to the Labour movement is not at all clear, but no study of the relationship can be complete without an examination and evaluation of the work of these ministers. And if, towards the end of the period under consideration, the relationship of the churches to the Labour movement appears to be less strong, it will be necessary to ask whether this was, in part, due to the publication of Albert Schweitzer's *Von Reimarus zu Wrede*,[23] in which Schweitzer argued that Jesus shared the views of his time by thinking of the Kingdom of God as an eschatalogical event and not something to be realized in this world, an argument that undermined the intellectual basis of much of the New Theology, with its emphasis on this world.

Intellectual impulses, important though they may have been, were not, however, the only reasons why Nonconformists became interested in the Labour movement. Ever since the Religious Census of 1851 had shown that, with the possible exception of the Roman Catholics, the churches had lost touch with the working classes to a greater extent than had been realized, attempts had been made to attract the masses. At first this involved the establishment of Missionary societies and new theological colleges which would train ministers specially suited to the conditions and needs of the working classes. But the churches could not engage with the working classes for their spiritual and moral welfare without also becoming aware of the social problems so inhibiting to the fullness of life which their gospel proclaimed. In the 1870s the Salvation Army had come into existence and its approach, which combined spiritual concern with social welfare, was emulated by most denominations, whether or not they shared the simple evangelical faith of the Salvationists. Congregationalists and Unitarians established Settlements on the pattern of those pioneered by the Anglicans, whereby middle-class churchmen, many of them students, resided in the poorer districts of the large cities and attempted to relieve the conditions of the poor. Unemployment was a particular problem in the mid-1880s. The churches could not fail to be aware of it. Those who were not working in the industrial areas read in their newspapers of demonstrations and public disorder in London, particularly in 1886, and might occasionally be embarrassed in their Sunday worship by unemployed people filing into churches as part of demonstrations arranged by branches of the socialist societies. The so-called Social Question became the main topic of addresses given to the denominational assemblies in the late 1880s and early 1890s. Nonconformists made some attempts to find solutions to the problem of the unemployed. Settlements, PSAs and the Salvation Army organized Employment Bureaux, by which news of jobs was announced. H. V. Mills, the Unitarian Minister at Kendal who had seen the worst effects of unemployment in Liverpool, wrote a book entitled *Poverty and the State*,[24] in which he suggested a solution might be found by establishing Home Colonies, and this was followed by a short-lived experiment at Starnthwaite, Westmorland, in which the socialist pioneers, Katherine Conway and Dan Irving, were also involved. However, those in the churches who were concerned for the plight of the unemployed must have soon become aware that such small experiments, even if successful, could only relieve the problem for a few, and they must have been attracted by the programme of the ILP, which included legislation for an Eight-Hour Day as a means of reducing unemployment on a much wider scale. Whatever the theological viewpoint of Nonconformists, practical policies for the relief of social ills must have been very attractive, but they must have seemed particularly so to those who found theological sanction for them in the New Theology.

There was, of course, much resistance to the emergence of Labour amongst Nonconformists, which resulted from the strength of the historical alliance with the Liberal Party. Indeed, a Nonconformist Anti-Socialist Union was formed at Baptist Church House in 1909. But there is considerable evidence of support for the new Labour Party. Given this interest of Nonconformists in the new Labour movement, the question arises as to what kind of response it met with from the Labour leaders. Many of them had been influenced by early experiences in Noncon-formist chapels or the Sunday Schools, where they had learned the skills of public speaking and committee procedure. Some of them continued as lay preachers, even whilst engaged in political propaganda. They coloured both sermons and political speeches with biblical imagery, which came as naturally to speakers as to listeners. Kenneth Brown has suggested that Labour pioneers may have exaggerated their Noncon-formist connexions in their efforts to win the votes of Nonconformist Liberals.[25] It is probably true that these connexions may not in many cases have involved full chapel membership, but rather associations with the auxiliary societies, and that there was some element of putting a bit of 'Come to Jesus' in their speeches, but the connections were nonetheless real and the religious element of the speeches genuine. In the early years of the independent Labour movement religious and political aspirations were all of a piece, and it was not necessary, as it later became, to choose between the different cultures of party and chapel. The teetotal ethos of the early ILP and the social and educational activities of its branches was remarkably similar to the culture of Nonconformity, as it found expression in the north of England, not because it was necessary to curry favour, but because people in party and chapel had similar roots. Eventually, practical considerations made it necessary for individuals to choose how they apportioned their time and energies between religion or politics, but most probably they saw the two as part of one process which involved the Brotherhood of Man and the establishment of the Kingdom of God. Labour leaders were pleased to use the opportunities afforded them by sympathizers within the chapels and made particular use of the platform provided by the Pleasant Sunday Afternoon meetings of the Brotherhood Movement. It is also possible that because the PSAs were large associations of working men, organized into district wards for visiting,

22

the Labour leaders may have seen them as providing the basis of electoral registration societies, much in the same way as the chapels had been viewed by the Liberal Party.

It will be argued that in its early years the independent Labour movement welcomed the support of the Nonconformist churches, but that by the close of the nineteenth century the 'religious' element that had inspired and sustained the early Labour pioneers had waned with the advent of party machinery, and that after Robert Blatchford's rejection of religion in *God and My neighbour* (1903), the Labour movement preferred to distance itself from the churches in the interests of socialist unity, for there were those to be considered who had roots not in the ethical socialism of the ILP but in the quasi-Marxism of the SDF. It will also be suggested that the Labour movement became doubtful about the usefulness of associating with the churches because of the imperialism of many leading Nonconformists at the time of the Boer War, which contrasted with the pro-Boer attitudes of most socialists. The evidence for this section of the book is to be found mainly in the ILP Minutes, the Archive of the Labour Party, the Francis Johnson Collection, the G. H. Wood Collection and the pamphlet collections of the ILP and the Labour Party, which are comparatively untapped sources for all previous examinations of the relationship between Nonconformity and the independent Labour movement in the period of its emergence.

The evidence of Nonconformity's response to Labour has been partly provided by the work of Wearmouth, Mayor, Jones and Moore, but, with the exception of Moore's detailed study of Durham mining villages, there has been very little examination of the response of rank and file ministers and lay people at local level. The generalizations about how the Nonconformist alliance with the Liberal Party impeded Labour's advance do not sufficiently take into account the evidence of ministers and lay people who supported independent Labour's progress, sometimes at the cost of their own livelihoods. Such generalizations are frequently made on the basis of the support given to Liberal candidates in Bradford, where the Free Church ministers appeared on Liberal platforms which led to the formation of a Bradford Labour Church, while much of the evidence is diffuse and local, some of it having been described as 'fugitive'. But it is only by its discovery and evaluation that we shall better understand both how Nonconformity in its local expression responded to the new politics and the relationship between Nonconformist chapels and the branches of the socialist movements, the ILP and SDF. The biographical details of Nonconformist ministers known to have been speakers at Labour Church meetings should point to localities where a minister and his congregation were more sympathetic to Labour than the generalizations suggest. In Lancashire and Cheshire the Congregationalist, Rev. T. E. Leonard of Colne, the Unitarians Rev. Harold Rylett of Flowery Field, Hyde, and Rev. H. Bodell Smith of Crewe, (where the church was split and eventually closed because of his leadership of the local ILP branch), and the Rev. J. Bellamy Higham of Park Lane, Wigan, (who was dismissed for being a socialist), are amongst those on the west side of the Pennines who will be considered; as also will the circuit ministries in Chester and Manchester of the Rev. S. E. Keeble, the foremost Methodist socialist, and John Trevor, who began his Labour Church in 1891. In Yorkshire, where the Bradford platform incident gives the general impression that Nonconformist ministers were unanimous in remaining Liberals, the support of the New Theology men, T. Rhondda Williams and K. C. Anderson, and the campaigns of the Rev. J. Stitt Wilson, the American socialist evangelist, must be examined. At Keighley a young Swedenborgian minister, the Rev. S. J. C. Goldsack, was secretary of the New Church Socialist Society established in 1895; its treasurer and the editor of its journal, *Uses*, was T. D. Benson, who was later treasurer of the ILP. And in 1907 Victor Grayson, erstwhile student for the Unitarian ministry, was elected to Parliament for Colne Valley in a by-election on what has been described as a straight socialist ticket. His success has been partly attributed to the appeal he made to local Nonconformists.

It may also be possible to infer sympathy for the new politics from those Minutes of meetings of ministers' fraternals, which have survived. For example, a meeting of Unitarian ministers held at Bolton in February 1884 heard one of their company give a 'suggestive' address on 'Henry George's Views', and it is widely recognized that one of the routes leading from Radical Liberalism to Socialism was via the Land Nationalization movement, in which a number of prominent Nonconformist ministers were involved as officers and members. In both counties, finding evidence of whole congregations which supported Labour's advance will be far more difficult, and in most cases perhaps all that can be hoped for is either implicit support for a minister deduced from an absence of strained relationships that might have caused his departure, as was the case with J. Bellamy Higham, or examples of churches that were ready to allow their premises to be used for ILP or trades' union meetings.

It has, however, been suggested that the part played by the Salem Independent Methodist Church in the growth of the Nelson branch of the ILP is a case for systematic investigation.[26] The district of north-east Lancashire was distinctive in having two working-class Nonconformist denominations, the Independent Methodists and the Methodist Unitarians, the latter certainly having a history of support for Chartism, and this district might also yield examples of other congregations collectively supporting the growth of the ILP. If there is evidence of much Nonconformist support in north east-Lancashire, it will raise questions such as why this should have occurred so near to Burnley, where the leadership of independent Labour advance was mainly in the hands of the strong SDF branch led by Dan Irving. The assumption has generally been that whereas Nonconformists would have been repelled by the SDF's quasi-Marxism, the ethical stance of the ILP made socialism acceptable to Nonconformists, although some evidence suggests that in the early days the meetings of SDF branches, even in the London area, often had a 'religious' character similar to those of the ILP, and the differences in this respect may have been exaggerated.[27] Membership of the different socialist groups in the 1880s and 1890s cannot be taken as evidence of hard-line political stances, as some of the pioneers were members of more than one group, using them as debating societies for the new socialist ideas.

One reason for the affinity between Socialism and Nonconformity in the late nineteenth century may have been the fact that Labour pioneers of all varieties, including those claiming to be scientific rather than ethical, tended to speak of their Socialism in religious terms as a new-found faith. The term 'religion of Socialism' was widely used during the 1880s and 1890s, with even Ernest Belfort Bax, of the Socialist League and SDF, publishing collected essays under the title *The Religion of Socialism* in 1885. The religious character of Socialism in this period has been interpreted in three different ways. Firstly, it has been seen as a substitute religion, filling a gap left by declining orthodoxy and weaning the Northern working-class Liberals into secular, scientific socialism.[28] Secondly, it has been regarded as a moralising dress worn by socialists because of the peculiarities of British popular and middle-class culture – an apparel which did not necessarily proclaim the man. Thirdly, in Pierson's view, it was a line of fissure along which Marxist ideology cracked when it met class organization in national culture.[29] The message of Socialist propagandists couched in the familiar language of religious idealism appealed to northern Nonconformists in a way that scientific socialist theory did not. Even those who purported to reject religion adopted its language and style in the common usage of terms like 'evangelist', 'apostles', 'disciples', 'new-birth' and 'gospel'. The process of becoming a socialist was seen as involving 'conversion' to a radically different way of life, being ostracized for one's beliefs, and leaving family and friends for the brotherhood and fellowship of the new life.

Moreover, the advent of socialism in the early period was not only seen to involve the reconstruction of society, but also the regeneration of each individual life. The process of bringing in the new age would require sacrifice, and for this the pioneers must be sustained by a devotional life. So socialist meetings, even the most secular, often had the character of religious gatherings, with 'socialist' hymns, some of which were common to Nonconformity, and readings taken from such books as William Morris' *News from Nowhere*. Such developments could not fail to be noticed by the churches, some of whose members would secede to join the Labour Church, leaving behind others who would feel the pressure to make their congregations more progressive about the social questions of the day. In the reverse direction Labour leaders like Tom Mann, Keir Hardie and Ben Tillett showed considerable interest in the churches, eagerly accepting every opportunity to address the annual assemblies of the various denominations. Tillett particularly delighted in haranguing his middle-class audiences for their failure to provide the kind of churches that would attract the working classes, and Mann even toyed with the idea of taking Holy Orders. Blatchford, in the *Clarion*, prodded and coaxed the churches, provoking responses and interaction from both Established and Nonconformist churchmen. In the period when socialism was commonly referred to as being a 'religion', many individuals in the Labour movement had relations with the churches which were closer than they later confessed. It is remarkable how few autobiographies of Labour leaders who were prominent as speakers at Labour Church services make any mention of the Labour Church movement or of John Trevor its leader, whose role in the developments which led to the formation of the ILP has received scant acknowledgement. Perhaps they did not, with hindsight, consider the opportunities afforded by the Labour Church and the Nonconformist churches to have been very significant for the advance of the independent Labour cause, but their almost unanimous silence seems to suggest that for some reason they became less prepared to acknowledge the closeness of relations in the earlier period.

Stephen Yeo has argued that until the mid-1890s, during the period of the 'making of socialists', there was no necessity to choose between politics and religion, the one being to many socialists simply the extension of the other, albeit taking unorthodox forms. There was tremendous energy and activity, but still time for cultural activities, fellowship and personal growth. Speakers did not confine themselves to the materialism of political programmes, but would also adopt topics that would edify and encourage. It was a time of powerful vision, but there was a short-sightedness about how the change to Socialism would be achieved. Yeo delineates the period of the 'religion of socialism' as 1883–1896 and suggests that it was displaced by the growth of party machinery for the achievement of electoral representation.[30] Even if Yeo's 1896 cut-off date is rather early, bearing in mind the continuing success of the Socialist Sunday School Movement,[31] the decline of this kind of socialism does seem to stem from mid-decade and may have been partly a result of the bitterly disappointing results at the 1895 General Election, when, expecting to find itself well represented in the new Parliament, the Labour movement's twenty-eight candidates were all defeated. But the decline of the Labour Church, the principal institutional expression of the 'religion of socialism', after 1895 appears to confirm his conclusion. One reason for the decline of the Labour Church was the difference of opinion about its purpose, Trevor insisting on its spiritual role and Fred Brocklehurst, whose supporters gradually took control, seeing it as little more than an agency for electoral success and part of the party machine. In this period, when the 'religious' element was in decline, it would not be surprising to discover the churches taking less interest in the Labour movement, and one aim of this book is to evaluate the evidence for this.

By the turn of the century, and even a little earlier, the Labour movement faced the problem of how a Socialist society was to be established. The major thrust of Labour advance since the establishment of the ILP in 1893 had been amongst those who rejected revolution as the means, and who saw the way ahead through parliamentary democracy. This necessitated the establishment of a party machine co-ordinated by the Labour Representation Committee, formed in February 1900. Five years had elapsed since the disappointing results of the 1895 General Election, and the movement was resuming its propaganda and election-eering work. The part that Nonconformist sympathizers could play in this was severely limited by the fact that most Labour meetings were held on Sundays. Although Nonconformist ministers had a great deal of freedom in the application of their weekday time, they were heavily committed on Sundays, usually to two services and Sunday School work in the afternoons. J. Ramsay MacDonald, the secretary of the LRC, regarded this as a serious handicap when ministers offered their support as speakers.[32] In the case of laymen who were active in Labour propaganda work, previously unnecessary choices now had to be made between chapel and party; for it was impossible to keep up regular chapel attendance and also be present at the meetings of the party machine and active as a propagandist. The 'lapsed Methodist' is a phenomenon of the developing Labour movement, and the lapse may partly be explained by the practical impossibility of being active in two movements whose activities took place at the same time.

Relations between Nonconformity and the Labour movement were further strained by the cultural divergences that occurred as the Labour movement endeavoured to become a mass party. The cultural similarities between Nonconformity, particularly in Lancashire and the West Riding, and the meetings of the early socialist societies, particularly the ILP, have already been noted. These are epitomized in the common attitude to the 'Drink' question shared by the chapels with their strong Temperance traditions, and the ILP clubs from which alcohol was banned in the early years. But, as the Labour movement sought to expand, it had to reach out to a popular culture centred in the public houses and workingmen's clubs. Nonconformists, who had grown up in the teetotal traditions of the chapels, were ill at ease in this different culture and it must have reduced the possibility of a more active commitment by some chapel sympathizers. The ILP dropped 'the pledge' as a condition of membership early in the new century. Temperance traditions in the chapels were weakening, but were still sufficiently strong to make chapel people feel uncomfortable wherever there was public drinking.

27

The Anglo-Boer War drove another wedge between the Labour movement and the churches. The war caused a remarkable re-alignment of friendships and hostilities amongst British socialists, but on the whole their sympathies were with the Boers. It deeply divided Nonconformity, but, more importantly, some prominent Free Church ministers and laymen adopted imperialistic attitudes which were not forgotten by the Labour leaders. Amongst Methodists, the war caused a split between Hugh Price Hughes and S. E. Keeble, the latter ceasing to write for Hughes' *Methodist Times* and commencing his own short-lived, Manchester based, *Methodist Weekly*, which, because of its pro-Boer stance, as much as its pro-socialism, lasted only two years. Similar conflicts occurred in most denominations. On the Labour side there is evidence that in the early years of the new century the movement was cool in its reception of offers of co-operation and assistance from the churches, and it will be argued that the attitude of prominent Free Churchmen to the South African crisis proved for some years to be a obstacle preventing closer relations between Nonconformity and the Labour movement.

Relationships were further strained, but this time it was the churches who were outraged, when in 1903 Robert Blatchford, who had popularized ethical socialism in his paper, *The Clarion*, reviewed a new edition of Haeckel's *Riddle of the Universe*, saying 'the book demolishes the entire structure upon which the religions of the world are built. There is no escape from that conclusion. The case for science is complete.' Alex. Thompson, 'Dangle', the paper's co-founder, has described how it fell like a bombshell on the *Clarion's* readership, commencing 'the fiercest religious controversy ever known in journalism.'[33] Blatchford followed it in similar vein with *God and my Neighbour*. Critical correspondence flowed into the *Clarion's* office throughout the following year, including many letters from ministers who deplored this attempt to sever the roots of British socialism, which they believed were in religion as much as in scientific socialism. R. J. Campbell and T. Rhondda Williams were amongst the correspondents. Destructive though it was, Blatchford's onslaught attracted much attention from the churches, who were now forced to take the Labour movement seriously. Campbell, minister of the City Temple, who already had a reputation as a great preacher, began to turn towards socialism in 1904. At the same time his New Theology was developing naturally into the Social Gospel movement, and in 1907 the League of Progressive Thought and Social Service was formed 'to work for a social reconstruction which will give economic emancipation to all workers, with fullest opportunities and the most favourable surroundings for individual development; and establish a new social order based upon co-operation for life instead of competition for existence'.[34]

The New Theology movement thrived from 1908 until 1911 and provided theological grounds for moving towards Socialism. It gave confidence to those in the churches to break with the deeply established Liberal politics in which they had been reared. Campbell established a hostel for young men, called Pioneer Preachers, who were attracted to his movement, and who spoke in the London area wherever platforms and pulpits were available to them. Many eventually became ministers, and at least one, R. W. Sorenson, became a Labour MP. Campbell's theology caused widespread controversy and many pulpits were denied to him, forcing him to speak at Labour movement meetings instead, yet the movement was widely known and responsible for encouraging many in the Free Churches to support Labour's advance. Finally, in 1910, as a result of New Theology influences, the Congregational Union followed the other Nonconformist denominations by creating its Social Service Committee, making social-unionism the medium of its social concern, and diverting attention from the more radical solutions suggested by socialists. Not only was Nonconformist interest in socialism contained by its internal social-unionism, but additionally the social policies of the 1906 Liberal government, which included free school meals for poor children, a school medical service and old age pensions, must have made many Nonconformists feel that the Liberals were dealing seriously with the Social Question. Moreover, the intellectual basis of the New Theology had also been partially undermined by Schweitzer's contention, in 1910, that Jesus had shared his contemporaries' view of the Kingdom of God as an other-worldly event. Nonetheless, the now somewhat dated influence of the New Theology continued to filter through to the regions, and it remained for some years a force attracting chapel goers to Socialism, particularly in South Wales.

Alongside this development of a more social theology, great advances were being made in the organization of labour. Between 1906 and 1914 the Trade Union movement, now more closely allied with the emergent Labour Party, was growing in numerical strength; its membership doubled. The last of the large unions, the Miners' Federation, affiliated to the Labour Party in 1909. But the alliance was crippled politically by the Osborne Case in 1909, when its financial basis was temporarily destroyed by a court injunction not to allow dues to be used for political purposes, foremost amongst which was the payment of the Labour MPs' salaries. Yet in spite of these setbacks, perhaps because of them, the power of the unions was increasing. Not only had membership risen , but for some time unions had been amalgamating. Tom Mann had recently returned from Australia, where labour was already better organized, and created the Transport Workers' Federation in November 1910. Soon after he had returned to England, Mann had made a brief visit to France to learn at first hand about the emerging Syndicalist philosophy. On his return he started the publication of a monthly journal, the *Industrial Syndicalist*, and formed an Industrial Syndicalist Education League, to agitate for the consolidation of sectional or craft societies into large single unions for each industry, with the purpose of using general strikes as a means to achieve political change. However, while syndicalists and those who sympathized with their methods played a significant part in four major stoppages, their influence was small in the unprecedented level of industrial disruption between 1911 and 1914. The annual number of stoppages recorded by the Labour Department of the Board of Trade, which had not exceeded six hundred since 1901, climbed through 872 in 1911 to a peak of 1,459 in 1913. The strikes involved miners, seamen and dockers, cotton weavers, jute workers, carters, cab drivers, tube and metal workers, transport workers and construction workers, with newspapers reporting several violent incidents, including the killing of two dockers at Liverpool.[35]

To many in the Nonconformist churches, inspired as they were by traditions of class-conciliation rather than class-conflict, it must have appeared, mistakenly, that the Labour movement as a whole was flirting with revolution and betraying its commitment to Parliamentary democracy. Additionally, the social unrest caused local revivals of the Labour Party and consequent threats to the Liberals. In these circumstances Nonconformists were even more cautious about supporting Labour. And before there was time for reappraisal of the extent of Syndicalist influences in the movement, Nonconformists were too preoccupied with the national and often tragic personal events of World War I to give much time to either support for or opposition to the Labour campaign. This book argues that Nonconformists were not only subject to the general intellectual impulses which played a part in converting Liberal radicals into Socialists, but that there were also specifically theological impulses directing them towards socialism. But it also suggests that these impulses, powerful though they were, were not in themselves sufficient to make Socialists, and it was only when confronting problems of unemployment and poverty, (as they sought to re-establish contact with the masses), that the most socially concerned members of the Free Churches found themselves supporting the policies of the independent Labour movement, as popularly expressed by the ILP. The strength of Nonconformity's historic alliance with the Liberal Party as an impediment to greater support for the emerging Labour movement will not be in question, but it will be maintained that active Nonconformists, and those whose backgrounds were in the chapels and Sunday schools, played a significant role in the emergence of the Labour movement, especially when compared with those subject to purely secular traditions, and that this was responsible for a type of socialism less concerned with class-conflict than might otherwise have been the case. It will also be suggested that whilst Methodism might eventually have nurtured a majority of Nonconformist Labour MPs, its support for the emergence of the independent Labour movement during the early years was no more, and perhaps less significant than that of the denominations

30

of the Old Dissent. The emphasis on the middle-class character of Nonconformity as a reason for its failure to play a more prominent role in the Labour movement will be seriously questioned, particularly in respect of Lancashire and the West Riding of Yorkshire, where Nonconformity had a large working-class following and the ILP made most headway. The book seeks to demonstrate how the relations of the churches with the independent Labour movement, which may be described as never more than thin, were subject to fluctuations caused by such issues and events as the decline of the 'religion of socialism', the building of the party machine, the South African War, Blatchford's rejection of religion, Liberal social measures, and the Syndicalist influences, thought to underlie the widespread strikes of 1911 and 1912. The overriding objective, however, is to explain how Nonconformity's historic alliance with the Liberal Party, its largely middle-class membership and, above all, its individualistic Evangelical theology, prevented close relations with the emergent Labour movement, and to demonstrate that what support there was for Labour came mainly from Nonconformist modernists, who rejected Evangelicalism in favour of a reconstructed 'New Theology'.

Notes

1. E. Halévy, 'La Naissance du Methodisme en Angleterre', *La Revue de Paris*, August 1906, pp.519–39 and 841–67. *v/Semmel.*
2. S. H. Mayor, *The Churches and the Labour Movement* (Independent Press, London, 1967), p.355.
3. H. Pelling, *The Origins of the Labour Party* (Macmillan, London, 1954), p.128.
4. Mayor, *op. cit.*, p.355
5. R. F. Wearmouth, *Methodism and the working-class movements of England* (Epworth, London, 1937); *Methodism and the Struggle of the Working Classes 1850–1900* (Backus, Leicester, 1954); *The Social and Political Influence of Methodism in the Twentieth Century* (Epworth, London, 1957).
6. Wearmouth, *op. cit.*, vol. 3, p.253.
7. S. H. Mayor, 'Some Congregational Relations with the Labour Movement', *Congregational Historical Society Transactions*, August 1956, 18 (1), pp.23–35.
8. S. H. Mayor, 'Organised religion and English working-class movements, 1850–1914', PhD Thesis, Manchester, 1960.
9. Mayor, *The Churches and the Labour Movement* (Independent Press, London, 1967).
10. R. J. Campbell to Keir Hardie, 5 January 1907, Archive of the ILP, Series III, *The Francis Johnson Correspondence*, 1888–1950, 1907/2, Harvester Press, Microfilm.
11. See A. J. Ainsworth, 'Religion in the Working Class Community, and the Evolution of Socialism in Late Nineteenth Century Lancashire: A Case of Working Class Consciousness', *Histoire Sociale*, Vol. 10, 1977, pp.154–80.
12. Mayor, 'Some Congregational Relations with the Labour Movement', p. 23.

13. Mayor, *The Churches and the Labour Movement*, p.355.

14. *Methodist Recorder*, 2 May 1907.

15. P. d'A. Jones, *The Christian Socialist Revival* (Princeton U.P., New Jersey, 1968).

16. E. J. B. Kirtlan was minister at Kingsley Park Wesleyan Chapel, Northampton, where he published a lecture entitled *Socialism for Christians* (Pioneer Printing and Publishing Co., Northampton, 1906). The lecture had been given at Regent's Square Chapel on 22 May 1905, and previously to Methodist congregations in the Channel Islands, Leicester and Newcastle on Tyne.

17. R. Moore, *Pit-men, Preachers and Politics* (Cambridge U.P., London, 1974), p.3.

18. *Bradford Observer*, 10 December 1890, 13 April 1891, 28 April 1891.

19. See H. Pelling and F. Bealey, *Labour and Politics, 1900–1906*, (Macmillan, London, 1958); also P. Joyce, *Work, Society and Politics* (Harvester, Brighton, 1980).

20. J. Hill, 'Working Class Politics in Lancashire 1885–1906, a Regional Study in the Origins of the Labour Party', unpublished PhD Thesis, University of Keele, 1969, p.433.

21. D. W. Bebbington, *The Nonconformist Conscience* (George Allen and Unwin, London, 1982), p.13.

22. A. Harnack, *Das Wesen des Christentums* (Berlin, 1900); English translation, T. B. Saunders, *What is Christianity?* (Benn, London, Fifth Edition, 1958; First English Edition, 1901).

22. A. Schweitzer, *Von Reimarus zu Wrede* (Mohr, Tubingen, 1906); English translation, *The Quest for the Historical Jesus* (A. & C. Black, London, 1910).

24. H. V. Mills, *Poverty and the State* (Kegan Paul, London, 1886, 1889).

25. K. D. Brown, 'Nonconformity and the British Labour Movement: A Case Study', *Journal of Social History*, VIII, 1975, pp.113–18.

26. H. McLeod, 'Religion in the British and German Labour Movements c.1890–1914: A Comparison', *Bulletin of the Society for the Study of Labour History*, Vol.51, No.1, 1986.

27. G. Lansbury, *My Life* (Constable and Co., London, 1928), pp.78–79.

28. E. Hobsbawm, *Primitive Rebels* (Manchester U.P., Manchester, 1959).

29. S. Pierson, *Marxism and the Origins of British Socialism* (Cornell U.P., Ithaca, 1973).

30. S. Yeo, 'A New Life: The Religion of Socialism, 1883–1896', *History Workshop Journal*, 4–6, 1978–79.

31. F. Reid, 'Socialist Sunday Schools in Britain 1892–1939', *International Review of Social History*, 1966.

32. J. R. MacDonald to J. Belcher, 20 December 1905, Archive of the LP, Series III, General Correspondence and Political Records, 28/11–13 (Harvester Press, Microfilm).

33. Alex. Thompson, *Here I Lie* (George Routledge and Sons, London, 1937), p.105.

34. R. J. Campbell, *Primitive Christianity and Modern Socialism*, Progressive League Series No. 1, London, n.d., p.2 (advertisement).

35. H. A. Clegg, *A History of British Trade Unions since 1889, vol.2, 1911–1933* (Clarendon Press, Oxford, 1985), p.24.

Chapter 2

Theological and Intellectual Impulses towards Socialism

The years which preceded the emergence of the independent Labour movement were ones of considerable intellectual ferment in all areas of thought. Impulses towards socialism were increasing in strength and came from several quarters, although the evidence does not suggest that these, alone, were sufficient to convert Liberal Radicals into Socialists. In the 1880s, the membership of the new socialist groups, the Social Democratic Federation, Socialist League and The Fabian Society, remained very small, and radicals were content to pursue Labour's cause in alliance with the Liberal Party.[1] Nonetheless, these impulses played a significant part in the making of Socialists and must be reviewed before evaluating the impact upon the churches of the industrial and social conditions of the working classes, this appearing to have provided the catalyst for wider but limited support for a new independent Labour party amongst members of the Nonconformist churches.

For convenience, the impulses which suggested Socialism to certain ministers and members of the Nonconformist Churches can be broadly categorized, on the one hand, into the self-generating ones produced by the development of theology and, on the other, into the secular intellectual influences which Nonconformists shared in common with society at large.

Theological

From the mid-nineteenth century onwards English religion was being shaken at the foundations. The assault upon it was both external and internal. Externally, it was a triple attack from the natural, biological and social sciences, whilst the internal threat came as a result of the application of historical methods to the study of the Bible. As early as 1830 Sir Charles Lyell's *Principles of Geology* had conclusively shown that Archbishop Ussher's (1580–1656) dating of the Creation at 4004 BC must be pushed back millennia to conform with the geological evidence of the earth's stratification and the fossils of plants and animals that existed millions of years before Christ. With this discovery the account of creation as recorded in *Genesis* had to be rejected in favour of a scientific explanation. In the biological sciences, the publication of Darwin's *Origin of Species* (1859) was even more disturbing, for it not only undermined the Biblical doctrine of the Creation of man, but also the doctrine of the Fall, and, against the traditional established order of creation and society, it suggested the concept of development and progress. T. H. Huxley, the scientist and writer, gave popular currency to Darwin's views by writing books and giving public lectures in support of the theory of evolution. The new social sciences pioneered by Marx, Comte and Spencer, also cast doubt upon traditional religious interpretations by rejecting the Biblical view of man as having dominion over the beasts of the field, in favour of one which viewed him as the victim of heredity and environment, with common characteristics more important than his individuality; a creature who could be manipulated economically.

Moreover, these new discoveries were not only being discussed in centres of learning, but, emerging as they did at a time when popular education was creating a public avid for books and papers, they soon became topics for discussion in the average middle-class Victorian home where they cast doubt upon simple evangelical faith. They also received considerable coverage in the churches, for it was necessary to raise them in order that they might be countered, and this was often done in ways that seemed unconvincing. The result was widespread questioning of established views, not only of the Bible, but of the ordering of society based upon traditional interpretations. These external, implicit criticisms which science was making of the way in which religion understood the creation and social order were confirmed from within by churchmen themselves when they began to apply the methods of literary and historical criticism to the Biblical records. The development of historical studies in theology, especially in Germany, led to internal questioning of the most central doctrines of orthodox Christianity, including the Incarnation. The Higher Criticism, by which scholars attempted to get behind the legendary accretions of the Biblical texts, led to the publication of new 'lives' of Jesus, which portrayed him as a Galilean prophet intent on the establishment of a just social order. The most radical of these, Strauss' *Leben Jesu* (1835), was translated into English by Marianne Evans ('George Eliot'). Also widely read were Ernest Renan's *Vie de Jesus* (1863) and Seeley's *Ecco Homo* (1866). The effect was to suggest that Christianity was not simply about saving souls for a future life, which appeared to be the central concern of nineteenth century Nonconformity, but the application of Christ's teaching to personal relationships, extended to include social organization. It is not surprising, therefore, that Socialism appeared to provide the way in which Christianity could be applied to industrial and economic conditions. Indeed, several of the Nonconformists who gave their support to the early independent Labour movement did so precisely because they believed Socialism to be 'applied Christianity'. This was particularly true of the Rev. S. E. Keeble, the foremost Methodist socialist of the period.[2]

The spiritual upheaval which the new scientific and theological learning caused both churchmen and chapel-goers is mirrored in the novels of the period, widely read at the time although now largely forgotten. Mrs. Humphry Ward's *Robert Elsmere*, which appeared in 1888, tells of the doubt of a former Oxford don and Anglican clergyman who resigns his living because he can no longer subscribe to the creeds of his church. Elsmere then begins a process of theological construction along Modernist lines which leads to the foundation of a new religious group, The Order of Brotherhood, to work for social amelioration in the London slums. It clearly reflects the Settlement Movement, which was one of the routes by which churchmen and nonconformists found themselves drawn more closely to Labour's advance.[3] More directly relevant for this book, because they chronicle Nonconformist doubt and theological reconstruction, are William Hale White's *The Autobiography of Mark Rutherford*[4] and *The Deliverance*[5]. These tell of 'Rutherford's' rejection of the Calvinist faith of his upbringing and the discovery of a re-interpreted historic Christianity; a religion of ideas and truths exemplified in Jesus, but a religion stripped of supernaturalism; a religious way which would reconcile faith with intellectual honesty and issue in practical compassion. The works are semi-autobiographical and describe the crisis of faith which was not uncommon in White's generation. They must have struck chords in many who were experiencing similar doubts, and provided them with confidence to reconstruct their faith along more liberal and practical lines, a process which frequently seems to have gone hand in hand with a rejection of orthodox Nonconformity's preoccupation with individual sin, and the adoption of a more collectivist way of thinking about the purpose of religion.

It was from amongst those who felt these crises of faith most acutely that there arose those within Nonconformity who were most sympathetic to an independent Labour movement. For example, John Clifford, the foremost Baptist Socialist, who as a youth in Leicester had been influenced by William Lovett's moral force Chartists, wrote in his notebook of the disturbance that the scientific and theological revolution caused him at the age of eighteen. 'Questions came to me as to the reality of the basis upon which Christianity rests. Is Christianity historical? Are the teachings of Jesus true? What is miracle, and what is its place in the life of the world? Questions like this surged in on me in my nineteenth year, and for a considerable period – some six or seven months – I was living in a land of darkness and of drought, where the spirit found no nourishment, and where anxiety followed anxiety, apprehension followed apprehension'.[6]

A few denominations made some positive responses to the onslaught of the new knowledge. Broad Church Anglicans, who had come under the influence of F. D. Maurice and the Christian Socialists of the 1850s, Unitarians and, to a lesser extent, Congregationalists, showed some signs of adjusting their faith to accord with the new scientific and theological insights, but until the end of the nineteenth century Nonconformity as a whole remained threatened but almost unmoved by them, prefering to bury its head in the ground and to continue with its traditional Evangelical role of saving souls.

Nineteenth-century Nonconformity was overwhelmingly Evangelical. This was not only a result of the growth of Methodism, but also because, with the exception of the Unitarians, the denominations of the Old Dissent had absorbed the Evangelical spirit of the New Dissent. It was concerned with man's sinful nature and how the individual was to be saved. As the century progressed, its outlook was restricted to a narrow moralism and an overriding concern about personal moral behaviour and salvation. It is true that there was a social side to Evangelical faith. Anglican evangelicals were to the forefront of social reform during the 1830s and 1840s, particularly in the agitation for the Ten-Hour Act to limit the hours children could work in the factories. Shaftesbury, who led the Factory Movement, was the leading Anglican Evangelical layman of his day. One of the motives was that children should have more time for spiritual exercises in the home and Sunday school, although there was no one single motive for supporting the agitation. However, the Nonconformist evangelicals were less involved with social concerns than their Anglican counterparts, and by the 1880s the dominant tendency in all branches of Evangelicalism was an other-worldly concern for souls. The influence of F. D. Maurice and the Christian Socialists of the 1850s, who had suggested that the Kingdom of God must encompass nothing less than the whole of creation, and religion be intimately concerned with the fate of all mankind and the condition of men in the secular world, had barely touched Nonconformity. There were, of course, varying degrees of Evangelicalism. It was strongest in the sects that were the product of the Evangelical Revival itself, Wesleyan Methodism and its secessions into Independent, New Connexion, Bible Christian and Primitive Methodism. Amongst the Churches of the older Nonconformity, (the denominations with origins in the seventeenth century), the Baptists became most Evangelical, the Congregationalists less so, and the Unitarians, whose traditions were essentially in the Enlightenment, resisted it almost entirely, although at the popular level of Sunday Schools their people probably shared much of the general religious culture of the period.

In its concern for personal salvation Nonconformist religion was individualistic. It emphasised personal sin as the cause of evil. John Trevor, the founder of the Labour Church, who had been brought up amongst Johnsonian Baptists, told how, as a child, he had lived under the constant fear of Hell, and how his primary concern was to escape from it.[7] The more evangelical a sect, the less likely it was to be concerned with social conditions, at least until bad social conditions were standing in the way of the saving of individual souls. If there were social evils they were the product of individual sin, and it was there, and there alone, that the problem could be tackled.

Within Nonconformity those who reacted against this individualism were the people most likely to lend their support to a more collectivist view of how society should be organized. In the early 1890s the reaction found expression in the Labour Church movement, which began with the formation of the Manchester and Salford Labour Church by John Trevor, a Unitarian minister, in 1891, and which spread mainly in the textile regions of Lancashire and the West Riding, alongside the developing Independent Labour Party.[8] Trevor expressed the reaction in the first of his Labour Church tracts, *Theology and the Slums*, in which he explained that the churches had 'a desire to save individual souls for another world, but the idea of getting rid, once and for all, of our cesspools of misery on earth was not dreamed of. They worshipped devoutly on Sunday, and on Monday went on with their work, and accepted the social order.'[9] Trevor's criticism was that the churches saw slums as the product of social evils, whereas he, and others who were sympathetic to the rising tide of socialist opinion, believed 'there was a social responsibility also, and denounced the conditions of life as themselves responsible for social evils.'[10] It might, therefore, be assumed that the greatest support for the emerging Labour movement would come from the most Evangelical denominations, where the reaction to individualism was greatest; but this was not so. Trevor himself had become a Unitarian before founding his Labour Church. However, whilst he had freed himself from a narrow Calvinism, he had not escaped from the economic individualism that was even more a characteristic of middle-class Unitarianism than of most Nonconformist sects. Amongst Nonconformists who supported Labour there was a leftwards movement theologically. Several Congregationalists became Unitarian, including J. H. Belcher, the secretary of the Christian Socialist League, and J. Kirkman Gray, first Secretary of the Unitarian Union for Social Service. And those who remained associated with the more Evangelical branches of Nonconformity were generally, theologically as well as politically, the most advanced in their thinking. If there is an explanation of 'the lapsed Methodist' syndrome in early Labour support, it may lie in the difficulties of combining the narrowly individualistic faith of Evangelicalism with collectivist politics. Members of the less Evangelical branches of Nonconformity were not subject to these opposing tensions to the same degree. Contrary to much Labour and Nonconformist historiography, which incorrectly gives Methodism such a prominent role, this may account for what appears to be the greater participation of Congregationalists and Unitarians in the socialist organizations of the 1890s, particularly in the Fabian Society, the Labour Church and the ILP, especially in Lancashire and the West Riding.

During the first decade of the twentieth century the reaction against individualism within Nonconformity found greatest expression in the New Theology movement. Its leaders were the Rev. R. J. Campbell, Congregationalist minister at the prestigious City Temple, a convert from the Church of England to which he eventually returned in 1915; and, in the north, the Rev. T. Rhondda Williams and the Rev. Dr. K. C. Anderson, respectively ministers of Greenfield and Horton Lane Congregational churches at Bradford, 'the cradle of the ILP'. The movement appears to have sprung up quite independently of the earlier reactions to the individualism of Nonconformity, which a decade before had been organized into John Trevor's Labour Church. In many ways it was the popularization in England of the Liberal Christian theology stemming from the work of Adolf Harnack at Berlin. Not only in his scholarly work on dogmatics, but more widely in his popular lectures, *What is Christianity?*, Harnack had emphasized the centrality of the idea of the Kingdom of God in the teaching of Jesus, and suggested it was to be realized in the achievement of a just social order here on earth.[11] It clearly had a strong affinity with Socialism, which was attempting to replace the competitive spirit of Capitalism with its new vision of a social order based upon the common ownership of the means of production, distribution and exchange. The New Theology was immanentalist. As opposed to a transcendent God, or a God incarnate in one human life two thousand years ago, it stressed the Divinity immanent in contemporary life. It was concerned with the religion *of* Jesus not the traditional religion *about* Jesus. In fact, it rejected as anachronistic most of the tenets of orthodox Nonconformity, 'the Fall, the scriptural basis of revelation, the blood-atonement, the punishment of sin, heaven and hell', which Campbell regarded as 'not only misleading but unethical' and the reason why the masses were drifting from the churches. He argued that the New Theology was 'the religious articulation of the social movement', the theology of the Labour Movement, 'whether the movement knows it or not'.[12]

In 1904 Campbell, already a popular preacher, attacked the workers in a *National Review* article for their failure to observe Sunday. As a result he was asked to repeat his charges at a mass Labour meeting, where he discovered how ignorant he was of the Labour point of view. Thereafter he was in close touch with the more prominent Labour leaders. At the end of 1906 he publicly declared for Socialism by preaching a sermon on *Christianity and Collectivism* from the pulpit of the City Temple, which was widely commented on in the newspapers, bringing forth the condemnation of Congregationalists both for his heretical views and his politics, although the City Temple congregation stood by him.[13] The association of the New Theology with the Labour movement was apparently not only rhetorical, for Keir Hardie approached Campbell to consider standing as a Labour candidate, to which he replied that he did not care a fig about entering Parliament and could have done so long ago as a member of either of the orthodox parties if he had wished. Yet Campbell could see the incongruity of his preaching, remarking that 'the acquiescence of the people is rather remarkable' since 'the City Temple represents the quintessence of the bourgeois spirit. With Nonconformity as a whole it is otherwise. My back has been to the wall for years.' He went on to say how he was doing his best 'to destroy the unethical doctrines and ideals of the churches' and expressed his conviction 'that the New Theology (which is the gospel of the kingdom of God) and the Labour movement are the same. The same spirit is behind both.'[14]

In the north of England, where the major thrust for independent Labour representation came with the formation of the national ILP at Bradford in 1893, after the Manchester and Salford Independent Labour Party had been formed a year earlier, Campbell's two New Theology lieutenants, the Rev. T. Rhondda Williams and Rev. Dr. K. C. Anderson, were settled in Bradford. Williams arrived there in 1888 to become minister of the Greenfield Congregational Church, Manningham. By his own admission he was at that time 'what would be known as an orthodox evangelical'.[15] His address at the recognition service 'would have left no doubt in any mind. Orthodox visiting ministers present that evening would have discerned a faithful brother who would be valiant in defence of the true gospel'.[16] And with the exception of one member, the Rev. Dr. Duff, Professor of Old Testament at Bradford College, the Greenfield congregation shared this view, having 'no vision of what was then known as the modernist position.'[17] It was at the Ministers' Fraternal that Williams met 'men who spoke of things Biblical and Theological in a way that left me in utter darkness.' Anderson, who had come to Bradford from a pastorate in the USA, 'drove a plough through the fields of orthodoxy cutting them up in a bewildering fashion.'[18] Another member, James Fotheringham, a lecturer to the upper forms of the Boys' and Girls' Grammar School, had been intended for the Baptist ministry, but did not enter it on account of his heretical opinions. Dr. Duff, the Old Testament tutor at the Congregational theological college, had for some years been teaching his subject on the lines of the Higher Criticism, and congregations listening to his students preach on their Sunday visits to Yorkshire Congregational Union chapels were inclined to complain that they heard too much about Amos and Hosea, and not enough about Jesus. (In the company of these men of advanced views Williams found that his 'old theory of the Bible simply went to pieces on the indisputable evidence').[19]

This brought about a crisis of faith which seemed to signal his departure from the ministry, but Anderson reassured him that he would work his way to a reconstruction of faith and find himself in possession of a larger truth than he had ever known. He did so along similar lines to many other Nonconformists who supported Labour, and it took the form of a reaction against Nonconformity's preoccupation with saving the individual. He recounted some years later how 'in mission services, almost invariably, attention is given to individual salvation to the exclusion of the tremendous need for social salvation, and to individual sin without considering social sin, in the grip of which so many individuals are helpless. If a missioner broadens the basis and widens the range of his appeal he is very soon up against opposition.'[20] Williams did widen his range and shortly after reading an anonymously-written publication, entitled *Commerce and Christianity*, he began a series of sermons on topics of social concern. In addition to one bearing the title of the seminal work it included 'The Coming of Man in the Nineteenth Century', 'Did Christianity Transfer the Ideal from Earth to Heaven, and if so, Why?', 'The need of a New Industry in Bradford – the Manufacture of City Councillors' and 'The Modern Interpretation of Salvation by Faith'. They were published in 1902 under the title *The Social Gospel*. With such preaching, which was common amongst New Theology men, Williams encouraged his hearers at Greenfield and the wider readership 'not to limit their work to the business of saving souls.' 'The economic, the social and the spiritual conditions are so interrelated that we can never draw clear boundaries for each.'[21] 'So called secular questions are therefore soul-questions.'[22] Against the pietism that was characteristic of so much Nonconformity, he argued that 'it is no descent from our high vocation to seek to apply the principles of our religion to concrete civic wrongs and to organize an effort to realize brotherhood'.[23] Even staunch Liberals within the Greenfield congregation were mildly tolerant of his views[24] and appear to have caused no disruption until 1907, when W. E. B. Priestley (later Sir William Priestley, MP) and W. H. Boothroyd left the Greenfield church as a consequence of the support which Williams gave to William Leach, a Labour candidate in the Bradford City Council Elections of that year.[25] However, many years later, Williams admitted that, in the early years of the century, the relations between Labour men and the churches had been extremely difficult, and it may not be insignificant that he left Bradford, for Brighton, in 1909, when the New Theology controversy was still arousing bitter opposition within the churches. But Williams's influence was by no means confined to Bradford. He engaged in extensive mission campaigns in various cities and was particularly popular in South Wales, where he spread the New Theology and Social Gospellism by preaching in his native Welsh.[26]

K. C. Anderson, who had encouraged T. Rhondda Williams in the reconstruction of his faith along New Theology and Social Gospel lines, had come to Bradford from the United States in the late 1880s and became very sympathetic to the Labour cause. He was minister of Horton Lane Congregational Church and in 1891 was one of a deputation of five Nonconformists, ministers and laymen, who made the first of several attempts at conciliation in the strike at Manningham Mills. The others were the Rev. C. W. Skemp, P. Bland, W. Sugden and E. Halford.[27] The strike was caused when, in December 1890, the workers were informed by placard of large cuts in their wages – a result of the McKinley Tariff, at a time when the firm had just announced record profits. Although not organized in a union the workers were helped by most trade unions in the area and the prolonged dispute caused much bitterness between masters and workmen in the neighbourhood. This was bound to strain relationships in the Nonconformist chapels where employer and employee were frequently members of the same society, and the churches were drawn further into the dispute by the decision of some clergy not to allow the strikers to leave collection boxes for their relief in the churches. Only five Bradford churches responded to the strikers' financial appeal.[28] Opposition to the strike came also from the Bradford Nonconformist Association, which in June 1891 had been formed to unite the Bradford congregations. At the meeting to celebrate the Association's first anniversary, in June 1892, a motion was proposed calling on Nonconformists to support Illingworth and Caine, the Liberal candidates, at the General Election of 1892, in which Tillett was the Labour candidate for West Bradford. The decision infuriated Labour supporters and from the body of the hall, Fred Jowett, a member of Anderson's Horton Lane Congregational Church moved the following amendment:

> That this meeting, regarding Ald. Tillett at least as good a Nonconformist as Mr. Illingworth (cheers and a voice 'Bosh'), and as a faithful follower of Jesus Christ (loud cheers), hereby expresses its strong disapproval of the attempt of the Committee of the Bradford Nonconformist Association to put a Labour candidate for the Western Division of Bradford at a disadvantage in the eyes of the Nonconformist electors.

The amendment was defeated and the meeting ended in confusion, with Jowett warning that:

> ... if the reverend gentlemen (on the platform) would persist in opposing the Labour movement there would be more reason than ever to complain of the absence of working men from their chapels (loud cheers), and the labourers would establish a Labour Church ... and they would cheer for Jesus the working man of Nazareth (cheers).[29]

Within two months the Bradford Labour Church had been founded, with Jowett as its chairman. This left Anderson almost isolated in his support for Labour at Horton Lane Congregational Church, which included many of the town's most prominent Liberal Nonconformist businessmen, and it is not surprising that in 1893 he left Bradford for Dundee, though not before startling his congregation by saying 'the socialist indictment against modern society is a true bill; we cannot answer the charge'.[30]

On account of their heretical views, the preachers of the New Theology found that many pulpits were closed to them. When Campbell addressed the annual assembly of the Lancashire Congregational Union, in 1907, on 'The Ministry of Reconciliation', it was only because the invitation had been issued before the New Theology controversy flared into prominence in the autumn of 1906, and it proved inconvenient to withdraw it despite considerable opposition to his coming.[31] At the 1908 assembly of the Lancashire Congregational Union an attempt was made to counter the criticisms which the New Theology adherents were making of the churches' indifference to labour, when an afternoon session was devoted to a paper by George Shillito of Park, Ramsbottom on 'The attitude of the churches to social reform', in which the speaker 'dealt with the charges of Labour men, Socialists, Fabians and the rest'.[32] However, the pendulum appears to have swung the other way when, in 1909, Will Crooks MP was invited to speak. The Congregationalists appeared far from certain how they should align themselves following the advent of a third political party.[33] Both Campbell and Williams addressed the national assemblies of the Congregational Union in 1906, and it would appear that they were popular until it became evident that they were not only a threat to orthodoxy but also critical of the Liberal Party's failure to deal adequately with the grievances of Labour. With pulpits and church platforms increasingly denied to them, Campbell and Williams accepted invitations to speak at Labour demonstrations, appearing on the platform with Labour leaders like Keir Hardie and Robert Blatchford. With the object of linking their theological movement more closely with social reform, a series of summer schools was held in 1906 and 1907, the first at Montreaux and the second at Penmaenmawr. Campbell has been criticised for the 'cult' which surrounded him.[34] He was publicised with large photographs in journals, a large sale of autographed portraits and even an *R. J. Campbell Birthday Book*, which are said to have sickened his more socialist followers, but these things were not unusual amongst Nonconformist ministers and socialist pioneers of that period, and in Campbell's case too much should not be read into them. Nonetheless, he did attract to himself a number of disciples who were formed into a small brotherhood, including a couple of 'sisters', who were known as Pioneer Preachers.

From a hostel in Highgate, London, these young apostles of the New Theology assisted in the spreading of a modernist theology coupled with the message of social reform, speaking where they could find platforms, mainly in the London area. The members of the Brotherhood of Pioneer Preachers were drawn from the churches, and went on to careers in either the Labour movement or the churches. For example, R. W. Sorensen became the Member of Parliament for Walthamstow and eventually went to the upper house in 1965, to create a by-election for the return of Harold Wilson's defeated Foreign Secretary, Patrick Gordon Walker, which in turn resulted in a further defeat. Walker was history tutor at Oxford to Alan Bullock, later Lord Bullock, the son of the Rev. Frank Bullock of Bradford Unitarian Chapel. In a photograph of the Pioneer Preachers (with inset of Campbell) dated 1919, my father, J. Harry Smith, who went on to train for the ministry at Unitarian College, Manchester, stands next to Sorensen. Outside the Unitarian movement the Pioneer Preachers appear to have been almost unknown to Nonconformist and Labour historians, and deserve closer attention than they have so far received. The sources for their early history under Campbell's direction have not been located, but the records of the 'Pioneers' between 1911 and 1934, after the heyday of the New Theology, when they had been absorbed into the Unitarian movement, are at Dr. Williams's Library, London. Unfortunately, the minutes for the early years have suffered flood damage and are of little use and, in common with most Nonconformist records, the remaining years make almost no explicit references to political views or activity, except that with the advent of the First World War there was a difference of opinion over support for the war effort, which led to the resignation of one of the preachers.[35]

The opposition which Campbell met within Congregationalism led him to write to the *Christian World* and to his own periodical, the *Christian Commonwealth*, complaining of repression by church authorities of his New Theology followers, and he called for the establishment of a League of Progressive Thought and Social Service to encourage them. Campbell became its President, T. Rhondda Williams and J. A. Seddon, MP, vice-presidents, and the Rev. F. R. Swan, another Congregationalist and a strong ILP supporter, who had been active in the Colne Valley in 1907, the first organizing secretary. It thrived between 1908 and 1911, when the New Theology was losing its steam, partly as a result of the Congregational Union's establishing its own Social Service Committee in 1910, and partly because the theology became less extreme in a reorganized, broader-based Liberal Christian League, from which Campbell hoped to purge those who were prepared to go further than himself.

Within the Nonconformist churches, the New Theology won relatively few adherents, but there were many, even amongst those who resisted it, who were affected by analogous tendencies. It had most impact amongst Congregationalists in areas where the advance of Socialism was meeting with greatest success and where Nonconformity played a prominent part in the culture of a district, for example in South Wales, where Campbell's visits coincided with religious revivals, and in West Yorkshire textile towns. For those who were attracted by the Labour programme, who had either active or nominal associations with Nonconformity, it provided theological sanctions for the difficult but decisive step of breaking with the Liberal Party for a new allegiance to an independent Labour Party.

Contemporaneous with the New Theology movement and also arising out of Congregationalism, albeit in the USA, were the campaigns of the American socialist-evangelists, J. Stitt Wilson and his brother, Ben, who preached their message in the manner of the chapels. Wilson, who has been described as 'the most powerful figure that ever appeared' in English Christian socialism, was remembered in South Wales as 'a champion orator', 'walking backwards and forwards on the stage', 'holding the audience in suspense' and then 'shaking them with a single word'.[36] An early visit to London in 1899 was cut short by family illness. But a campaign lasting several months in 1900, when he made the Rev. R. Roberts' Brownroyd Congregational Church his headquarters, drew large crowds. Roberts had joined the ILP in the late 1890s, but rejoined the Liberal Party in 1902 after failing to persuade Fred Jowett to co-operate with the Liberals, though he later returned to the ILP just before the First World War. Wilson lectured to Labour Churches, Quaker Meetings and ILP audiences, climaxing the campaign by speaking every night for three weeks and holding two meetings at St. George's Hall, Bradford, attracting 4,000 people on each occasion.

The outcome of Wilson's intensive campaign was that, immediately after his departure, a meeting was held at Brownroyd Congregational Church to inaugurate a Social Crusade Circle. In his inaugural address, James Fotheringham, the grammar school teacher, whose intention to enter the Baptist ministry had come to nothing on account of his heretical views, referred to the 'difficulty of defining the boundaries of either politics or religious matters' and of how 'to a large extent the political bodies kept to politics, the churches to religious and charitable matters'. But, 'if the goal of the social effort was to establish the Kingdom of God on earth', then 'the churches should help in this social crusade.' The purpose of the Social Crusade Circle was to draw the churches and the Labour Party closer together by identifying the goal of collectivist policies with the coming of the Kingdom of God, thus countering the charges often made against Socialism, that it was anti-religious. Moreover, the following principles, objects and methods, which were adopted by the Social Crusade Circle on the proposal of Dr. McDonald and Mr. Arthur Priestman, allow no concessions to the chapels' traditional attachment to the Liberal Party, in their insistence that the community should own and control the production and distribution of wealth:

PRINCIPLES. – 1. That the end of society is to secure the proper good of all its members. 2. That it is the duty of each member of a society to help others to this good. 3. That the production and distribution of wealth in a community, and all its laws and customs, are good only as they make for this greatest good. 4. That what the community needs for the attainment of this good it ought to own and control. 5. That the goal of social effort is to establish this good in an order of life which shall be the Kingdom of God on earth.

OBJECTS. – 1. To bring about a better understanding of these principles. 2. To use all righteous means to secure their application to social life. 3. To educate the people as to the essential character of our present social and industrial life, and in connection therewith to arouse the social conscience concerning the wrongs and injustices of the present competitive system.

METHODS. – 1. Members of the circle shall seek to forward its aims - (a) by lectures and addresses, (b) by the uses of the Press as occasion may arise, (c) by civil, personal, and other efforts, (d) by jealously safeguarding freedom of speech.[37]

At the invitation of the Social Crusade Circle, in 1907 the Wilsons returned to Bradford, from where their campaigning reached out to Glasgow, Halifax, Leeds and South Wales, well into 1908, and was accompanied by a propaganda sheet, *Social Crusade*.[38]

The primary reason for the revival of the Social Crusade at this time was probably to combat the propaganda of the newly formed Anti-Socialist Union, which, with its accusations that Socialism was anti-religious, made church and chapel-goers cautious about supporting the Labour movement. Indeed, at Halifax, where, at the invitation of the local ILP branch, a four-week campaign was extended for a further month,[39] the argument that socialism was not anti-Christ was the main emphasis of the lectures which Wilson gave at the Grand Theatre, where his addresses followed selections rendered by the Clarion Vocal Union and the Copley and Skircoat Band. Repeatedly he asserted that 'if they wanted to know what Socialism meant they must ask what was the mission of Jesus – to preach good news to the poor, to bind up the broken spirited, to proclaim deliverance to captives, to open the eyes of the blind, and to see to the bruised. The business of Christianity was to deliver truth to the poor until there were no poor, to bind the broken-spirited until there were no broken-spirited, to proclaim liberty until everyone was free, to carry light into every household until humanity was delivered from its captivity'. After instancing how people worked at the rate of two pence per hour making articles of clothing to save enough to keep them out of a pauper's grave, Wilson declared that if Jesus Christ was on the earth and supported a system that compelled people to work for this pittance they would repudiate him. It was their duty to abolish the social conditions that were bruising the people.[40]

One of the features of the Wilson crusades was to raise consciousness of the growing Labour movement's strength by drawing together the socialist groups of an area for a large meeting. At Halifax, the campaign ended with a demonstration in Savile Park, including a half-mile long procession led by Clarion cyclists, followed by the Trades Council with a huge banner.[41] Whereas Campbell and Williams had only begun to preach socialism to a broader audience after their New Theology had been rejected by the churches, the Wilsons went directly to working-class audiences. Nonetheless, the message was still delivered using religious imagery, which appealed to workers in the strongly Nonconformist districts, whether or not they were actively connected with the churches. Socialism was advocated in deeply religious terms, and the call was for a commitment that was of a religious nature. The titles of Stitt Wilson's speeches, which were subsequently published, included: 'Moses – the greatest of labour leaders', 'The Messiah Cometh, riding upon the ass of Economics' and 'The Message of Socialism to the Church.'[42] The preaching was messianic in tone; it proclaimed the coming of a new age. 'We wish to avoid any merely theological or ecclesiastical issues' and 'to arouse the social energies of the people' and to 'place that power as a dynamic behind the Socialist programme', said Wilson. Nor was there any doubt about what Wilson's vision of the new age was intended to replace: 'This campaign is intended to be a straight attack upon the capitalist system , as unChristian, unjust and cruel, and responsible for the perpetuation of poverty in the midst of superabundance'.[43] Wilson went further than the New Theology movement and it was perhaps his extreme views that led Campbell's Progressive League to adopt an increasingly moderate stance. As if critical of the New Theology, Wilson declared, 'The Messianic age does not come primarily with a New Theology or a new code of ethics, but with a new social vision.'[44]

Not all Nonconformist support for the emerging Labour movement came, however, from the theologically most progressive denominations. Methodism, for instance, did not embrace Modernism, played no part in the New Theology movement and was virtually untouched by it. Indeed, even the Rev. S. E. Keeble, the foremost Methodist Socialist, rejected Campbell's New Theology as inadequate for Labour's needs. But Keeble, who had not been born into a Methodist home, and who had been a City businessman before entering the Methodist ministry, shared with other Nonconformist Socialists the rejection of the pietism which was characteristic of evangelical Nonconformist religion, which regarded any concern with public affairs as a worldly deviation from the true concerns of the faith. At Leeds he was forced to defend himself against complaints that he had spoken about so worldly a subject as housing on a Sunday afternoon,[45] and at Sheffield members of the Brunswick congregation complained to the superintendent minister that he had preached politics in the pulpit.[46] Of the Methodist movement in the 1870s, Keeble wrote, many years later, that 'The Church had no special interest in social problems, being engrossed in the problems of the individual.'[47] Social Gospellism did, however, find expression in Methodism through Hugh Price Hughes' Forward Movement, which was an attempt to re-establish the Church's contact with the working classes, through the establishing of Central Halls, Pleasant Sunday Afternoons and the development of the Nonconformist Conscience concerning social issues. Keeble identified himself with the Forward Movement. Between 1889 and 1895 he contributed a column entitled 'Labour Lore' to Hughes' paper, *The Methodist Times*, in which he dealt with labour problems, and before long revealed his Socialist sympathies. He attacked bad employers as 'human vampires' who forced girl employees to work a fourteen-hour day in defiance of the Factory acts, 'Christian' employers who demanded Sunday work from tailors, and 'coal owners whose base profit-mongering ... is the source of all our woe.'[48] Methodist ministers were urged to abandon their neutrality and support the Hull Dock Strike.[49] Keeble supported the formation of the ILP as 'the party of the future as the Liberal Party has been the party of the past and is that of the present.'[50]

Unusually amongst the Christian socialists, Keeble was widely read in economics. In October and November 1889 he became the first known Methodist to read and summarize the English edition of *Kapital*, which he described as 'a piece of massive, virile reasoning ... a masterly study of the economic development of human society.' But, whilst he regarded Marx as 'a great pioneer of the emancipation of the masses of Europe from economic slavery', to be 'held in honour by all humane-minded men',[51] and *Kapital* as a 'wonderful book', he regarded it as 'marred by materialist philosophy, Hegelian jargon, and economic errors'.[52] His own book, *Industrial Daydreams*, published in 1896, was the first Methodist work on Socialism. In it he introduced his readers to the leading ideas and figures in the history of Socialism, arguing that 'if Socialism will only eliminate all morally obnoxious features, as well as economic fallacies, from its programme, Christianity will clasp hands with it; for a purified Socialism is simply an industrially applied Christianity'.[53]

The book was well received by reviewers, only one out of nine was hostile, but the members of Keeble's own Wesleyan Methodist denomination failed to purchase it and the author had to buy back from his publisher 267 copies of the first edition of 475 copies.[54] Nor did his newspaper, *The Methodist Weekly*, win more than a small readership. Founded as a result of Keeble's differences of opinion with Hughes over the latter's anti-Boer imperialism at the outbreak of the Anglo-South African War, the paper was unpopular with Methodists not only for being pro-Boer but for its support of the new Labour Representation Committee in the Commons. It first appeared in November 1900, but lacked strong financial backing. A year later only 4,500 out of 10,000 shares had been sold, and in March 1902 Keeble took over the editorship in a financial crisis. Unwilling to sacrifice his principles, Keeble saw his Manchester-based paper expire in August 1903 because it was 'too progressive and independent for popularity'.[55] It had, however, for three years acted as a vehicle for socialist ideas amongst Methodists. However, official Methodism remained wedded to the Liberal Party and Keeble was a rejected prophet. Nevertheless, he remained a Methodist minister, living long enough to see the return of the 1945 post-war Labour government.

The itinerant nature of the Methodist ministry was perhaps a factor that enabled a Socialist minister to remain in the Methodist Church, where he and the congregations would know that it was only a matter of time before Conference sent him to another 'station'. The situation of Methodist laymen who supported the Labour movement was rather different. Being settled in a circuit for much longer periods than the ministers, they often found that relationships with staunch Liberals were likely to be strained beyond breaking point, thus making it impossible to continue their chapel membership without acrimony. Also, compared with the independence of the other Nonconformist churches, Methodism exerted authority through its circuit system and central organization, which forced upon lay Methodist socialists a choice between their church and their party, one which was less necessary in the independent and freer ethos of other denominations. Methodism, as a result, played a minor role in the emergence of the Labour Party; too small to justify the popular aphorism that 'there is more of Methodism than Marxism in British Socialism', even though there is a possibility it might be strictly correct. The fact is that neither Methodism nor Marxism played more than very minor roles in Labour's emergence. But Keeble's contribution was significant and distinctive because of his grasp of economics. His socialism rested upon his wide reading of seminal works, including Marx, which could not be said of most Nonconformist socialists. Considering that much of his ministry was in Methodist circuits in the textile districts of Lancashire and the West Riding, it is somewhat surprising that, compared with ministers of other denominations, he did not play a more active role in the formation of the ILP. This may partly be explained by the unsettled nature of the Methodist ministry, and partly by the fact that theologically he had little in common with the modernist Nonconformists who were so prominent, particularly in Bradford. He never joined a political party or spoke at ILP or Labour Church meetings. His influence was essentially intellectual, through *Industrial Daydreams*, which had a decisive influence upon his limited readership, some of whom would become leaders in the new party. Philip Snowden's membership of the Labour movement has been attributed to the influence of Keeble's articles, although Snowden made no reference to them in his *Autobiography* and there does not appear to have been one source for his change of ideas. However, when Ethel Snowden stayed with the Keebles on a visit to North Wales in 1912 and brought home a copy of Keeble's book as a gift for her husband, in acknowledgment Philip replied:

> The early articles in the book are those which appeared in "Great Thoughts" about nineteen years ago, and which were responsible for first turning my mind to the study of Socialism. I have been grateful to you through all the intervening years and I am delighted to know you personally by deputy.[56]

Outside the mainstream of Nonconformity some distinctive theological impulses towards Socialism were generated within the small New Church founded on the teachings of Emmanuel Swedenborg, and these were propagated by the New Church Socialist Society founded in 1895, with the Rev. S. J. Cunningham Goldsack of Keighley as its secretary. The relaxed theology of the New Church was nearer to the modernism of the New Theology than to that of orthodox Nonconformity and a social theology supportive of Socialism was developed from Swedenborg's doctrine of Use, by which he meant service to others that unifies the creation. The weakness of the New Church Socialist Society was that, like the Socialist Quaker Society, which had some influential members at Dalton Hall, a residence for Manchester University students, it had little influence outside its own denomination, but it is significant for this study that the centre of New Church strength was in Lancashire and the West Riding where the ILP emerged.

Secular

In addition to generating its own theological impulses which played a part in taking its politically radical adherents beyond Liberal Radicalism to Socialism, Nonconformity was also subject to the general secular impulses which were broadly supporting that direction, and it is now necessary to review these in order to fully evaluate the Nonconformist response to the emerging independent Labour movement. It will be suggested that not only did Nonconformity absorb these influences, but also that Nonconformist chapels played a significant part in the dissemination of literary influences amongst working men, albeit often unwittingly as part of their social concern to improve educational standards.

Positivism was the most distinctive intellectual tendency in England between 1860 and 1880, and Royden Harrison has suggested that of all the influences on the Labour Movement those of the English exponents of Auguste Comte's philosophy were decisive.[57] It could not fail to have an effect upon young men training for the ministry, for the simple reason that Comte's system rested upon a repudiation of theology. In its first form, the *Philosophie Positive*, he had repudiated 'religion' also; but in the final phase, the *Politique Positive*, Comte had attempted to graft onto the system a non-theological 'religion of humanity'. At Manchester New College, London (later to become Manchester College, Oxford), Philip Wicksteed, a young man of outstanding ability who was training for the Unitarian ministry, came under the influence of the leading English exponent of Positivism, Professor Edward Spencer Beesly, Professor of History in the University of London and warden of University College Hall. Wicksteed had intimate talks with Beesly and acquired ' a deep attraction for him which for years remained powerful.'[58] Writing to his father, Wicksteed declared, 'I have at present no intellectual sympathy with Positivism, but I have far more practical and quite as much moral sympathy with the real Positivists (including Congreave, Beesly, Bridges and Harrison) as with any people and men in theology.'[59]

Several of the English Positivists had backgrounds in Evangelical faith. Beesly, Bridges and Harrison had been together at Wadham College, Oxford, where Richard Congreave, who was at one time considered to be the rising star of the Evangelical Party within the Established Church, was their tutor. Frederic Harrison, barrister, was the nominee of the five leaders of the 'Conference of Amalgamated Trades' (the 'Junta') for membership of the Royal Commission to investigate the whole subject of unionism after alleged cases of intimidation in 1866. Dr. Bridges, a Poor Law inspector, who, like Beesly, was the son of an Evangelical clergyman, was highly critical of the administration of public assistance by northern manufacturers. Their adoption of Positivism was partly in reaction to an excessive concern of the Anglican evangelicals with individualism and personal salvation, a characteristic, which, as we have seen, they shared with many Nonconformists who found the emerging socialism attractive. Beesly, in particular, was no merely academic figure, but a Radical reformer who freely put his formidable powers of learning at the service of unpopular causes. Together with the other English Positivists, he was partly responsible for the campaign from 1861 to 1871 which led to the establishment of the legal status of Trade Unions, by the Trade Union Act 1871. This in the face of the strong middle-class opposition that was the outcome of the Sheffield Outrages and the Manchester Riots of 1866, in which trade unionists had resorted to intimidation to maintain control over the labour market. They also promoted the idea of an independent labour party. Their concern for the working men would certainly have appealed to Wicksteed, who, when he addressed the Triennial Meeting of the National Conference of Unitarian, Free Christian, Presbyterian and other Non-subscribing churches, in 1891, on the subject of 'The Church and Social Questions', declared that 'all questions of industrial organisation are to be regarded simply and without qualification from the point of view of the worker' and that 'all who do not in the strictest sense "make" their living must stand or fall by the simple test of whether they make life more truly worth living to the hewers of wood and the drawers of water.'[60]

Positivism also introduced Wicksteed, already a distinguished Biblical and Dante scholar, to the 'science of society' for which Comte had coined the name 'sociology'. As a result, in 1890, Manchester College established the Dunkin Lectureship in Social Economy with a £3,000 bequest from Mrs. Joanna Dunkin of Southampton, a sister of the Rev. Edmund Kell, with Wicksteed as the first occupant of the position, which he held several times, in turn with other distinguished economists.[61] It represented a new departure for the social sciences to be included as part of theological education, and for young men training for the ministry to be introduced to the 'Social Question' before having practical experience of it when they left the College for their first pastorates. One of Wicksteed's students was John Trevor who served for a year as his assistant at Little Portland Street Chapel, London, before accepting an appointment as minister of Upper Brook Street Chapel, Manchester. From here, in 1891, he seceded to form the Labour Church, which, Trevor said, 'rested on Wicksteed's broad shoulders'. Wicksteed's interest in the Labour Church movement outlasted Trevor's; in the early days of the movement he frequently travelled to Manchester to address Labour Church services, and through his interest the social concerns of Positivism filtered into the Labour movement through the Labour Churches, which, being without theology, were akin to Comte's 'religion of humanity'. Positivism, which rejected theology, may not have penetrated far into Nonconformity, but there is evidence that it deeply interested many Unitarians, and the example of the social concern of its English exponents had a significant effect in encouraging some Nonconformists to treat the problems created by Capitalism seriously.

Wicksteed's most direct intervention into the socialist debates of the period was his article 'Das Kapital: A Criticism', in *Today*, October 1884, in which he disputed the Marxian labour theory of value and as a result converted G. B. Shaw to Jevonian value theory.[62] Wicksteed was critical of socialist theory, but at the same time supportive of its social ideals, a position which many Nonconformists would have shared. He could see the advantages of market processes, but had a keen awareness of their darker side. In a sermon at Little Portland Street, *Our Prayers and Politics*, 1885, he spoke of the 'commercial instinct … which may be a priceless blessing or an incalculable curse to the world, which gives scope to some of the largest and most stable of human virtues, and tempts to some of the basest vices.'[63] When Wicksteed told John Trevor, who was about to leave London for Manchester, that he could see no reason to stop him from being a socialist, Trevor said, 'It must not be inferred from this that Mr. Wicksteed is a Socialist'.[64] Wicksteed himself asserted that 'I am sometimes supposed to be a socialist by my friends who are not Socialists, and am generally not considered one by my friends who are.'[65]

Among the Unitarian ministry, Philip Wicksteed was by no means alone in lending his support to the social idealism of the emerging Labour movement. James Martineau, the philosopher, divine and the leading Unitarian figure of his day, a Tory, resigned his membership of Little Portland Street as a result of Wicksteed's sympathy for the new democracy and moved to Bedford Chapel, only to find the Rev. Stopford Brooke tainted with the same socialist sympathies. Brooke drew considerable attention because in 1880, when chaplain to Queen Victoria, he had converted to Unitarianism from Broad Church Anglicanism. A member of the Fabian executive, Brooke, in a paper to a meeting of the London Unitarian Ministers in 1893, demanded of his colleagues 'fearless preaching' on contemporary topics, and, believing the political future to be in the hands of the Labour movement, suggested that 'the whole future of the Unitarian body lay in taking the side of the people as opposed to the privileged classes.'[66] Brooke, like Wicksteed, and not a few other Unitarian ministers, was a popular speaker at Labour Church meetings; nor was it unusual for Unitarian ministers to be members of the Fabian Society.

In the early 1880s the ideas of Henry George, an American who had published *Progress and Poverty* in 1879, attracted widespread attention in England. Since the mid-Victorian economic expansion had slowed in the 1870s many in the middle classes had been concerned about the distress caused by unemployment and wage cutting in the manufacturing industries. Now, the plight of the poorly organized agricultural workers added a further dimension to the distress and focused attention on the land. George advocated a single-tax on land as a cure for economic ills, arguing that the origin of land values was primarily to be found in the growth of society as a whole and not in the virtue of individual landowners. His campaigning visits to Ireland and Scotland, the areas of greatest distress, helped to publicize and popularize his views. George was not a Socialist, but his views, and the Land Nationalization Society – founded in 1881 'to restore the land to the people and the people to the land' – which developed from them, are widely recognized as one of the routes by which Liberal Radicals were transformed into the Socialists of the 1890s. His writings and lectures were part of the early political education of many of the leaders of the new independent Labour movement. Keir Hardie and many other Socialists with backgrounds in Nonconformity have testified to the importance of George's views in their political development. When W. T. Stead conducted a survey of the literary influences on the Labour members of parliament elected in 1906, he concluded that 'Henry George had left a deep impression upon the mind of the British workman.'[67]

Georgeist theories were widely discussed and commented upon in secular and religious papers. Wicksteed wrote a series of articles for *The Inquirer*, in 1884.[68] According to R. F. Rattray, he had first read *Progress and Poverty* on the Glasgow to London train, on the recommendation of the Rev. Alexander Webster, the Glasgow Unitarian minister prominent in the formation of the Scottish ILP. Wicksteed felt 'that if the book was true, there would be a revolution in England: if the book were not true, it must be answered'.[69] He wrote to George in both 1882 and 1883. In the letter of 29 October, 1882, he told Henry George that he had opened 'a new heaven and a new earth', thanked him for his 'freshly enkindled enthusiasm' and said the book had given 'the light I vainly sought for myself'. In February of 1884 the Bolton and District Ministers' Fraternal (Unitarian), which prior to 1878 had heard a paper on 'Christian Communism' by the Rev. A. Rushton, and one on 'Religious Communism' by the Rev. A. Lazenby, heard one of its members, the Rev. Bannister give a 'very suggestive address on Henry George's Views, which received much discussion'.[70] The general sympathy which this group had with labour issues is evident from several papers and discussions between 1884 and 1914.

Indicative of the interest of Nonconformists from a broad range of denominations, excluding Methodism, in the Georgeist and Land Nationalization movements is the list of vice-presidents of the Land Nationalization Society on a letter-head dated 1900. Amongst others it includes: Rev. Stopford Brooke (Unitarian), W. P. Byles (Congregationalist), Rev. Dr. John Clifford (Baptist), Charles Wicksteed and the Rev. Philip Wicksteed (Unitarians).[71] In many of the socialist debates between 1880 and 1914 the involvement of Nonconformists was only tangential, but as regards the Land Nationalization movement it was direct and overt.

The Victorian age had been used to the exposure of social distress in the novels of Elizabeth Gaskell and Charles Dickens, but the 1880s saw for the first time the publication of some investigations into the social conditions in which many of the working class lived. By present day standards of social enquiry they cannot, with the possible exception of Charles Booth's work, be regarded as satisfactorily systematic, but they did attempt to gather the facts, even if they were sometimes presented in cavalier manner. These could not be ignored by Nonconformists, if for no other reason than that the social investigators came from their own ranks, and in some instances, like Charles Booth, from their most respected Capitalist families. A Congregationalist pamphlet, *The Bitter Cry of Outcast London*, was published in 1883; followed by Salvationist William Booth's *In Darkest England and the Way Out* in 1890; and a few years later by Charles Booth's massive and painstaking study of the metropolitan poor in *London Life and Labour*. The authorship of *The Bitter Cry*, which was written for the London Congregational Union, has been a source of some confusion, but Peter d'A. Jones suggests it is the work of the Rev. W. C. Preston, using material gathered under the supervision of the Union's secretary, the Rev. Andrew Mearns, in a survey of East London poverty.[72] Using the facts provided by others, Preston, an outstanding journalist with experience of editing local papers and direct experience of urban poverty in Lancashire, produced a brilliant pamphlet, which led many in his own Church and beyond to question whether Capitalism might not be replaced by some system that would eradicate such evils. It also led many in the churches to engage in Settlement work and other agencies for the amelioration of the distress, and these brought them, as never before, into closer contact with the life and conditions of the urban poor. This concern in the churches for the the Social Gospel was primarily aroused by their reading of the literature of social investigation, which was a new feature of the times.

The Pleasant Sunday Afternoon movement, which was loosely linked with Nonconformity, deserves attention because it may have unwittingly been responsible for the dissemination of some of the literary influences which impelled working men towards support for an independent Labour movement. It grew from an initiative taken in 1875 by John Blackham of

53

Ebenezer Congregational Church, Hilltop, West Bromwich, to attract working men by replacing the dull bible class with a meeting that would be 'brief, bright and brotherly'.[73] It met with success and after ten years, though the movement remained a local one, it was estimated that 100,000 men were meeting in classes within a radius of ten miles of West Bromwich.[74] After 1885, as a result of co-operation with the Young Men's Christian Association, the movement spread to Derby, thence via Nottingham and Leicester to other strategic centres of population.

The most marked development came in 1890 when Blackham addressed the Congregational Union of England and Wales at Hull, on 'The Work and Witness of the PSA Movement'.[75] As a result, still more PSAs sprang up, mainly, but not exclusively associated with Congregational churches. At the Annual Conference of the Lancashire Congregational Union held at Ashton-under-Lyne in March 1897, the Rev. Fred Hibbert could report that every Sunday afternoon there was in his church a congregation of 1,000 to 2,000 men and that during the three years of his PSA's existence they had distributed 11,760 volumes of good literature as prizes to the men.[76] The PSA gradually established a variety of auxiliary agencies – Labour bureaux, Penny Banks, Savings Clubs, Temperance Societies, Ambulance Classes, Flower Shows, Sick and Burial Societies, Popular Saturday Night Concerts and Helping Hand Funds, but the Book Prize Award Scheme was a feature from the beginning. At Ebenezer Congregational Church, West Bromwich, Blackham had told the first 120 men he attracted to the PSA: 'If you will come every Sunday, I shall give you a tract, and all who bring eight tracts at the end of two months shall have a book.'[77] The success of the movement soon outstripped the ability of Blackham's friends to finance the purchase of books, even at the discounted rate, but it was continued by the agreement of the members to pay a half-penny per week. At the Patricroft Congregational Church PSA, in 1904, 24 attendances were required for a First Class Prize, 18 for a Second Class Prize and 12 for a Third Class Prize.[78]

Through the scheme working men had access to literature they were unable to afford. The choice of titles for prizes was very broad, and although a bible or hymn book could be chosen they appear at the bottom of the list from which members at Patricroft were invited to choose. The list includes works by Bunyan, Dickens, Shakespeare, George Eliot, Burns, Tennyson, Scott and Carlyle, and many of the titles reported to W. T. Stead for his article 'The Labour Party and the books that helped to make it'[79] are those which had had a significant influence upon the Labour members elected to Parliament in 1906. Stead wrote that the culture of these early Labour leaders was derived from 'the chapel, from that popular university the public library, or still more frequently from the small collection of books found in the home of the poor.'[80] He noted three striking features from the 45 replies received from the 51 Labour members. First, the frank manner in which they acknowledged their indebtedness to the Bible, a noteworthy fact indeed for a party committed to secular education. Secondly, Dickens had more influence on them than any other novelist. Thirdly, Henry George had made a deep impression upon them. In addition, it appeared that 'Ruskin and Carlyle, Mazzini and John Stuart Mill have all influenced many; but the "Pilgrim's Progress", "Robinson Crusoe", Burns, Shakespeare and Scott still stand first.'[81] Of course, it was not possible to obtain through the PSAs explicitly political propaganda, such as a working man might obtain through the Clarion movement or ILP, but several of these authors and titles were obtainable as PSA prizes, and are now widely regarded as having been influential for the transformation from Liberal radicalism to Socialism. The reasons why relationships between the PSAs and the Labour movement grew closer remain to be traced, but their origins lie in the fact that Nonconformist chapels unwittingly provided for working men some of the literature that suggested socialism.

Secular impulses alone were considerable and forceful, and it is surprising that they did not produce greater formal commitment to Socialism than is reflected in the relatively tiny memberships of the Socialist societies that emerged in the 1880s. In addition to sharing these impulses with society at large, Nonconformists were subjected to theological impulses which suggested that the Kingdom of God was to be realized here in a just society, which approximated to the Socialist vision of Brotherhood. It is, therefore, even more surprising that the emerging independent Labour movement met with such a limited response from the Nonconformist Churches, and in many instances was fiercely resisted. The fact is that the failure of the independent Labour movement to attract wider and more rapid support was a result of the historic view which the middle and working classes, and Nonconformists in particular, had of the Liberal Party as 'the friend of the people', which would eventually emancipate Labour, just as it had previously emancipated Nonconformity from its civil and religious disabilities. An alliance committed to civil and religious liberty would not, it was thought, stop short of liberating society from the human distress which was a product of the Capitalist system. While they could still believe this there was every reason not to dissolve the traditional alliance of Nonconformity with the Liberal Party, or to embark upon the formidable task of establishing a third parliamentary party on a limited franchise. It was only in the late 1880s, in a climate of deepening economic depression and industrial unrest, that faith in the Liberal Party began to founder. It did so, initially, in the textile areas of Lancashire and the West Riding of Yorkshire, where the denominations of Old Dissent were especially strong. The introduction of the McKinley Tariff resulted in wage cutting, unemployment and widespread distress. Strikes failed to bring any improvements and the refusal of the Liberal Party to appoint working-class candidates highlighted, as never before, the need for independent

Labour representation. It was inevitable that Nonconformists, whose chapels played a cultural as well as a religious role in the community, should have become involved in the developments that led to the establishment and growth of the Independent Labour Party founded at Bradford in 1893. In the interest of the historic alliance with the Liberal Party, Nonconformity in general resisted the formation of the independent Labour movement. However, the few ministers and laymen who did support it were those who most of all had been touched by the theological and secular intellectual impulses which have been reviewed. Generally, they were of the Old Dissent, not Methodists; and, with the exception of an isolated Methodist or two, they were Modernists. Yet, for all their quantity and strength, it was not theologies, intellectual influences, or even economic theories, that triggered off wider support for an independent Labour movement, but the distress of working people and the loss of faith in the ability of the Liberal Party to relieve it.

Notes

1. For figures, see H. Pelling, *Origins of the Labour Party* (Macmillan, London, 1954), p.44, and P. A. Watmough, 'The Origins of the SDF', *Bulletin of the Society for the Study of Labour History*, No. 34, 1977.
2. Michael S. Edwards, *S. E. Keeble* (Wesley Historical Society, Chester, 1977).
3. Mrs. Humphry Ward, *Robert Elsmere* (Smith, Elder, London, 1888).
4. W. H. White (Mark Rutherford), *The Autobiography of Mark Rutherford* (T. Fisher Unwin, London, n.d.). (1881)
5. W. H. White (Mark Rutherford), *The Deliverance* (T. Fisher Unwin, London, n.d.). (1885)
6. Sir James Marchant, *Dr. John Clifford, C.H.* (Cassell and Co. London, 1924).
7. J. Trevor, *My Quest for God* (Labour Prophet Office, London, 1897).
8. See L. Smith, 'John Trevor and the Labour Church Movement', Huddersfield Polytechnic MA Dissertation, 1986.
9. J. Trevor, *Theology and the Slums*, p.2.
10. *Ibid.*, p.3.
11. A. Harnack, *Das Wesen des Christentums* (Berlin, 1900); English translation: T. B. Saunders, *What is Christianity?* (Benn, London, Fifth Edition, 1958). First English edition, 1901.
12. R. J. Campbell, *The New Theology* (Chapman and Hall, London, 1907).
13. P. d'A. Jones, *The Christian Socialist Revival: 1877–1914* (Princeton U.P., New Jersey, 1968), p.422.
14. Letter, R. J. Campbell to J. Keir Hardie, 5 January 1907, Archive of the LP, Series III, *The Francis Johnson Correspondence*, 1907/2.
15. Cuttings from articles by the Rev. T. Rhondda Williams, *Bradford Telegraph and Argus*, 1937.
16. *Ibid.*
17. *Ibid.*
18. *Ibid.*
19. *Ibid.*

20. *Ibid.*
21. *Ibid.*
22. *Ibid.*
23. *Ibid.*
24. Greenfield Congregational Church, Deacons' Minutes, 20 June 1904.
25. *Ibid.*, 27 November 1907; *Yorkshire Daily Observer*, 8 October 1907.
26. T. Brennan, E. W. Cooney and H. Pollins, *Social Change in South West Wales* (Watts & Co., London, 1954), p.27.; Jones, *op. cit.*, p.426.
27. *Bradford Observer*, 10 January 1891; W. D. Ross, 'Bradford Politics 1880–1906', unpublished PhD Thesis, University of Bradford, 1977, p.203. Also K. Laybourn, 'The Manningham Mills Strike: Its importance in Bradford History', The Bradford Antiquary, New Series, Part XLVI, 1976.
28. *Bradford Observer*, 14 July 1891.
29. *Ibid.*, 14 June 1892.
30. A. Fenner Brockway, *Socialism over Sixty Years* (G. Allen and Unwin, London, 1946), p.31.
31. W. G. Robinson, *A History of the Lancashire Congregational Union 1906–1956* (Lancashire Congregational Union, Manchester, 1955), p.72.
32. *Ibid.*, p.74.
33. *Ibid.*, p.70.
34. Jones, *op. cit.*, p.430.
35. Minutes of the Pioneer Preachers Committee, 16 June 1915, Archive of Pioneer Preachers, 1912–1934, Dr. Williams's Library, London.
36. Brennan, Cooney and Polins, *op. cit.*, p.149n.
37. *Bradford Observer*, 10 April 1900.
38. Jones, *op. cit.*, p.428.
39. *Halifax Evening Courier*, 27 April 1908.
40. *Ibid.*, 9 March 1908.
41. *Halifax Guardian*, 30 May 1908.
42. Jones, *op. cit.*, p.427.
43. *Ibid.*, p.428.
44. *Ibid.*, p.429.
45. Edwards, *op. cit.*, p.15.
46. *Ibid.*, p.15.
47. *Methodist Recorder*, 28 December 1939.
48. *Methodist Times*, 18 February 1892 and 17 August 1893.
49. *Ibid.*, 20 April 1893.
50. Quoted by Edwards, *op. cit.*, p.20.
51. S. E. Keeble, *Industrial Daydreams* (Elliot, Stock, London, 1896, 2nd Edition, 1907).
52. *Ibid.*, p.34.
53. *Ibid.*, p.152.
54. K. S. Inglis, *Churches and the Working Classes in Victorian England* (Routledge and Kegan Paul, London, 1963), p.295.
55. *Methodist Weekly*, 6 November 1902.
56. P. Snowden to S. E. Keeble, 26 February 1912, photocopy in S. E. Keeble archive (John Rylands University Library of Manchester); Edwards, *op. cit.*, p.21; *Methodist Recorder*, 28 December 1939.
57. Royden Harrison, *Before the Socialists* (Routledge, London, 1965), p.251.

58. C. H. Herford, *Philip Henry Wicksteed* (Dent, London, 1931), p.43.

59. *Ibid.*, p.43.

60. *The Inquirer*, 25 April 1891, p. 275.

61. V. D. Davis, *A History of Manchester College, Oxford* (G. Allen and Unwin, London, 1932), pp. 102, 173, 183 and 195.

62. See Herford, *op. cit.*, Appendix II for text of Wicksteed's Review of *Das Kapital*, G. B. Shaw's Reply and Wicksteed's Rejoinder.

63. P. H. Wicksteed, *Our Prayers and Politics* (Swan, Sonnenschein, Le Bass and Lowrey, London, 1885), p.3.

64. Trevor, *Quest*, p.220.

65. P. H. Wicksteed, *The Social Ideals and the Economic Doctrines of Socialism* (National Conference Union for Social Service, London, 1908), p.2.

66. London Unitarian Ministers' Meeting, Minutes, 20 November 1893 (Dr. Williams's Library).

67. W. T. Stead, 'The Labour Party and the Books that helped to make it', *The Review of Reviews*, 1906, p.582.

68. *The Inquirer*, 2, 16, 23 February 1884.

69. *Ibid.*, 9th March, 1946, pp.66–7.

70. Bolton and District Ministers' Fraternal, Minutes, 4 February 1884 (Lancashire County Record Office, Preston).

71. Letter, M. T. Simm to J. Keir Hardie, 29 January 1900, Archive of the ILP, Series III, *The Francis Johnson Correspondence*, 1900/55 (Harvester Press Microfilm).

72. Jones, *op. cit.*, pp. 413–417.

73. J. W. Tuffley, *Grain from Galilee: The Romance of the Brotherhood Movement* (Headley, London, 1935), p.11; See also Clyde Binfield, *So Down to Prayers* (J. M. Dent and Son, London, 1977), pp. 211–212.

74. Tuffley, *op. cit.*, p.14.

75. *Ibid.*, p.19.

76. I. H. Wallace, *The Brotherhood Movement at Patricroft* (The author, Eccles, 1971), p.1.

77. Tuffley, *op. cit.*, p.11.

78. *Patricroft Congregational Magazine and P.S.A. Record*, Prize List, 1904.

79. W. T. Stead, *op. cit.*; See also D. E. Martin, 'The Instruments of the People?: The Parliamentary Labour Party in 1906' in D. E. Martin and D. Rubinstein, *Ideology and the Labour Movement* (Croom Helm, London, 1979), pp.125–146, and D. E. Martin, 'Ideology and Composition' in K. D. Brown, *The First Labour Party, 1906–1914* (Croom Helm, London, 1965) pp.17–37.

80. *Ibid.*, p.568.

81. *Ibid.*, p.582.

Chapter 3

Nonconformity and Social Reform

In the climate of economic depression which followed the end of mid-Victorian prosperity in 1873, middle-class intellectuals, many of them members of the Nonconformist churches, were brought closer to the conditions of the working classes in programmes of social reform. It was this engagement during the 1880s and the failure of charitable and philanthropic remedies adequately to relieve the condition of the urban poor that was ultimately to lead to wider support for the political remedies suggested by the programme of the Independent Labour Party in the early 1890s. Whereas the intellectual impulses previously described were not in themselves sufficient to bring about conversion to Socialism, they aroused the social consciences of many middle-class Nonconformists and sent them to do philanthropic work in the urban slums, where they came face to face with problems of wage cutting, unemployment and slum dwellings, which, in turn, made them realize that nothing short of Socialism could bring relief on the necessary scale.

The engagement of Nonconformity with the working classes in post-1880 social reform movements was not entirely new, although it had a new element – a concern for social justice. It had begun with the attempt which churches of all denominations made to attract the working classes after the depressing revelations of the 1851 Religious Census, which showed that working people were absent from the churches in even greater numbers than had been thought. The 1850s and 1860s saw the proliferation of Home Missionary Societies and Home Missionary Colleges to train ministers drawn from the artisan class who, with some experience of the working and social conditions of the agricultural and urban poor, would better be able to attract them to mission churches. The re-engagement with the working classes at this stage was fired almost entirely by evangelical zeal to win souls who would reap the benefits of salvation in another world, and, no doubt, as part of the consolidation of the social control that had helped to bring Chartism to an end. The exceptions were a few philanthropic endeavours, such as the Domestic Mission Societies founded by the Unitarians in the 1830s and 1840s, to promote self-help and mutual aid amongst the needy, and where the mission was the point at which class barriers should be breached and rich and poor learn from each other for the realization of civic community. There was, of course, less evident need for philanthropy between 1850 and 1880, than there had been during the trade recessions and high unemployment that followed the Napoleonic wars and the agricultural crises of the 1840s. By the 1870s the mid-Victorian expansion of industry and the benefits that flowed from Empire were improving the social conditions of most workers, and there was no lack of immigrants from the country to the towns, to escape the vagaries of agricultural work. There was, as always, the need for charitable concern for the mentally and socially inadequate, but beyond this Nonconformists saw little reason for social reform, or to question Capitalism, which was increasingly bringing benefits to the able-bodied in all classes. Under these conditions the motive for evangelical philanthropy was simply to raise the social conditions of the most needy only that they might be prepared to receive the spiritual redemption that Evangelical faith offered. Circumstances changed, however, when the boom ended in the 1870s. Generally it was the middle classes who suffered through a notable decline in their returns on industrial investment. On the whole, the lot of the workers tended to improve as real wages increased. However, the repeated and deepening trade recessions of the 'seventies, mid-'eighties and early 'nineties resulted in wage cutting and widespread unemployment, with consequent poverty and distress, at which point the most theologically progressive Nonconformists were moved to takes steps for Social Reform on the grounds of social justice.

At first sight, it might appear that Nonconformists were less socially radical than Anglicans. Until 1905, when the Wesleyan Methodist Union for Social Service was founded, and within a few years quickly followed by the formation of similar Unions in the other Nonconformist denominations, Nonconformity had no groups resembling the Christian Social Union founded by Anglicans in 1889, or the even earlier Guild of St Matthew, founded in 1877 by the Rev. Stewart Headlam, curate of St. Matthew's, Bethnal Green, which brought together Anglican socialists. However, as Dr. Inglis has observed,[1] it would be rash to draw comparisons about the late advent of the Social Unions which in the new century were to co-ordinate efforts for social reform within the Nonconformist denominations, without taking into account the structural differences between Nonconformity and the Church of England. The established custom within the Church of England was that any group of people with a programme could form a society with impunity as long as it presented no threat to doctrinal orthodoxy or ecclesiastical authority. In the polity of Nonconformity, the establishment of anything like the Christian Social Union was virtually impossible until the beginning of the twentieth century, for different reasons. On the one hand, in the Methodist bodies – Wesleyan, New Connexion, Primitive and Bible Christian – such a group could only be established by the will of the Conference, which was unlikely to authorize any sectional society that only represented the will of a minority. On the other, in the Churches organized on the principle of the independency of each congregation – those of the Baptists, Congregationalists and Unitarians – it was notoriously difficult to achieve any common organization. When in fact these denominations did form Social Service Unions it was partly a result of the greater centralization that became necessary because of the decline of Nonconformity. By 1905, the Free Churches were working more closely together in the National Council of Evangelical Free Churches, and the formation of the Methodist Union for Social Service was an example quickly followed by other denominations. It has also been suggested that the late emergence of the Nonconformist Social Unions was part of a process by which the growth of small, more radically Socialist groups within Nonconformity was subverted.[2] To evaluate the advocacy of social reform amongst Nonconformists during the 1880s and 1890s it is, therefore, essential to examine the efforts of individual campaigners.

In the 1880s, the earliest development in the approach of Nonconformity to the poorer classes was the foundation of the Salvation Army by William Booth. Unlike the other examples of Nonconformist efforts for social reform, (shortly to be considered), which sprang more directly from a desire for social justice, in the Salvation Army the philanthropic concern was only gradually adopted by a body that had commenced with a purely evangelical purpose. Booth was brought up in the Church of England, but drifted into Wesleyan Methodism. In the 1840s, as a young man, he had some association with the Chartist Movement in the Nottingham area, where he heard O'Connor speak in 1842. By 1854 he had transferred his allegiance to the Methodist New Connexion, and in turn resigned from this in 1862, probably because he found the Wesleyans and then the New Connexion too socially exclusive and entirely unsympathetic with his desire to bring the Nottingham poor into their chapels.

In 1865 Booth turned his attention to the East End of London, where in a tent at Mile End he began the Christian Mission. Harold Begbie, Booth's biographer, has highlighted the naivety of the narrowly Evangelical approach.[3] Begbie suggests that Booth was vocal about the moral degradation and spiritual destitution of East London, but said not a word about the economic degradation and the physical destitution, and was blind and deaf to the political question. Nonetheless, the work flourished: the tent was replaced by a succession of buildings, until a permanent home was secured by the purchase, in 1868, of a market-hall on Whitechapel Road. By 1875 about a dozen branches had been established in various poor districts of London and the work had spread to other areas of the country, as far afield as Stockton, Middlesbrough and Cardiff. The nick-name 'Salvation Army', suggested by the contemporary war scare over the Eastern Question, gradually displaced the duller official title, as so often the case in the emergence of Nonconformist sects. In the mid-1880s a change came over Booth's outlook, and instead of confining himself to purely evangelical efforts, he began to see the need for measures of social relief work. In this Booth was influenced by the Congregationalists, the Rev. J. B. Paton of Nottingham and the journalist W. T. Stead, and it was sometimes suggested that Booth's book, *In Darkest England and the Way Out*,[4] contained more of Stead than Booth.[5] The work expressed sympathy with what socialists wanted to achieve, but, said Booth,

> whether it is Henry George's Single Tax on Land Values, or Edward Bellamy's Nationalism, or the more elaborate schemes of the Collectivists, my attitude to them all is the same. What these good people want to do, I also want to do. But I am a practical man, dealing with the actualities of to-day. I have no preconceived theories, and I flatter myself I am singularly free from prejudices. I keep my mind open on all these subjects; and am quite prepared to hail with open arms any Utopia that is offered me. But it must be within range of my finger tips. It is no use to me if it is in the clouds.[6]

Nonetheless, the first section of *Darkest England* was concluded with a bitter attack on those who are 'determined to bring about by any and every means a bloody and violent overturn of all existing institutions', who would oppose his scheme.[7] And to commend it to those of Evangelical sentiments, he asserted in 'the most unqualified way that it is primarily and mainly for the sake of saving the soul that I seek the salvation of the body'.[8]

The Salvation Army's programme of social relief began with the provision of sleeping accommodation and food for homeless and unemployed men in exchange for work, in London, in 1888, and was a response to the large-scale demonstrations of the unemployed that were widespread during 1886. The Darkest England Scheme, outlined in the Booth's book, dated from 1890 and went much further with the provision of a system of Labour Bureaux, operating on a national scale to provide information about the availability of work. This was a feature widely imitated by other social agencies of Nonconformity, particularly the PSAs. During the first year 15,697 unemployed and 14,045 vacancies were registered, and by 1897, 81,831 unemployed had been registered and 69,119 had been found jobs.[9] The development was significant in considerably extending the relief of the Salvation Army to the settled unemployed with families, whereas the 18,039 men who received accommodation in what Booth called 'elevators' must have been mainly single men, many of them vagrants. The task of directing the unemployed to work was further extended when the Salvation Army set up a department of Emigration, a solution that was viewed with considerable criticism by early socialists.[10] In 1891, in response to the report of a Commission on Sweating, Booth opened a match-factory, paying workers four pence per gross instead of two and a quarter pence or two and a half pence paid by Capitalist manufacturers.[11] Another venture, which was part of the 'Back to the Land' solution to the problem of the unemployed, was the establishment of a home colony at Hadleigh in Essex. A farm of 800 acres was purchased in 1891, and later extended by the purchase of a further 2,400 acres. Favourably mentioned in the 1909 Poor Law reports, the colony admitted 6,870 persons in the course of its twenty-one years' existence.[12]

The social relief work of the Salvation Army set an impressive example and at an early date was imitated by the formation of similar agencies in other denominations, particularly amongst Anglicans rather than Nonconformists, perhaps for the same reasons that have been considered in respect of the late appearance of the Nonconformist Unions for Social Service. The Church Army was begun in 1881 by Wilson Carlile and F. S. Webster; at Richmond, Surrey, the vicar of Holy Trinity, Evan Hopkins, began the Church Gospel Army; and in Bristol the Church Mission Army was commenced by Canon Atherton.[13] Then, as now, the the Salvation Army won wide respect for its sincere and urgent concern for the destitute. It was studied with interest and respect by many who did not share Booth's simple Evangelical theology; by Broad Church Anglicans, Modernist Nonconformists and Secularists. There were, however, critics. John Trevor, who observed the work of the Salvation Army on a visit to London only a few weeks before forming his Labour Church in Manchester in October 1891, was impressed by what he saw, but believed the Evangelical theology to be inappropriate for a theology of the Labour movement.[14] Most socialists regarded Booth's work as palliative, and diverting attention from the need for fundamental political changes for the eradication of poverty. A major criticism of his schemes to provide relief employment was that they tended to undercut the market and to create as well as relieve destitution, a fact which he failed to appreciate because of his ignorance of economic theory and his remoteness from the world of organized labour. Booth, who recklessly spent money in the mistaken belief that it could be recovered, was also criticized for the inefficient management of the finances of the 'Darkest England' scheme. Autocratic in his rule of the Salvation Army, in the words of his biographer 'he was a monarchist, a constitutionalist, a conservative, and certainly not a lover of radicals or socialists; he kept his eyes averted from the political problem, he never once was tempted to make himself the leader of revolution, the captain of an angry and avenging democracy; his whole emphasis was on religion, and the only war he understood ... was the war against sin.'[15] In such attitudes lay the weakness of the Salvation Army as a vehicle for permanent social change, however impressive the temporary relief work. The system was based upon sympathy, not on justice. In the naive Evangelicalism of Salvationist preaching there were virtually no echoes of the prophetic call of the eighth-century (BC) Old Testament prophets for justice and social righteousness, such as were frequently heard from modernist Nonconformists with more worldly theologies. While it might have noble work to do amongst the residuum, the Salvation Army had neither the theology, nor the economic and political awareness required for real co-operation with the main stream of workers in their quest for democracy, and its role in the emergence of a Labour movement intent on permanent change was thereby restricted.

By contrast most middle-class Nonconformists gained their practical understanding of the condition of the working classes through the Settlement Movement. The usual pattern of a settlement was a building in a poor district, which served as a social and educational centre, and sometimes as a religious centre. It included a hostel to which under-graduates came to live and work alongside the working classes. The first settlement, that of the Ancoats Brotherhood, founded by Charles Rowley in Manchester in 1877 was not connected with any religious denomi-nation. It differed from the organization of other settlements in that it was not confined to University men, but welcomed the service of any suitable person, although it had close links with the Victoria University of Manchester and in time became generally known as the University Settlement.[16] The Settlement Movement, in general, was an Anglican initiative, though it was eventually taken up by most Nonconformist denominations, with the somewhat surprising and noteworthy exception of the Unitarians, which is perhaps explained by their earlier involvement in Domestic Missions.

Its origins lie in the 1860s, when J. R. Green (1837–1883), the social historian, had chosen to live for nine years in East London as Vicar of Stepney, with the intention of building a settlement house. The idea did not come to fruition, but one of Green's young associates, Edmund Holland, founded the Charity Organization Society in 1869, with the intention of rationalizing the resources of overlapping charities. Although it was eventually heavily criticized by Socialists for dispensing a degrading form of charity, the Charity Organization Society did provide a training ground for some brilliant young University students, including Henry Scott Holland, founder of the Christian Social Union, and Arnold Toynbee, who in 1879 visited the East End under the Society's auspices, and whose death in 1883 resulted in the main stream of settlements modelled on Toynbee Hall, founded by Cosmo Gordon Lang, J. A. Spender, F. S. Marvin and Samuel Barnett in Toynbee's memory, with Barnett as the first warden. Toynbee Hall was opened on 10 January, 1885. Although it sprang from the Christian Socialist movement at St John's College, Cambridge, the idea of a College mission was rejected in favour of a broader basis that could include the co-operation of Non-conformists, a decision which must have encouraged Free Churchmen to become involved in the Settlement movement, eventually setting them up in association with their own theological colleges.[17] At Toynbee Hall, middle-class intellectuals not only came face to face with the plight of the industrial worker, but had an opportunity to learn more about the questions agitating the working classes. Conferences were held on such subjects as old-age pensions, friendly societies, co-operative credit banks, the extension of trade unions, Labour homes and farms, co-operation, the unemployed, strikes and, of course, Socialism.[18] One on the 'Utility of strikes' was reported in the Settlement's annual report for 1890:

> Lord Herschell presided, and the discussion was carried on by members of the Hardwicke Society, with Mr. Tod, a dock director, on the one side, and by representative trades-unionists on the other, including several members of the Dockers' Union ... An interesting and useful interchange of views took place between men who do not often have a chance of meeting. Lord Herschell summed up the discussion in a speech of balanced discrimination, in which, while emphasising the losses, both material and moral, which strikes cause, and the grave responsibility which rests on all those who advocate them, he admitted that under many circumstances they were justifiable, and also that the altruistic form of labour contest, called the "strike on principle," might become necessary.[19]

Nor did the settlers stand outside the conflicts between Capital and Labour. In 1888, they sent a committee to meet the managers of Bryant and May about the terrible conditions of employment,[20] which, eventually, led to the brief strike by a few hundred matchgirls, encouraged by Annie Besant. And, at the outbreak of the Dock Strike in 1889, Barnett, who had been on holiday in Switzerland, immediately came home 'to support the strikers in their demands for better organization of unskilled labour, aiding by relief those who would have been, without it, starved into unrighteous submission'. The Strike Committee, including John Burns, Ben Tillett and Tom Mann, were entertained to supper at Toynbee Hall on 21 September, 1889.[21] Thus, the Settlement was associated with the emergence of the New Unionism, which was attempting to organize the hitherto unorganized unskilled labourers and to extend Unionism amongst the skilled and semi-skilled. The 1890 Annual Report of Toynbee Hall spoke highly of the value of trade unions, and revealed that many of the new unions were holding their meetings at the Settlement, including the Tailoresses' Union, Women Cigar Makers', Stick Makers', Tailors', Cutters' and Pressers', Railway Servants', Furriers', Shop Assistants', Fellowship Porters' and Dock Labourers'.[22]

Among Nonconformists the Settlement ideal was taken up mainly by Congregationalists. The Browning Settlement at Walworth rapidly became a trade union and labour headquarters, led by the Rev. F. H. Stead, the brother of the journalist, W. T. Stead.[23] In 1890, Mansfield College, Oxford, the foremost training college for Congregational ministers, established the Mansfield House Settlement at Canning Town, where Percy Alden, the warden, was joined the following year by his brother-in-law, Will Reason. The success of the Mansfield College experiment led, in 1892, to the establishment of a Women's Settlement, also in Canning Town.[24] But, apart from Rowley's Ancoats Settlement, the settlement idea took some time to spread to the north of England. In Manchester, the students of Lancashire Independent College established a settlement at Hulme in 1898, and, in view of the encouraging development, G. H. Parker was permitted to undertake the duties of warden during the last year of his College Course.[25] This appears to have been a student initiative without much encouragement from the College authorities, although the Annual Report presented on 8 January 1899 did direct 'the attention of all friends of the College to this useful work now being carried on, and the valuable experience it affords to those who will hereafter have to deal with the great social needs of our population and its claims upon the ministry of all the Churches'.[26] At Bradford, where the tutors were much more alive to the development of the political climate that was to lead to the independent Labour movement, and where the preaching of T. Rhondda Williams and K. C. Anderson was sympathetic to Labour's advance, the Yorkshire United Independent College inaugurated the Cambridge Place Settlement in 1902.[27] There, in the slum district of Wapping, two students lived on the church premises and engaged in social work. They visited crowded homes, opened a soup kitchen and organized clubs and sports for children and young men. It showed the concern of the college for the social problem and 'gave invaluable experience to young men who were to enter the Christian ministry not as "gentlemen" separated from their people but sharing the lives of ordinary folk'.[28]

Yet the rather late formation of the Cambridge Place Settlement may give the impression that the Yorkshire United Independent College was slow to respond to the social questions of the day, and this would be far from the truth. During the academic year 1893–94, when Bradford was host to the inaugural conference of the ILP, Yorkshire United Independent College introduced into its curriculum a course entitled 'Christian Economics'. In each of the three terms the Rev. Professor Elkanah Armitage, MA, lectured on Political Economy, Economic History and Social Reconstruction. Although he remained a Liberal and orthodox, Armitage was a man of broad social sympathies who had, in the 1880s, introduced his Rotherham congregation to the theories of Henry George. Four days after reading *In Darkest England* in November 1890, he arranged for General William Booth to take breakfast with the Bradford students, and in the 1890s he was an occasional visitor at Labour Church services. For the third term of the course the textbook was Graham's *Socialism Old and New*, and in the June examination students were asked nine questions covering such matters as the different senses in which the word Socialism is used, the life and work of Lassalle, Marx's doctrine of surplus value, and the effect of competition in the various departments of economic activity.[29] The external examiner, J. M. Keynes, M.A., D.Sc., of Cambridge, commented that 'the students had taken much interest in the topics under discussion, and considering the wide range covered by the course their attainments were satisfactory'. He went on to say, 'it may be hoped that they will be led to carry their economic reading further, and in any case a basis has now been laid which will enable them to form a far better judgement than they otherwise could do upon the social questions which more and more force themselves upon the attention of Christian ministers.'[30] Yorkshire United Independent College may have been rather late in giving practical expression to its social concern in the establishment of the Settlement at Cambridge Place, which continued until 1917, but it wasted no time in responding to the ferment of ideas that gave rise to the ILP, by the adaptation of its curriculum to cover the questions being widely debated amongst working men, and nowhere more vociferously than in Bradford.

Not unlike the settlements, although more closely combining the features of both church and settlement, were the Institutional Churches that became a prominent development of Nonconformist activity in the late 1880s. Sellers has suggested that these developed first by accident, then by design, as a response to working-class alienation.[31] In the 1830s and 1840s the Unitarians founded Domestic Missions for philanthropic purposes. Then, from the mid-nineteenth century, Congregationalists and Baptists gradually superimposed social work of a philanthropic, 'improving' or culture dispensing variety on their original evangelistic activities.[32] The process accelerated in response to the secular currents. Social surveys highlighted the poverty that made it impossible for working people to be associated with 'respectable' chapels, the growth of suburbs made life increasingly home-orientated, and the rise of popular entertainment necessitated the development of counter-attractions in the churches. Meetings of the PSA type, with an afternoon lecture to attract working men, were launched by H. S. Brown, a Baptist minister in Liverpool, as early as 1854.[33] Gradually each church became surrounded by satellite clubs, which has been the pattern of Nonconformist church life in urban areas ever since. Sellers makes the interesting point that it was a process by which the chapels secured cultural dominance over their neighbourhoods.[34] The existence of so many clubs and societies associated with Nonconformist chapels, and the extensive surviving physical evidence of complexes of chapel and Sunday School buildings in the midst of nineteenth century working-class housing should at least suggest that the middle-class character of Victorian Nonconformity may have been exaggerated. But although Nonconformists did make significant responses to working-class alienation, the chapels, in general, succeeded mainly in attracting the labour aristocracy, and had less success with the unskilled.

In the 1880s, however, more ambitious projects to attract working men were begun by leading Baptist and Congregational ministers who were sympathetic to Labour's advance. Dr. John Clifford at Westbourne Park Baptist Chapel, London, had an Institute that became the intellectual and organizational centre of the surrounding district, from which various types of social welfare work were carried on.[35] At Queen's Park Congregational Church, Dr. Charles Leach, who had been converted to Socialism after a debate with Keir Hardie at Bradford in 1892, and who joined the ILP in 1893, had a church which seated 1,500 and an Institute to seat 650. Membership of the various auxiliary societies totalled 2,659, and Leach claimed over 3,000 attendances each week in the winter months.[36] Percy Alden, the warden of the Mansfield House Settlement, was another exponent of the social club church. In 1904 he suggested that the ideal church for East London 'would have space to seat 1,000, a good organ, a platform instead of a pulpit, chairs instead of pews, class rooms, games rooms, with a workingmen's club attached, free medical benefits, free legal aid, a maternity club, lads' and girls' clubs, a band, a glee club, a "coffee palace" and adult education classes.'[37] Silvester Horne achieved pre-eminence amongst Congregationalists in this field, encouraging the growth of the Institutional Church movement by the publication of a short book, *The Institutional Church*, in which he suggested ways that would get results in competition with music halls and theatres.[38] At Whitefield's Chapel, Tottenham Court Road, London, Horne provided accommodation for social and educational clubs, and a billiards room with a bar for non-alcoholic drinks. The institutional churches not only met with considerable success in providing forums for the discussion of the social question and relating it to the Social Gospel that was the product of Modernist theology, but also like the Settlements, they brought middle-class Nonconformists into closer contact with the problems of the urban poor, as they came into working-class areas from the more affluent districts to help administer the institutional churches.

A feature not only of the Settlements and the Institutional Churches but of all Nonconformist chapels in any way touched by the Social Gospel were the Pleasant Sunday Afternoon meetings of the Brotherhood Movement. The origins of the Brotherhood Movement and its influence in spreading socialist intellectual influences through its book prize scheme have already be noted in chapter two, but it is now necessary to examine its contribution to social reform. Sylvester Horne, one of the movement's keenest supporters, told Arthur Porritt, before his last trip to America in 1914, that he intended neither to return to the ministry nor to remain in public life but to devote himself to this movement.[39] Although the PSAs were often begun by members of Nonconformist chapels, they were only loosely connected with them and frequently proceeded to secure their own premises. At Hyde, Cheshire, a PSA meeting was commenced in 1894 by a number of young men connected with the Water Street Wesleyan Sunday School,[40] whilst at neighbouring Ashton-under-Lyne the first meeting of the PSA was in 1891 at Albion Chapel

(Congregational).[41] Hyde erected a purpose-built property in 1907,[42] and Ashton purchased an old chapel in 1922, renamed it Brotherhood Hall and had it dedicated by Arthur Henderson, the most prominent Labour Member of Parliament connected with the movement.[43] PSA meetings spread rapidly after 1890, mainly in association with Congregational churches, after their founder, John Blackham, had been invited to address the Annual Assembly of the Congregational Union of England and Wales meeting at Hull.[44] Not surprisingly, as they sought to attract those for whom the conventional forms of Nonconformist worship had little appeal, the meetings became concerned with the social issues agitating their members. The Book Scheme was an attraction to working men eager for wider education. At Ashton, which had 1,400 members drawn exclusively from the working and operative classes, the first annual report recorded 3,086 books distributed. Unemployment was widespread and an early innovation at Ashton-under-Lyne was a Labour Bureau to help members find employment.[45] Nor is it surprising that working men who attended PSA meetings in the northern textile towns should have invited those who were suggesting political remedies for economic distress to speak to them at their Sunday Afternoon meetings, which apart from a hymn and a prayer were otherwise secular in character, or that Labour pioneers should have readily accepted invitations from what was virtually the largest organization of working men.

In spite of the opinion of a section of the movement who in 1909 thought it was neglecting the evangelistic intentions of its founder and becoming too concerned with social reform, the National Council was, until 1914, vigilant about a wide range a social issues, including Unemployment, Minimum Wage, Discharged Prisoners, Sweated Labour, White Slave Trade, War, Tuberculosis, Poverty, Housing and Town Planning, and a Weekly Rest Day.[46] The movement played an important role in the agitation for Old Age Pensions, which began when a PSA meeting arranged by the Rev. F. H. Stead at the Browning Hall Settlement, Walworth, on 20 November, 1898, heard the Hon. William Pember Reeves, Agent-General for New Zealand, expound the provisions of the measure passed in New Zealand to give 7s. a week to every needy applicant over sixty-five years of age. Between 1898 and 1908 the PSAs were to the fore of the agitation for pensions. Their slogan 'Prayer and Postcards' linked religion with political pressure. F. H. Stead used to say, 'pray for this measure and send a post card to your sitting Members urging them to hatch something in the way of Old Age Pensions.'[47] The PSA movement provided a kind of half-way house between religion and politics. It was only loosely connected with the Nonconformist chapels, although many ministers supported it. The concerns of its working-class membership were similar to those of the emerging independent Labour movement.

Whereas the Labour aristocrats of the older trade unions were of the social stratum that found its way to the chapel, the members of the New

Unions that were formed during the last decade of the nineteenth century could find their religious and social needs met, if they felt the need, in a Labour Church coupled with an ILP branch and Club, but, more likely, it would be at a PSA meeting. The PSAs certainly retained their religious character, often of a rather sentimental kind, but, gradually, as they acquired their own premises, the links with Nonconformity weakened, whilst relations with the Labour and trade-union movements grew stronger. At Hyde, the Society of Engineers had the use of a small room every day from 9 till 12 and from 2 till 5, and the use of the large room every alternate Monday evening.[48] Labour Members of Parliament were prominent amongst the speakers at PSA meetings. K. D. Brown has provided evidence to show that of the nine preaching Labour Representation Committee men elected to Parliament in 1906, only three occupied the pulpit in conventional churches, the rest spoke at PSAs.[49]

A few Nonconformist ministers and laymen also played a prominent role in the formation of Social Reform unions early in the 1890s. R. F. Horton of Lyndhurst Road Congregational Church, Hampstead, who lectured on the Unemployed, the Housing Question and the Eight-Hour Day, formed his listeners into a Social Reform League which campaigned for sanitary improvements.[50] Lapsed Wesleyan members of the Labour Church joined a similar body at Holbeck, Leeds. At Bradford, the theologically radical wing of Congregationalism was instrumental in forming the Bradford Social Reform Union sometime around 1892. The initiative was taken by T. Rhondda Williams of Greenfield Congregational Church who had no confidence that the churches themselves would act in the interests of social reform.[51] The Rev. Robert Roberts of Frizinghall Congregational Church, and the Rev. Ceredig Jones, the Unitarian minister at Chapel Lane, were also active in this organization. Williams's pessimism stemmed from the fact that he alone amongst representatives of the churches had supported the provision of free school meals for indigent children when Bradford became the first municipality to introduce them in advance of the Education (Schools Meals) Act.[52] Under the guidance of a School Board attendance officer, Williams made a visitation of the town's slum dwellings, where he saw for himself 'the terrible conditions that prevailed', and through his sermons and the Social Reform Union focussed attention upon them. The Social Reform Union was also concerned about the problem of unemployment and sent delegates to the meetings of the the Bradford Unemployed Emergency Committee.

Originally the Committee had been a sub-committee of the Bradford Fabian Society, but the failure of its repeated attempts to gain public attention by open-air meetings, demonstrations and deputations to the Mayor and Board of Guardians led to a decision to extend the scope of the committee, and to ask the Social Reform Union, the Trades and Labour Council and the Independent Labour Party to send three delegates each, and to invite three from the unemployed themselves.[53] The new committee met for the first time on 20 December, 1893, and immediately began to agitate for a solution to the problem of unemployment. Requests for relief works and a bureau to register the unemployed went unheeded, so the committee itself undertook a census of the unemployed by means of a house-to-house canvass. Twenty unemployed men were paid a guinea a week to conduct the survey at a total cost of between seventy and eighty pounds.[54] They found that 9,869 Bradfordians were wholly unemployed, 11,944 partially unemployed, and there were 36,745 dependants of the unemployed, a total of 58,558, or 27.1 per cent of Bradford's population of 216,000.[55] Having determined the size of the problem, the Committee again approached the Mayor of Bradford with a request that a conference of all persons interested in social questions be called to discuss the best means of dealing with the problem. When this was refused, with no more than a offer to open a subscription list, the Committee, itself, called a conference, held in the Central Hall on 5 May, 1894, at which thirty-six organizations of all shades of political and religious opinion were represented.[56] It was decided that 'the best way to deal with the Unemployment Problem was by means of Farm Colonies and Municipal Workshops, and by getting people back to the land.'[57]

However, Tom Mann, a member of the Amalgamated Society of Engineers, who in 1886 had published a pamphlet entitled *What a Compulsory Eight Hours Working Day Means to the Workers*, and who was attending the Conference whilst in Bradford for a Labour Day demonstration, was quick to suggest that 'far before the labour colony there was needed an eight-hour day'.[58] Later that year the Committee produced its *Manifesto*, which was thoroughly collectivist in rejecting any schemes for home colonies like those of the Salvation Army, Church Army and The Home Colonisation Society, which were individual attempts to deal with a problem which 'the community alone can satisfactorily deal with.'[59] Its programme recommended the adoption of a general eight-hour day, or 48-hour week in all industries;[60] the adoption of a public works scheme, similar to the Mansion House Scheme of the London County Council at Abbey Mills allotments, Stratford, East London;[61] and the municipal provision of properly managed 'elevators'[62] like those instituted by General Booth, in which loafers and the improvident might be given accommodation in exchange for work. The Committee was, however, at pains to point out that they regarded the manifesto's programme as no more than a palliative for a problem that could only be solved by 'a complete reorganisation of our industrial system' on 'a collective basis, or, in other words, in the collective ownership of all the means of production and exchange, to be controlled by a democratic state in the interests of the entire community.'[63] How many of the delegates of the thirty-six organisations of all shades of political and *religious* opinion which were represented at the Conference

71

would have gone along with such a forthright declaration of socialism is impossible to say. But there can be little doubt that the Congregationalist ministers, Williams and Roberts would, as well as some of their followers.

Unusual amongst the settlements was that established by Mrs. Humphry Ward under the auspices of University Hall, London, of which Philip Wicksteed became the warden. It did similar work to the other settlements, but was explicitly based on theological modernism, and its educational programme was largely concerned with spreading the new theological ideas amongst the working classes. This, however, was a short-lived venture, perhaps because Wicksteed had too many other interests as minister, University extension lecturer and Labour Church supporter, to give it enough of his time. Although he and other Unitarians were drawn into the work of the settlement movement through this non-denominational modernist initiative, Unitarians, on the whole, were not prominent in Settlement activities. Their Domestic Missions were doing similar work, so that the establishment of settlements would only have duplicated the kind of activity in which they had long been engaged. Their social reforming zeal, as it touches upon the development of the Labour movement, was in the 1880s and 1890s directed towards the attempts being made to find solutions to unemployment through 'Back to the land' and Land Nationalization schemes. They were strongly represented in the Land Nationalization Society, established in 1881 to 'Restore the Land to the People and the People to the Land'; Stopford Brooke and Philip and Charles Wicksteed were vice-presidents of the Society.[64]

As part of the 'back to the land' movement the work of Herbert Vincent Mills, the Unitarian minister at Market Place Unitarian Chapel, Kendal, deserves attention to explain the process by which the emerging Labour movement came to reject Utopian schemes in favour of political programmes for the relief of unemployment. Mills' social reforming zeal appears to have been exercised independently of his fellow Unitarians. He was of a different class than Stopford Brooke and the Wicksteeds. Born at Accrington in 1856, after serving an engineering apprenticeship he was trained for the ministry by the Unitarian Home Missionary Board at Manchester (1876–1879), and at Owens College (1877–1879). Brief ministries at Bolton and Colne were followed by three years (1884–1887) at Hamilton Road Church, Liverpool, where he gained first hand experience of the plight of the urban unemployed.[65] He described how, when visiting some destitute poor on a cold December morning, he had found in 'a certain house a baker out of work, and next door to him a tailor out of work, and next door again a shoemaker in the same plight'.[66] Mills noted that none of them had a proper pair of shoes or decent suit, and all were anxious to get bread, but none of them would stir themselves to use their skills, because they could not sell their products in markets overstocked with cheap machine-produced articles. From that moment,

Mills began to believe that the poverty of England was capable of reform along communitarian lines, whereby, for example, the shoemaker, tailor and baker would make goods for each other, regardless of the market.

But where was he to begin? With experience as a Poor Law Guardian, Mills looked to the reform of the workhouse system. In his book *Poverty and The State* (1886)[67] he suggested the replacement of the existing scheme of enforced idleness in mainly urban workhouses by a network of 4,000 rural farm colonies on 2,000 acre sites,[68] which would provide employment in healthy surroundings in which the poor would escape the moral degradation so often the product of living in urban slums, or idling away their hours in workhouses. He believed that as many a 4,000 people could be occupied with employment in each 'home colony':[69]

> In short, we must constitute our own market, we must co-operate not only to produce and distribute, but we must co-operate also to consume our produce ... we must grow our own wheat and oats, and potatoes and fruit; we must raise our own cattle, grow our own flax, spin and weave our own wool and linen, and grind our own corn. And I believe that, having such diversity of occupations, we shall always be able to occupy a man out of employment at the particular work he can do best.[70]

Mills envisaged that on a home colony four hours work a day would be 'more than enough' to provide the necessities of a comfortable life. Workmen would commence at 9 o'clock, take lunch at 1 o'clock and resume work between 2 o'clock and 4 o'clock, and a further hour a day would be required for participation in government and administration of the colony.[71] To gather information about the implementation of his idea for self-sufficient communities, Mills visited the Beggar Colonies at Frederiksoord, Veenhuizen and Ommerschans, Holland, in August, 1886,[72] and the remote island community of St. Kilda in August 1888.[73] In 1887, he became minister of Market Place Unitarian Chapel, Kendal, and that same year founded the Home Colonisation Society to publicize his vision.[74] By 1892 there was widespread support for farm colonies as a solution to unemployment, and private subscribers had promised £1,000 to Mills, who was prepared to give his services as manager free of charge for seven years if a colony could be established. In March, 1892, Starnthwaite Mill, a mile north of Crosthwaite, and a few miles from Kendal, was purchased, and in November, 1892, the nearby 127 acre farm at Brow Head was added to it.[75] The estate, which included corn-mill, saw-mills, blacksmiths' forge, joiners' workshop and an area for peat-cutting, was intended for between forty and fifty people; it quickly became known as the 'Westmorland Commune'.

Amongst the earliest colonists were John More and Richard Binfield, two unemployed ostrich feather cleaners from Kentish Town, members of the London SDF.[76] Mills appears to have been equivocal in his support for Socialism, but he was, himself, at this time a member of the Fabian Society and the SDF, which seems to have been a source of recruitment for the new colony in which all 'would sit down at the same table and live in common.' When Robert Blatchford, editor of *The Clarion*, visited the colony soon after its formation in 1892, he wrote enthusiastically of this Utopian experiment set in countryside 'as convenient, quiet and pleasant as a man could wish for'.[77] Katherine St. John Conway was secretary of the Home Colonisation Society, with the task of selecting the first intake of eighteen adults from hundreds of applicants. Amongst those she chose were SDF members, Dan Irving and Enid Stacy;[78] and it was Irving who in the spring of 1893 wrote a letter to *The Clarion*, entitled 'Trouble at Starnthwaite', in which he accused Mills of having misled the colonists into thinking they were joining a democratic community, when in fact Mills' autocratic control made it 'an out-door workhouse conducted on more arbitrary lines than any known in Bumbledom'.[79] In *The Clarion*, Blatchford sided with Irving, regretting that he had been misled by Mills, and hoped that Socialists would not be misled in selling themselves into slavery.[80]

Katherine St. John Conway, however, defended the experiment. She admitted that there are been misunderstanding about the Socialist nature of the colony, but argued that the rebels' claim to democratic rights had to be subordinated to a system that secured for the workers the whole product of their labour, their material comfort and absolute freedom outside work.[81] Believing unemployment to be the most urgent problem socialists faced, she remained committed to home colonisation as the only sound remedy to the problem. Her view was widely shared amongst those engaged in social reform movements in the settlements and churches, and farm colonies, including Starnthwaite, continued in one form or another into the early years of the twentieth century. However, the trouble at Starnthwaite received widespread publicity, and made socialists wary of trying to establish Utopian communities within a capitalist society. It highlighted the need for reforms of society on a much wider scale, for which nothing less than Parliamentary representation would be necessary, if there was not to be revolution. Nonconformists, particularly if actively engaged in supporting the 'Back to the land' movement, must have watched with regret the problems associated with H. V. Mills' experiment and begun to realize that isolated reformers could never do more than relieve for a few the distress which was a product of the competitive system. Such schemes could not even touch the tip of the problem and the removal of urban workmen to Utopian schemes in remote rural districts was an unlikely solution.

Methodists, in general, shared the conservative Evangelical attitude to social reform, viewing the relief of social hardship as worthy of support only if its recipients were likely converts. As the head of a Wesleyan mission in Liverpool said, 'Of course we have helped thousands of people who have been in distress, but never until we have assured ourselves that their religious professions or intentions were sincere.'[82] There were, however, a few who rejected the old idea that Methodism should not become involved in politics and that poverty was the fruit of sin. Their responses took form in the Forward Movement, which 'may best be understood as a gradual and increasing protest against the attitude of complacency and conventionalism; and as an attempt to translate into practical life the essential teaching of Christianity'.[83] To reach the working classes, the movement created Central Halls, which, in a less developed form, were the equivalent of the Settlement Movement within Congregationalism and other Churches of the old dissent. The movement had three leading personalities, Hugh Price Hughes, J. Scott Lidgett and S. E. Keeble, who represented what Dr. Inglis has described as the 'new evangelicalism'.[84] They remained theologically conservative but absorbed secular influences leading them towards Social Reform, greater State intervention, and in the case of Keeble, to a thoroughly collectivist view of how society should be organized. They were, however, an even smaller minority in Wesleyan Methodism than the modernist social reformers amongst the other Nonconformist denominations. Compared with the responses to the social distress of the period reviewed above , there is much less evidence of Methodists being involved in Social Reform movements which were not linked with evangelism. And evidence appears to be particularly sparse for Lancashire and the West Riding of Yorkshire.

Dr. Inglis has suggested that, amongst Nonconformists and Anglicans generally, doctrinal opinions were crucial in determining attitudes to social reform, rather than denominational affiliations.[85] Evangelicals, of either church or chapel, were largely indifferent to social reform in the period under consideration, whereas those who took a more optimistic view of human nature were more concerned. The latter were either Unitarians and Swedenborgians, or they were Congregationalists and Baptists whose personal, spiritual quests had led them to reject Evangelicalism, whilst remaining members of essentially Evangelical communions. All, to a lesser or greater degree, were theological Modernists. This was certainly true of Lancashire and the West Riding, and particularly of Bradford, where there was a concentration of New Theology men.

The way in which a liberal doctrinal position provided an impetus to support for social reform, and eventually for the emerging independent Labour movement, needs further clarification, because it was not the only doctrine to provide such a basis. Inglis has drawn attention to the odd spectacle of 'near-agnostic pastors and ritualist parsons speaking on the same platform' to agitate for social reforms.[86] The common ground between the apparently very different 'High' Anglicans, with their emphasis on the sacraments, and modernist Nonconformists, with an immanentalist theology, lay in the fact that both regarded the material

75

world as an object for sanctification, whereas Evangelicals, whether they were Anglicans or Free Churchmen, viewed matter and spirit, body and soul, as antithetical and rejected the world. The equation between support for social reforms and a developing religious liberalism is less certain in the case of Wesleyans, who insisted they remained true to their Evangelical traditions. Keeble dismissed the New Theology, declaring, in 1907, that 'A New Theology that denies sin, grace, redeeming love, and the new birth cannot suffice for the spiritual necessities of the Labour Movement.'[87] Nonetheless, his Evangelical doctrine was tempered by broad interests and sympathies:

> I have ever held that Methodists are too narrow, that our sympathies and culture should be wide – that Christianity does not really call for perpetual meditation on heaven, but delight in nature, poetry, art, science, literature and human life. Nothing human – nay nothing at all in nature – is alien to the Christian. I have never held the hard doctrinal notions of many of my brethren, never held the hard mechanical theories of verbal and plenary inspiration ... nor the gross revolting theories of eternal punishment. My sympathies have ever been modern.[88]

But the problem for the 'new evangelicals' was that in order to remain within the orthodoxy of their doctrinal traditions, they were more inhibited from practical involvement in social reform movements than were New Theology adherents in the freer organization of the churches of the Old Dissent. This perhaps explains why Keeble, who wrote prolifically in support of reform and the collectivist organization of society, was not to any great extent practically involved in independent Labour politics, even when stationed at circuit ministries in the textile areas, where agitation for social reform was occupying Labour supporters and their sympathisers in other Nonconformist churches. The engagement of these middle-class liberal Nonconformists in social reform movements took many forms. Frequently, as in the Settlement Movement, it afforded direct experience of living amongst working people in urban slums, where the reality of the facts revealed in social surveys was confirmed. Often, as in the establishment of employment bureaux and the 'Back to the land' movement, it was concerned with the central problem of unemployed labour in a capitalist economy subject to trade cycles. Intended primarily as a charitable and philanthropic response to distress, it developed into a concern for social justice; then, when it became evident that piecemeal reforms and the work of isolated reformers could do no more than scratch the surface of the economic and social problems in the industrial urban areas, it developed into a sympathy for fundamental changes in the organization of society along Collectivist lines, and to closer relations with the emerging independent Labour movement. Links between Nonconformist social reformers and the early Socialists were, however, always tenuous. In a society still widely indifferent to the distress of the unemployed, the Labour movement could not oppose schemes like Starnthwaite, which brought relief to a few. Yet it soon realized that to support them would have diverted attention from the real solution. The limitations of philanthropy and the failure of communitarian experiments were, in the end, to emphasize the need for a political programme.

Notes

1. K. S. Inglis, 'English Nonconformity and Social Reform', *Past and Present*, Vol. 13, April, 1958, p.73.
2. Peter d'A. Jones, *The Christian Socialist Revival, 1877–1914* (Princeton University Press, Princeton, 1968), pp.455, 456.
3. H. Begbie, *The Life of General William Booth*, 2 Vols. (Macmillan, London, 1920), I p.71.
4. William Booth, *In Darkest England and the Way Out* (International Headquarters of the Salvation Army, London, 1890).
5. S. Mayor, *The Churches and the Labour Movement* (Independent Press, London, 1967), p.51.
6. William Booth, *op. cit.*, p.79.
7. *Ibid.*, pp.80–81.
8. *Ibid.*, p.45.
9. Mayor, *op. cit.*, p.51.
10. Salvation Army, *Letterhead*, 4 August 1909, Archives of the ILP, Series III, *The Francis Johnson Correspondence*, 1888–1959, 1909/272 (Harvester Press Microfilm).
11. Mayor, *op. cit.*, p.51.
12. *Ibid.*, p.51.
13. *Ibid.*, p.50.
14. J. Trevor in *New Era*, February, 1892.
15. Begbie, *op. cit.*, II p.22f.
16. Mayor, *op. cit.*, p.53.
17. H. O. Barnett, *Canon Barnett, His Life, Work and Friends* (John Murray, London, 1918), Cheaper edition, 1921, pp.308–313.
18. *Ibid.*, p.450.
19. *Toynbee Hall Report*, 1890.
20. Barnett, *op. cit.*, p.457.
21. *Ibid.*, p.458.
22. *Toynbee Hall Report*, 1890.
23. Jones, *op. cit.*, p.82.
24. W. T. Pennar Davis, *Mansfield College, Oxford* (Independent Press, London, 1947), pp.23, 24.
25. Lancashire Independent College, *Annual Report 1899*, p.11.
26. *Ibid.*, p.11.
27. K. W. Wadsworth, *Yorkshire United Independent College* (Independent Press, London, 1954), p.159.
28. *Ibid.*, p.160.
29. Yorkshire United Independent College, *Annual Report, 1893–94*, p.27;

Clyde Binfield, *So Down to Prayers* (J. M. Dent and Sons, London, 1977), pp.221–222.

30. *Annual Report, op. cit.*, pp.30, 31.
31. I. Sellers, *Nineteenth Century Nonconformity* (Edward Arnold, London, 1977), p.46.
32. *Ibid.*, p.47.
33. *Ibid.*, p.46; J. W. Grant, *Free Churchmanship in England, 1870–1940* (Independent Press, n.d.), p.176.
34. Sellers, *op. cit.*, p.49.
35. Grant, *op. cit.*, p.176.
36. Queen's Park Congregational Church, *Letterhead*, 20 August 1894, Archives of the ILP, Series III, *The Francis Johnson Correspondence*, 1885–1950, 1894/184 (Harvester Press Microfilm).
37. Jones, *op. cit.*, p.70.
38. C. S. Horne, *The Institutional Church* (James Clarke and Co., London, n.d) (1907).
39. A. Porritt, *The Best I Remember* (Cassell, London, 1922), p.56; Grant, *op. cit.*, p.178.
40. T. Middleton, *The History of Hyde and its Neighbourhood* (Higham Press, Hyde, 1932), p.399.
41. Ashton-under-Lyne Pleasant Sunday Afternoon, Notice of Meeting, (Tameside Public Library).
42. Hyde Pleasant Sunday Afternoon, Minutes, 12 March 1907. (Tameside Public Library).
43. Ashton-under-Lyne Pleasant Sunday Afternoon, Minutes, 1922. (Tameside Public Library).
44. J. W. Tuffley, *Grain from Galilee: The Romance of the Brotherhood Movement* (Headly, London, 1935), p.17.
45. Ashton-under-Lyne Pleasant Sunday Afternoon, *Annual Report*, 1892. (Tameside Public Library).
46. Tuffley, *op. cit.*, p.72.
47. *Ibid.*, pp.74–76.
48. Hyde Pleasant Sunday Afternoon, Minutes, 26 January 1913. (Tameside Public Library).
49. K. D. Brown, 'Nonconformity and the British Labour Movement: A Case Study', *Journal of Social History*, VIII, 1975, pp.116–118.
50. Inglis, *op. cit.*, p.76.
51. Cuttings from articles by the Rev. T. Rhondda Williams for *Bradford Telegraph and Argus*, 1937 (Bradford Public Library).
52. *Ibid.*
53. Bradford Unemployed Emergency Committee, *Manifesto*, 1894, p.3.
54. *Ibid.*, p.4.
55. *Ibid.*, p.5.
56. *Ibid.*, p.5; *Bradford Observer*, 7 May 1894.
57. *Manifesto*, p.5.
58. *Bradford Observer*, 7 May 1894.
59. *Manifesto*, p.5.
60. *Ibid.*, p.11.
61. *Ibid.*, p.12.

62. *Ibid.*, p.13.
63. *Ibid.*, p.16.
64. Land Nationalisation Society, *Letterhead*, 1899.
65. Unitarian College, Manchester, *Register of Students 1854–1929* (Manchester, 1929), p.31.
66. H. V. Mills, *Poverty and The State* (Kegan Paul, Trench and Co., London, Second Edition, 1889), p.2.
67. *Ibid.*
68. P. C. Gould, 'The Back to the Land Experiment at Starnthwaite, Westmorland (1892–1900)', *The Journal of Regional and Local Studies*, Vol.6, No.2, Autumn, 1986, p.19.
69. Mills, *op. cit.*, p.192.
70. *The Clarion*, 11 June, 1892.
71. Mills, *op. cit.*, p.131; Gould, *op. cit.*, p.19.
72. Mills, *op. cit.*, pp.145–163.
73. *Ibid.*, pp.164–171.
74. Gould, *op. cit.*, p.19.
75. D. Hardy, *Alternative Communities in Nineteenth Century England* (Longman, London, 1979), pp.112, 113.
76. Gould, *op. cit.*, p.19.
77. *The Clarion*, 11 June, 1892.
78. Gould, *op. cit.*, p.20.
79. *The Clarion*, 1 April, 1893.
80. *Ibid.*
81. Gould, *op. cit.*, p.21.
82. Rev. Charles Garrett in *Methodist Times*, 29 April, 1886, quoted by Inglis, *op. cit.*, p.76.
83. C. E. Gwyther, 'Methodist Social and Political Theory and Practice, 1848–1914', unpublished University of Liverpool MA Thesis, 1961, pp.114–115.
84. K. S. Inglis, *Churches and the Working Classes in Victorian England* (Routledge and Kegan Paul, London, 1963), p.308.
85. Inglis, *Past and Present, op. cit.*, p.83.
86. *Ibid.*, p.85.
87. *Methodist Recorder*, 2 May 1907, p.16.
88. S. E. Keeble, Diary 1889, cited by Gwyther, *op. cit.*, p.131.

Chapter Four

Labour Responses

Social reformers in the Nonconformist churches varied in their degrees of affinity to the emergent Labour movement, from Liberals who were attracted by Georgeist single tax theory to those who supported land nationalization, and a smaller number who were prepared for thoroughly collectivist solutions. The extremely limited range of Nonconformist support for reforms that would ameliorate Labour's condition was outmatched by a large body of opinion that thought it was no part of the churches' role to be concerned about such matters. Thomas Green, a Congregationalist, expressed the view that 'the secular element in church life' was threatening 'to hide Jesus Christ by confounding the Gospel with a comprehensive and material benevolence'.[1] To another Congregationalist, social Christianity seemed unnecessary because of the 'self-acting machinery of civilised society, by which capital is compelled to minister to the necessities of labour and poverty, irrespective of goodwill'.[2] Many more in the Nonconformist churches continued to share the widely held view of the minister disparagingly quoted by Philip Snowden in *The Christ that is to be*, a popular and influential Independent Labour Party tract aimed at converting Christians to socialism: 'Socialism could not rid the world of the poor any more than it could of little children and weak people who were a constant appeal to our solicitude and love. Poverty was more than it seemed to be. It had a great religious purpose to serve in the world.'[3] Wherever such views were held Nonconformists were not inclined to welcome the discussion of politics, and certainly not the politics of the new democracy, for this disturbed the traditional alliance of Nonconformity with the Liberal party created throughout the nineteenth century from the Whig/Liberal support for the removal of Dissenting disabilities. Neither, in the early 1890s, were more than a few Nonconformists sympathetic to the idea of independent Labour representation, a position highlighted in Bradford at the 1892 General Election when most of the town's Nonconformist ministers appeared on the platform at a meeting in support of Alfred Illingworth, Ben Tillett's successful Liberal opponent in Bradford West.

An early response to the largely hostile position which Nonconformity, as a whole, adopted towards working-class aspirations for Labour representation took the form of a secession. When John Trevor founded the Manchester and Salford Labour Church in 1891 it was an attempt to discover a solution to the problem which working men faced in their relations with Nonconformist chapels. It is true that from the early years of the nineteenth century many of the working class had ceased to have any connection with the churches; but in northern textile towns, particularly, the chapels, with their Sunday schools and other auxiliary societies, had generally been regarded as sympathetic to the condition of the poor and many working-class families had retained nominal associations, often maintained by the sending of children to Sunday school. However, it was for those working men who were still active in the churches that the problem arose most acutely. How could they continue to feel at home in chapels which, whilst happily welcoming them for the fulfilment of their spiritual needs, were quite unsympathetic and often hostile to their growing political aspirations?

Throughout the 1890s, the difficulty was overcome by the formation of Labour Churches. The Labour Church movement, which had its own journal, *The Labour Prophet*, spread rapidly nationwide, but mainly in the textile regions of Lancashire and Yorkshire, where the ILP had made most headway. Frequently the Labour churches existed side by side with ILP branches, with overlapping memberships. They attracted members from all denominations. The leaders included disaffected Unitarians, Quakers, Congregationalists and Wesleyan Methodists, but several whose backgrounds were Anglican. Labour Church dissatisfaction seems to have been with the churches generally, rather than Nonconformity in particular, but it was more likely to be directed against the chapels because they had traditionally been thought of as being sympathetic to the improvement of the economic and political status of working people, whereas the church had an accepted record of opposition. In Manchester, Labour Church members took a leading part in the formation of the Manchester and Salford Independent Labour Party, in May 1892. Trevor co-operated with Blatchford in the commencement of socialist Sunday Schools in connection with the Clarion movement's Cinderella Clubs. And when the unsuccessful strike at Manningham Mills, Bradford, led to the inaugural conference of the National ILP at Bradford in 1893, Trevor was responsible for a Labour Church service at St George's Hall attended by 5,000 people and addressed by Keir Hardie and George Bernard Shaw.

The complimentary nature of the Labour Church and ILP is emphasized by a resolution of the ILP's National Administrative Council in May 1894 advising 'that branches of the ILP wherever possible should run a Sunday meeting on Labour Church lines'.[4] The Sunday meetings provided a platform and a meeting point for Labour pioneers and ministers of religion who were supportive of independent Labour's advance, most of them either Congregationalists or Unitarians, but also a few High Anglican members of the Guild of Saint Matthew. Furthermore, the Labour Church did not only exist independently of the conventional Nonconformist churches, but there is some evidence, particularly amongst Swedenborgians, that 'Labour Church meetings' were held as part of a range of activities within an ordinary church.[5] After reaching a peak in 1895, when there were 54 congregations, the Labour Church movement suffered serious decline and by 1902 there were only 22 churches, most of these doing little more than provide a meeting ground for the different socialist groups – ILP, SDF and Fabian Society. The reason for the decline of the Labour Churches is not altogether clear, but suggestions have included the internal struggles between those, like Trevor, who regarded it as essentially concerned with the personal regeneration of Labour supporters and those, like Fred Brocklehurst, who became its second General Secretary, and who saw it as little more than an extension of the ILP's electoral machine. The 1895 General Election results were a disappointment. Despite high hopes, none of the ILP's 28 candidates was returned, (and even Keir Hardie, who had previously been Labour's lone voice in the Commons as the member for West Ham, lost his seat). It has been argued that this was a contributory factor. It may have been Trevor's own weak and ineffectual character which led to ossification. A year after his personal spiritual insight, that 'God was in the Labour Movement – working through it, as he had once worked through Christianity, for the further salvation of the world',[6] had led to the formation of the Labour Church, Trevor suffered a nervous breakdown and retired to Rulow, near Macclesfield, from where he published the *Labour Prophet*.[7]

Refusing, or unable to give his movement proper leadership, he saw it fall into the hands of those who had little concern about the personal regeneration which Trevor believed must go hand-in-hand with social reconstruction. And, just as the movement was suffering under the disappointment of the poor election results, he appears to have offended the moral sensibilities of those who shared his own view of the Labour Church by re-marrying within three months of the death of his first wife, Eliza, without a respectful period of mourning. When Trevor wrote to tell of 'the strange circumstances' that led to the marriage, but left further explanation until there should be an opportunity to meet,[7] Keir Hardie replied: 'You have given the movement such a blow as it will not recover from in a hurry, and if you really desire to serve it you will now best do so by resigning all connection with the Labour Church – otherwise the organisation will go to pieces'.[8]

Hardie's prophecy came uncannily true. The Labour Church movement was moribund by 1902. During the 1890s it had provided a meeting point for those with a wide variety of theological viewpoints who saw their religion and politics as part of a common hope, expressed on the one hand in terms of 'The Fatherhood of God and the Brotherhood of Man', and on the other in terms of the practical programme of the Independent Labour Party, with its Eight-Hour Day. It had united those of many denominations who whilst retaining a religious interpretation of life felt that there was no possible hope of persuading the conventional churches to support the Labour movement. Philip Wicksteed, the Unitarian minister and mathematical economist, 'on whose broad shoulders the Labour Church rested' and whose interest in the movement outlasted Trevor's, retained his charge of Little Portland Street Chapel but supported the Labour Churches not for any theological reason, but because social reaction reigned so firmly in the conventional churches, and its attackers were so relatively few that conquest from within was impossible. For about a decade after 1891, the mutual responses of the Labour movement and Nonconformity found greatest expression in the Labour Church Movement, whose heartland was virtually coterminous with that of the ILP. After that, any response which the Labour movement made to Nonconformist interest was made more directly simply because the Labour Church was no longer an effective organization.[9]

Before proceeding to evaluate the relations between Labour and the conventional Nonconformist churches, it is appropriate to consider, briefly, the 'religion of socialism' which produced mutual sympathies between Labour pioneers and their supporters within Nonconformity. The Labour Church movement was the most notable of several attempts to give institutional form to what was described as the 'religion of socialism'. The phrase had been used as early as 1885 in the peroration to the manifesto of the Socialist League, written by William Morris, and was used by many of the pioneers during the 1880s and 1890s.[10] It described the processes of conversion which many early socialists felt they had undergone in their call to a radically different way of life; it included the sense of social ostracism – the breaking with family and friends - which becoming a socialist frequently involved; and, above all, the sense of brotherhood in the fellowship of the New Life. The phenomenon was much broader than its institutional manifestations in such bodies as the Labour Church, the Brotherhood Church and the Socialist Sunday School Movement. It was by no means confined to the ILP ethical socialists, or to the areas where Labour advanced amidst strong traditions of religious Nonconformity. Even the meetings of the quasi-Marxist SDF often assumed a religious character. George Lansbury recalled his membership of the Bow and Bromley SDF branch where 'meetings were like revivalist gatherings. We opened with a song and closed with one, and often read together some extracts from economic and historical writings.'[11]

Early socialists also recognized the need for ritual. A few Labour Churches adopted ceremonies for the reception of infants, marriage and the burial of the dead, although only Leeds Labour Church was registered for marriages. But the tendency to ritual was present in less obviously religious sectors of the Labour movement. The Council of the Socialist League was urged to have a Christmas Tree in 1885 by Eleanor Aveling Marx, who asked 'Is not socialism the real "new birth", and with its light will not the old darkness of the world disappear?'[12] The adoption of a cultic style of expression was a significant characteristic of the 'religion of socialism'. Religious and anti-religious socialists equally gave form and colour to their speeches with the words 'evangelists', 'apostles', 'disciples', 'new birth', and suggested that socialism would create the 'New Jerusalem'. It was also common to publish collected essays under the umbrella-title *The Religion of Socialism*: Katherine St. John Conway and Bruce Glasier did it for the Fabian Society in 1893, the Socialist League and the ILP did it 1894, and Ernest Belfort Bax, the most anti-religious of Socialist League and SDF members, in 1885. Yeo has suggested that the period in which the Labour movement had the characteristics of a religious faith came to an end in 1896, after the total failure to win seats at the 1895 General Election, when it became necessary to develop the party machinery to secure Parliamentary representation.[13] Nonetheless, it continued in attenuated form until the advent of World War I, and in the case of a Labour Church and Socialist Sunday School at Hyde, as late as the 1950s. Although very different from conventional Christianity, there were enough similarities to stimulate mutual fascination between non-dogmatic Socialists and Free Churchmen, and conflict between the more doctrinaire sections of Nonconformity and the Labour movement.

Another important factor which determined the nature of relations between the emergent Labour movement and the Nonconformist chapels was the fact that a large number of the Labour candidates elected at the 1906 General Election claimed to be Free Churchmen, although it is not established that more than a few of them had retained active church membership. It is quite possible that a claim meant no more than some family association with a chapel, a baptism, or attendance at a Sunday School, possibly extending to the Adult class. The survey conducted by W. T. Stead for his article 'The Labour Party and the Books that have helped to make it' itself illustrates the problem.[14] Thomas Burt declined to allow any reference to religious affiliation to be included, adding 'I have struck out your entry under 'Religion,' as it might mislead. I am not a member – nor have I ever been – of the Primitive Methodist body. My father and mother were Primitives. I went to the P.M. Sunday school and chapel as a boy and youth. From the travelling preachers – who often came to our house – I derived intellectual stimulus, and benefit in other ways; but as I have said I never was a member of the denomination'.[15]

Yet Burt has been claimed by both Primitive Methodists and Unitarians. Clearly, on his own testimony, there was no actual affiliation but the acknowledgement of considerable Nonconformist influence. This may have applied to others who claimed more definite religious affiliations, but who could not afford to be so open about the truth of their purely nominal churchmanship because they had been returned as Lib-Lab members. This was a result of the unofficial agreement between Ramsay MacDonald and Herbert Gladstone, the Liberal Chief Whip, whereby Liberals did not oppose seats contested by the Labour Representation

Committee. These members owed their return to the co-operation of the Liberal/Nonconformist alliance, and their acknowledgement of Free Church roots may have been little more than a mark of respect. Burt, although a Lib-Lab candidate, was a miner's MP and less dependent upon the Nonconformist Liberals than many others. K. D. Brown has pointed to a discrepancy between the 18 MPs who claimed membership of Nonconformist churches and the eight listed in the denominational press.[16] The press mentioned Crooks, Gill, Hardie, Henderson, Hodge, Hudson, Jenkins and Taylor, but not Barnes, Clynes, Glover, Parker, MacDonald, Macpherson, Richards, Seddon, Shackleton and Wardle. But a number of the latter group are known to have had connections with Nonconformity. The discrepancy may, perhaps, be explained by the fact that the relations of Labour candidates were more likely to be with the Brotherhood Movement, an auxiliary of Nonconformity, rather than with its main stream, and therefore less likely to be reported in the principal denominational organs. Brown states that of the 9 LRC men who preached, only 3 did so within a traditional free church setting; the rest did so in the Brotherhood movement.[17] Another fact revealed by Stead's survey and Brown's analysis is that eight of the 18 claimed to be Methodists – five Wesleyans, two Primitives and one Free.

This may seem surprising in the light of previous chapters which suggest a relatively small role was played by Methodism in the early years of the Labour movement. The fact is that by 1906 the Labour movement was developing at the confluence of two streams, the socialist movement and the trades union movement, in which Methodism found it possible to play a greater role because it was more concerned with class conciliation than with class conflict. Significantly, many of the Labour candidates had served as trade union officials. Whether their claimed associations with Nonconformity were active or merely tenuous, the fact that almost two thirds of the Parliamentary Labour Party regarded themselves as Non-conformists created channels for at least limited co-operation with the Free Churches, as and when it seemed expedient.

The temperance movement provided another meeting point between Nonconformity and the ILP. From mid-nineteenth century onwards the chapels had developed a culture to oppose that of the public house. Band of Hope meetings grew in number in the 1890s as the production of beer increased, taking a larger proportion of working-class income, until it began to decline after 1900.[18] The Labour movement was divided over the question of whether drink was a cause of working-class poverty, or merely a symptom. Sometimes the process of becoming a socialist involved the realization that the roots of destitution lay deeper than the drink problem. As a member of the Evangelical Union in the mid-Lanarkshire coalfield, Keir Hardie, a strong supporter of the temperance movement, had believed that intemperance was the cause of much working-class distress. But by 1887 he had changed his view and believed that poverty could not be completely eradicated until the means of production was out of private hands. Nonetheless he remained a strong advocate of teetotalism, a commitment he shared with other leaders of the ILP. All four of the Labour MPs who sat in the Commons before 1906 – Hardie, Shackleton, Crooks and Henderson – had associations with temperance, as well as being Nonconformists. Of these, Crooks, a Congregationalist, Shackleton, a Wesleyan, and Henderson, a Congregationalist until sixteen then a Wesleyan, were actively involved in trying to persuade labour that drink was an enemy. They took a leading part in the Trades Union and Labour Officials' Temperance Fellowship, as did many other of the Labour members of parliament elected in 1906.[19] Henderson was its president and Shackleton the treasurer; MacDonald and T. F. Richards belonged to its executive committee; and among its vice-presidents were Barnes, Crooks, Duncan, Gill, Hodge, Snowden, J. W. Taylor and Walsh. For the first three years of its existence signing 'the pledge' was a condition of membership of the ILP. It reflected a continuing belief that drink was still a factor standing in the path of working-class emancipation, if not the fundamental cause of their bondage. And, in part, it was an attempt to give the emergent Labour party credibility and respectability, to show that working men could behave responsibly and were worthy of election to positions of influence and power. Significantly, when members of the party held divergent views, they were more often criticised for being intoxicated than for their opinions, as in the case of Hardie and Snowden's criticism of Victor Grayson for the speech that led to his suspension from the Commons.[20] But there were critics of the ILP's temperance tradition and 'the pledge' was abandoned for new members in 1896.[21]

This was, no doubt, partly a response to the depressing 1895 General Election results, and the realization that if the ILP was to make headway in securing Labour representation it would have to broaden its basis by more readily accepting the public-house culture of working-class life; and partly because of the necessity to raise funds by engaging in the sale of drink and tobacco at ILP clubs. Some, like Ben Tillett, were also critical of Labour MPs appearing on temperance platforms in the company of Liberals, thus blurring in the public's eye the image of the Labour movement as an independent party. Nonetheless, the party leadership remained committed to temperance and frequently joined with Nonconformists in the promotion of the temperance cause. On the other side, for Nonconformists, particularly in north-east Lancashire, attitudes to drink seem to have been crucial in determining the kind of Socialist advance they were prepared to support. Around Burnley, a stronghold of the SDF, Labour did not secure much, if any, Nonconformist support until the ILP emerged, with unequivocal teetotallers amongst its front rank leadership.

The Brotherhood Movement on the fringe of Nonconformity, with its Pleasant Sunday Afternoon meetings, provided yet another point of contact with the Labour movement. The Movement's part in spreading formative influences in favour of socialism through its book prize scheme has already been noted, and also the fact that it shared common objectives with the Labour movement in supporting measures for social reform, particularly the provision of Old Age Pensions. The PSAs also had links with the trades unions, who frequently made use of Brotherhood halls for their meetings and the payment of welfare benefits. Labour leaders responded to invitations to address Pleasant Sunday Afternoon meetings with the same readiness with which they had once responded to the opportunities provided by the Labour Churches, but with the benefits of a much larger and more enduring organization of working men. One important reason why the Labour leaders may have taken so great an interest in the Brotherhood Movement is that it was a large and efficiently organized association of working men. At Hyde, in the 1890s, the whole area served by the thriving PSA was divided into wards, with a committee to oversee visiting.[22] It could have been seen as providing an unofficial electoral registration society, as the chapels had once performed a similar function for the Liberal Party.

In areas where Nonconformity was not so hospitable to Labour pioneers, it was necessary to seek secular venues, but often the meetings nonetheless had a religious flavour. In South Wales, where the coalowners were strongly represented in the chapels, Keir Hardie was refused permission to speak in the vestry of Sharon Welsh Congregational Chapel in Aberaman, Aberdare.[23] In 1898, Willie Wright reported to the ILP's National Administrative Council that on Sunday afternoon, 7 August, 'we had a good meeting on Penydarren 'Tips' between Merthyr and Dowlais. The meeting was of a religious character, opened by Hymn, Lesson and Prayer, and Keir preached the sermon to a large and attentive audience.'[24] Wright went on to say how on the following Sunday he 'continued the work commenced on the Tips. A smaller but better audience; they wanted me to take up the work as a regular thing, weekly.' Of course, giving a religious character to political meetings on a Sunday may have been no more than a way of circumventing laws which would have prevented them, but it seems there was more to it than this. Many in the Labour movement believed that its roots ran deep, as deep as the Sermon on the Mount, and had enough respect for religious traditions not to disregard them in places where they were strong, and where sections of the working class still took inspiration from them.

In general, the leadership of the ILP responded positively to the development of socialist support within the churches, and in the late 1890s was encouraged by the formation of a number of Free Church socialist societies. In 1894, under the leadership of John Clifford, a distinguished Baptist minister and active member of the Fabian Society, the Christian Socialist League was formed out of The Ministers' Union, which declared that 'this country cannot accurately be called Christian so long as people in their collective capacity, by their social, industrial and commercial arrangements, practically deny the Fatherhood of God and the brotherhood of man'. Christ's teaching is 'directly applicable to all questions of sociology and economics', said the union. The union's president was Clifford; its vice president, J. Bruce Wallace, a Congrega-tionalist; and its secretary, J. H. Belcher, a former Congregationalist who had become Unitarian. The Union, under its openly socialist title of Christian Socialist League, (adopted by an almost unanimous vote), cut across denominational boundaries and co-ordinated Nonconformist support for the Labour movement between 1894 and 1898, during which time a number of important Free Church ministers left the Liberal Party and joined the ILP, including Dr. Charles Leach.[25] More sectarian was the Quaker Socialist Society (1898), which included Arthur Tuke Priestman, the prominent Bradford Quaker and socialist, and the New Church Socialist Society (1895),[26] whose journal, *Uses*, was edited by T. D. Benson. In November 1898 Priestman and Benson accepted the National Administrative Council's invitations to serve as trustees of the ILP Election Fund, and Benson eventually became treasurer of the ILP.[27] The denominational societies had limited influence on the Labour movement and were mainly concerned with trying to convert the members of their churches to socialism. The title of an article, 'The Building of the Bridge', which appeared in the organ of the New Church Socialist Society in 1898,[28] epitomizes the efforts being made by sympathizers within the churches at this time, to which many ILP leaders were pleased to respond encouragingly.

The relations between the Labour movement and sections of the Nonconformist churches, which seemed to be developing harmoniously as the nineteenth century drew to a close, suffered serious disruption in January 1903, when, in the *Clarion*, Robert Blatchford delivered a devastating onslaught on religion as part of a review of Haeckel's *Riddle of the Universe*, declaring that 'the book demolishes the entire structure upon which the religions of the world are built. There is no escape from that conclusion. The case for science is complete.'[29] The verdict incensed the largely northern readership of the paper, many of whom had strong associations with the Nonconformist churches. For a whole year the columns of the paper were filled with criticisms, including those of prominent socialist Nonconformist ministers, T. Rhondda Williams, R. F. Horton, S. E. Keeble and R. J. Campbell.[30] Some protested more in sorrow than in anger that the Labour movement should be so divided. A *Clarion* contributor, the Rev. Cartmel Robinson, wrote to Alex. Thompson (Dangle), 'Can you not prevail on Blatchford to cut this controversial wreckage loose and let it go? I am for Unity, but if it is on condition that I apostasize, then – !'[31] And Thompson could see why hundreds of the paper's readers shared Robinson's distress: 'Many leaders of Labour, especially amongst the Trade Union officials, had been local

88

preachers; most of them were more deeply rooted in Christianity than in Socialism.'[32] But Blatchford was unrepentant and reiterated his argument in a book, *God and my Neighbour*, which was followed by a series of articles entitled *Not Guilty or the Bottom Dog*, in which the theory of Determinism was pressed further. The *Clarion* staff was not altogether out of sympathy with religion, if it was of a Rationalist kind. Blatchford had co-operated with John Trevor when he founded the Labour Church, by speaking at Labour Church Services and advertising services free of charge in his paper. He had joined with Labour Church members to form a Sunday school in connection with one of his Cinderella Clubs, the aim being that 'it should be a place where children can be trained to think and not merely become Socialists or Labour Church members.'[33] But it was a conception of religion too progressive, at this stage, even for those who later became the leaders of the New Theology movement. For conventional Christianity the *Clarion* staff 'proposed to substitute a theology of Socialism, based on the expansive humanity of the Carpenter of Nazareth.'[34]

In the light of the subsequent theological developments in 1907, when Campbell and Williams were saying similar things under the banner of the New Theology, it is surprising that Blatchford caused such a furore, but even the more progressive elements in the churches were not ready for it and took more exception to it coming from someone outside organized religion than they might have done had it come from within. However, although in the short term relations between Labour and Nonconformity were seriously disturbed by Blatchford's outspoken rejection of religion, the conflict was widely reported and discussed, and questions of the affinities between the two movements were constantly brought to the attention of the Labour movement and the churches over a period of two, or more years. In the long term the '*God and my Neighbour* affair' probably did more to bring Labour and Nonconformity together than to separate them. Blatchford, at this time, was not only out of favour with those in the churches, but his attitude to the Boer War had not helped him in the Labour movement. Because he was not particularly interested in party organization, he was losing touch with the LRC leadership, amongst whom were some who saw that no advantage could be gained from being at odds with potential Labour voters who, whilst they might not be active in chapel life or agree with Nonconformist opposition to Labour representation, were sufficiently fair minded to admit that they owed much to chapel culture. This was particularly true of the strongly Nonconformist industrial districts, like Lancashire, the West Riding and South Wales, where Labour had most chance of an electoral breakthrough.

While Blatchford was alienating potential Nonconformist voters, other Labour leaders were courting the Liberal Nonconformists, and none more skilfully than one of the party's most outstanding propagandists,

Philip Snowden. Born in 1864 at Cowling, a West Riding weaving village situated only four miles from the Lancashire districts of Nelson and Colne, as a child Snowden 'witnessed the vigour of non-conformity, its Radical politics, its temperance zeal, its emphasis on self-improvement' which left a profound mark upon him as 'a life-long temperance enthusiast, attached to Radical icons, most notably Free Trade'.[35] He began work as a pupil-teacher and went on through an insurance office to become an Inland Revenue clerk, but in 1891 an illness left him crippled and unemployed. With time on his hands, Snowden became involved in the debates which surrounded the formation of the ILP in Bradford, and having been recruited by local Liberals to argue their case, he was converted to the views of his opponents and became a leading ILP propagandist, who, more than any other, adopted the style of an evangelical preacher. His likeness to the serious bearers of a redemptive faith of bygone days was recognized by a contemporary who described a 'frail figure, the grave firm features, the thin sensitive lips, the piercing eye, the somewhat ascetic kind of face – all go to make up a personality which may not have been rare in Puritan or Covenanting days, but which is all too seldom met with in our time.'[36]

When asked by W. T. Stead for his article, 'Books that have made the Labour Party', in 1906, Ethel, Snowden's wife gave his religion as Wesleyan.[37] But there seems little doubt that he abandoned his parents' formal attachment to Methodism at an early age, possibly soon after reaching the age of eight, when he failed to have a conversion experience at an evangelical meeting.[38] Writing for the *Labour Prophet*, the journal of the Labour Church movement, in 1898, Snowden described how this had led him to see the necessity for two salvations. He believed 'salvation from hell for original sin is getting out of date. With another generation of School Board education it will disappear altogether.' There needed to be personal salvation and social salvation, and they 'are like two palm trees which bear no fruit unless they grow side by side'. The individualistic faith of the churches had confined itself to the preaching of personal salvation as the cure for worldly ills, and 'it has done nothing, unless by accident, for the social amelioration of the people'. Yet he had 'seen everywhere men upon whom the principles of Socialism have had a remarkable effect in raising their personal character. Socialism has regenerated them in the truest sense'.[39] This type of commitment had given birth to the Labour Church movement, as a reaction to the individualism of the Nonconformist chapels and their preoccupation with personal salvation for a future life. But, although he appears to have abandoned the narrow theology of his childhood at an early date, Snowden retained strong local ties, and living for some years in Nelson, he courted and married Ethel Annakin, a local Wesleyan Methodist Sunday School teacher.[40] Here, where religion and temperance underlay all social and cultural life, Socialists were, *ipso facto*, compelled to adopt a positive attitude towards both. In doing so, in 1903, the same year as the *Clarion* was disrupting relationships between the Labour movement and Nonconformity, the ILP published a lecture by Snowden entitled *The Christ that is to be* under a text from Tennyson's *In Memoriam*:

> Ring in the valiant man and free,
> The larger heart, the kindlier hand;
> Ring out the darkness of the land,
> Ring in the Christ that is to be.[41]

The lecture is the most positive expression of the emergent Labour movement's attempts to win the support of Nonconformists, and in the range of its appeal is a remarkable example of Snowden's skill as a Labour propagandist. It includes theological ideas and religious terminology that would have appealed on the one hand to the liberal, near agnostic, and to the narrowly Evangelical nonconformist on the other. Snowden opened with a strong immanental bias. 'The life of Christ is the great example of human perfection'.[42] Despite all the inadequacies of the Christian Church and its role as 'the slave of rich men, and admitting every count in the indictment which the anti-Christian can bring against the Church', there still remains 'the great and potent fact that Christ has been the greatest influence in the world's history'.[43] This particular point would have had special appeal for those Lancashire and West Riding workers, who, whilst they did not recognize much true Christianity within the churches, and had ceased to attend, except for the so called rites of passage – baptisms, weddings and funerals – nonetheless continued to understand ethical behaviour in terms of Christ's teaching.

Snowden, from his own knowledge of the strongly Nonconformist textile districts, clearly recognized that working-class rejection of the churches did not mean that they had rejected religion. His estimate of Christ as differing 'in degree but not in kind from all great teachers' may not have satisfied some, but it was tempered by the qualification that 'in the life of Christ we find ... principles and truths more fully stated than in the life and teachings of any other master.'[44] Christ's law of sacrifice, love and cooperation is the foundation of all the great ethical religions of the world and of all schools of morality, and there is 'a sense in which all – Christian, agnostic and atheist – can accept him as a teacher able to make us wise unto salvation.'[45] United by this fact, 'the religion of the future will recognise ... the complete organic unity of the whole human race. And this religion will be a political religion ... which will seek to realise its ideal in our industrial and social affairs by the application and use of political methods.'[46] All this would certainly have appealed to theologically progressive Nonconformists, whose commitment to socialism was gradually developing. It could not have had much appeal for the Evangelicals, whose all sufficient scheme of redemption was based on the uniqueness of Christ, and who rejected politics. Yet, for all its progressive theological outlook, *The Christ that is to be* ends with Snowden expressing the socialist vision with a religiosity that would have appealed to Nonconformists at home with the terminology of an Evangelical revivalist meeting: 'the only way to regain the earthly paradise is by the old, hard road to Calvary – through persecution, through poverty, through temptation, by the agony and bloody sweat, by the crown of thorns, by the agonising death. And then the resurrection to the New Humanity – purified by suffering, triumphant through Sacrifice.'[47]

In the scope of one lecture, Snowden, with his outstanding propagandist skills, had achieved the almost impossible task of appealing to the broad spectrum of Nonconformity. And nowhere was this kind of material more useful than in pressing Labour's cause in the industrial districts where Nonconformity was intricately intertwined with all aspects of the local culture. The pamphlet's importance for the relations between Nonconformity and the early Labour movement has been widely recognized although its significance is partly missed by Jones who incorrectly attributes it to 1905, when in fact it was printed at Keighley in 1903. The earlier date not only suggests that Blatchford's onslaught on religion was not shared by important Labour propagandists, but also that the theological basis of R.J. Campbell's 'New Theology' movement, which emerged after 1904, was, even as early as 1903, the view of religion held by some Labour leaders, who believed electoral advantage could be gained by cultivating the common ground.

Labour pioneers may have used religious terminology naturally, given that they often had backgrounds in Nonconformity, but it seems more likely that in most cases they deliberately adopted it as a vehicle to carry the socialist message to the strongly Nonconformist areas. The effectiveness of Snowden's 'Come to Jesus' technique was widely recognized amongst propagandists. In the 1890s the chairman of a meeting at Wibsey, near Bradford, is said to have instructed his speaker, Fred Bramley, later secretary of the TUC:

> Now look here Fred. Tha' knaws they're an ignorant lot at Wibsey, so don't be trying any of that scientific socialism. We want no Karl Marx and surplus values and that sort of stuff. Make it plain and simple. Tha' can put in a long word now and then so as to make them think tha' knaws a lot, but keep it simple, and then when tha'rt coming to t'finishing up, tha' mun put a bit of "Come to Jesus" in, like Philip does.[48]

Victor Grayson, a former student for the Unitarian ministry, also made effective use of biblical imagery in his political speeches when he successfully contested the Colne Valley seat in 1907; and when he was defeated in 1910 it was by another Nonconformist preacher, Dr. Charles Leach, who had returned to the Liberal Party from the ILP. In the 1907 by-election campaign Grayson had received support from a number of clergymen and Nonconformist ministers. The editor of the local paper complained that 'The presence in the valley of men wearing the habiliments of the cleric may have had some effect on the election, but it will have more on the church. There is surely something lax in an institution when men ostensibly devoted to spiritual matters can so forget themselves as to promenade a town with a big red banner on which is "Socialism is God's Gospel for today". We know of no other place where the presence of these men would be tolerated – a prostitution of their high calling to associate God's gospel with modern Socialism.'[49] It would appear that candidates with backgrounds in Nonconformist preaching had a particular appeal in those constituencies where chapels and their ministers played an important part in the local culture, particularly amongst the somewhat isolated townships of the West Riding.

That these sympathetic approaches by the Labour movement did lead to an influx of Nonconformists into the Labour movement is suggested by a resolution of the National Administrative Council, in October 1904, under the heading 'Hymn Book', that 'J. Bruce Glasier compile a Songbook for the use of the Party and that T. D. Benson, I. O. Ford and Philip Snowden compile a song sheet'.[50] The idea was not new. The first edition of the Labour Church Hymnbook, published by John Trevor in September 1892, had a run of 10,000 copies, and more were needed before the end of the year. A second edition was published in 1898. As the Labour Church had only 54 congregations at the peak of its expansion in 1895, and because, with the exception of Manchester and Bradford, each with about 300 members, the membership of Labour Church congregations was small, it is clear that the Hymn Book was used more widely than for Labour Church services, by ILP branches and for other Labour movement gatherings. The Rev. Aubrey Martin, whose father was secretary of the Gorsemoin ILP branch, South Wales, just before the 1914 war, recounts that the first English hymnbook he ever saw was the Labour Church hymnbook.[51] One explanation of the need of a hymn book may be the choice which had to be made between attendance at church and participation in Labour movement meetings, most of which were held on Sundays. If it had been possible, some Nonconformists who were attracted into the work of the Labour movement might have preferred to continue to worship in their chapels, but sooner or later a choice had to be made, and the hymn, reading and prayer before the ILP branch meeting provided a truncated form of Sunday observance. K. D. Brown has drawn attention to Pierson's conclusion that Labour leaders in the West Riding of Yorkshire tended to abandon their church activity once they became involved in the Labour movement, though they were inclined to regard both in the same light – as a sort of moral crusade.[52]

However, because of their livelihoods, ministers could not so easily make a choice between church and party, although a few did. For example, the Rev. F. R. Swan, the Congregational minister at Marsden in the West Riding of Yorkshire, resigned his charge in 1907 to become a full-time speaker for the Colne Valley Labour League, which was followed by a further three months as full-time registration agent in Colne Valley. Swan became minister at Marsden in 1899, after studying at Paton College, Nottingham. The early years at Marsden appear to have been unexceptional, although by 1903, a member of the congregation had described him as 'a man before his time'.[53] Soon afterwards he became active in the New Theology movement, publishing a book entitled *The Immanence of Christ in Modern Life*,[54] and becoming the first organizing secretary of R. J. Campbell's Progressive League. But it was his increasing involvement in local politics that disturbed his congregation, although his marriage to Amy Cawthron, the daughter of a local confectioner, had not pleased them either.[55] In January 1907, Swan presided over a meeting on the 'Womens Movement and Socialism' addressed by Mrs. Pankhurst.[56] Later that month, as Grayson was being selected as candidate for the Parliamentary bye-election caused by the elevation of the sitting Liberal MP, Sir James Kitson, to the peerage, Swan chaired a mass meeting held in the Marsden Mechanics' Hall, under the auspices of the local Socialist party. A resolution was moved by Harry Tinker, 'that this meeting pledges itself to do all that lies in its power to vote for men to be sent to the House of Commons who will legislate for economic and industrial freedom for the voters'. In proposing the motion, Mr. Tinker said that it was the first time he had stood on a Socialist platform and 'some people thought that a Christian worker was overstepping the mark in supporting Socialism, but he believed it was a question of the future and they would have to face it'.[57] The following day, 27 January 1907, the minister announced his resignation at evening service, having informed the Deacons of it during the previous week. The conclusion must be that Swan wished to be free from all constraints to campaign for Grayson. The congregation did not ask him to reconsider his decision, as was customary in Congregational chapels, but accepted the resignation, 24 votes for, 6 against, 4 neutral;[58] 'they were glad to see him go'.[59] Yet the large crowd that gathered for his farewell service, when the back of an upstairs pew was damaged with the crush,[60] suggests he was popular in the district. Eventually for many years until his death in 1938, Swan was treasurer of the *Daily Herald*.[61] But generally, Nonconformist ministers tended to play a supportive, rather than an active role in Labour movement activities because they were severely limited by their Sunday duties. When J. H. Belcher, the former secretary of the Minister's Union, wrote from the Unitarian Church, Treville Street, Plymouth, to J. Ramsay MacDonald offering his services as an LRC candidate, he received the reply 'you are, of course, heavily handicapped because you cannot give us Sundays'.[62] The difficulties of transferring loyalties from chapels to the Labour movement did not go unnoticed, and by the publication of song sheets and the provision of a substitute for religious worship at the opening of meetings the transference was made a little easier.

The readiness of some Labour leaders to express their Socialism in the language of the chapels was an important factor that helped to bring the two movements closer together by 1905. Influences also developed which attempted to reconcile the old doctrines with the new social thought and suggested that Socialism was not as incompatible with chapel membership as Liberals liked to argue. For example, Campbell's 'New Theology' sought to widen the social content of religion. The movement had a strong influence in Wales where, coupled with the Religious Revival of 1904–5, it led not only to the invigoration of the devotional life of the chapels, but to concern for social questions broader than the traditional ones of Education and Disestablishment. Whilst, with the exception of John Clifford, English Baptist ministers showed less interest in the Labour movement than the other denominations, some of their Welsh colleagues were prominent among the pioneers of the Labour Party. The Rev. William Saunders of Pontycymer was for many years one of the most influential members of Glamorgan County Council, as was the Rev. Deywell Thomas, the English Baptist minister at Neath. The Rev. Herbert Morgan, who was for a long period Director of Extra-Mural Studies at University College, Aberystwyth, was one of 'the leading Socialist thinkers and a Modernist theologian.' The Rev. Daniel Hughes, minister at Calfaria Welsh Baptist chapel, Llanelli, was a well-known member of the ILP, whose Socialism produced a reaction when he moved to the English Baptist Church, Crane Street, Pontypool, which was 'full of solicitors, etc.' Hughes was allowed plenty of time to campaign on behalf of Welsh Disestablishment, but when he began to do propaganda work for the ILP, the congregation secured an injunction and locked the chapel door against him. His breaking of the lock with a sledge hammer did not improve relationships with the staunchly Liberal and respectable membership and he moved to the more tolerant Baptist Church at Machen, Monmouthshire, but apparently without the approval of the denomination, since his name ceased to appear in the Baptist diary. He served for many years as a Labour member on Monmouthshire County Council.

In industrial South Wales, where Liberal coalowners were prominent members of town chapels, a similar attempt to silence a minister's forthright expression of his socialism occurred. The Rev. Simon Jones moved from Pontypridd to the Unitarian Chapel at Swansea and was offered, by a coalowner, an increased stipend if he did not support the Labour movement. In the same church opposition to emergent socialism coloured relationships for many years. The Rev. R. J. Hall, who ministered there from 1922 to 1930, had the door slammed in his face by a woman member because of his political activities.[63] There were, however, congregations where active participation in the Labour movement was accepted and even encouraged, without serious divisions.

For a few years, between 1904 and 1907, an active member of a newly-formed Unitarian cause at Aberystwyth was David Ivon Jones. Brought up amongst Calvinistic Methodists, he joined the Unitarians under the influence of the Welsh Revival of 1904 and became secretary of the Aberystwyth meeting house in 1906. He has been described as a Christian Humanist, indeed 'more of a Humanist than anything else', and he always stressed the social and economic implications of the teachings of Jesus. Jones suffered from tuberculosis and was advised to emigrate to a more congenial climate for his health's sake. In 1906 he went to New Zealand, then in 1913 to South Africa. Having joined the Labour Party, he later became active in the Marxist wing of the international Labour movement. An unrelenting opponent of imperialism, he became secretary of the War on War League which was formed in 1914 and the editor of its journal, *The International*. Disillusioned with its pro-war attitude Jones left the Labour Party in 1915 to become one of the founders of the International Socialist League, the fore-runner of the South African Communist Party which was formed in 1921. He was elected to represent the South African Communist Party in the Communist International, and came into close contact with leaders of the international working class-movement, including Lenin. When his health deteriorated further, he was sent to a sanatorium in the Soviet Union where he died on 31 May 1924 and was buried at Norodevichye Cemetery, Moscow.[64] Pro-socialist ministers and laymen like David Ivon Jones could not have escaped the notice of Labour leaders, who, up to a point, were ready to co-operate with allies in the churches. Their views often provoked conflicts in chapels and denominations overwhelmingly Liberal in their political allegiance,

Moreover, the Labour leaders must have been encouraged to cultivate closer relationships with the churches because of the strong influence which Socialism appeared to be having during the first decade of the century upon those who were to be the next generation of Nonconformist ministers. Under the influence of the currently fashionable liberal theology, which emphasized the centrality of the Kingdom of God, to be realized on earth, theological students were apt to see no demarcation between religion and politics, and to anticipate the fulfilment of religious aspirations in political processes. This was particularly true in the denominations which most readily accepted modernist theological ideas. Theological students were inclined to adopt either political or ministerial careers as opportunities proved favourable and advantageous. It was not a question of choosing between religion or politics, for they regarded the two spheres as all of a piece.

Victor Grayson was a student at the Unitarian Home Missionary College, Manchester, from 1903–07, and resigned from the course only shortly before winning the Colne Valley seat as Labour candidate, without the support of the LRC, in the by-election of 1907.[65] Grayson was politically active whilst a student and influenced his fellow students, particularly S. E. Bowen, James Glynne Davies and D. R. Davies. Bowen described how they used to unlock the door of the college after it had been shut for the night to admit Grayson when he returned from speaking at ILP meetings. D. R. Davies eventually became minister of a Congregational church at Southport where he 'filled the place with left-wingers'.[66] After R. J. Campbell's return to the Anglican Church and his 'Pioneer Preachers' had been taken over by the Unitarians in 1911, the Unitarian Home Missionary College became the destination for the majority of the Pioneer Preachers on their way to careers as Unitarian ministers. But, whilst the Unitarian churches tolerated their political views, (they had always provided freedom for the expression of radical opinions), they can hardly be said to have embraced them. Students at Manchester College, Oxford, were also politically active in support of Labour, and R. V. Holt, later to become Principal of The Unitarian College, Manchester, was responsible for making arrangements for Keir Hardie's visit to the University of Oxford in March 1909.[67] The Labour movement must also have noticed that the Free Church Council, which had been formed in 1892 to represent the interests of Evangelical Nonconformity, was becoming more concerned with social reform, and in 1906 this led to the the Council's Social Questions Committee proposing a Scheme of Social Reconstruction pleading for a number of necessary and urgent reforms.

The rapprochement between sections of Labour movement and the Free Churches was, therefore, sufficiently close in 1905 for the ILP's National Administrative Council to expect that it might secure the co-operation of local Free Church Councils for a demonstration on behalf of the unemployed, which was to take place simultaneously in London and the provinces on 24th June. The Rev. R. F. Horton's Presidential Address to the annual conference of the National Council of the Evangelical Free Churches held in Manchester 'made reference to the relation of the Churches to the Working Classes and expressed an anxious desire that something should be done to bring the Churches into closer touch with the masses'.[68] The National Administrative Council must have been encouraged to seek the aid of the churches by these sentiments.

In July 1905, the National Council of the Evangelical Free Churches made a further response to this Labour initiative by arranging a special conference of the General Committee of the Council to meet repre-sentatives of working men's organizations. In his invitation to Ramsay MacDonald, the secretary of the Labour Representation Committee, the Rev. Thomas Law, secretary of the Council, said that 'some members of Parliament who are working men leaders have already consented to be present and take part', and that 'the conference will be perfectly private so that there can be free and frank expression of opinion on all matters'.[69] MacDonald's replies, however, illustrate the ambivalence with which even the section of the Labour movement most sympathetic to co-operating with the Free Churches, the ILP, viewed relations between

Labour and the Churches at this time. He was of the opinion that conferences were 'not particularly profitable because what we want to do is not meet and take part in something that is half conversation and half a speech, but rather, in much smaller gatherings, we should discuss certain underlying principles... Given a common outlook and understanding and all the rest will follow, but unless we have that common outlook sympathy may be professed and fine things said and done, but there will still be a want of organic relationship between us.'[70]

MacDonald's request for a list of those who would be attending the conference suggests that he had reservations about appearing in public with any labour and trade union leaders who, because of their associations with the Liberal Party, blurred the image of the Labour movement as an independent political force.[71] But the main uncertainty about the usefulness of co-operating with the Free Churches rested upon the imperialist stance taken by prominent Free Churchmen during the South African War. 'I might say', wrote MacDonald, 'that one of the reasons why I have almost given up hope that the Free Churches will help us very much is the attitude which your leading men, with one or two exceptions, took upon the war.' He referred to names on the letterhead of the National Council of the Evangelical Free Churches – Rev. J. G. Greenhough, R. W. Perks and Compton Rickett, MP, – and told Law 'if you seriously consider that a Christian organisation associated with these men can do anything for righteousness' sake, to say nothing of mercy's sake, I think you are very much deluded.' MacDonald doubted whether he would be able to attend the meeting because of another engagement, but if it were possible he would feel bound to say something on these lines, 'so that Free Churchman as I am by all my prejudices and inclinations, I should probably not be able to contribute anything very helpful to the discussion.'[72]

Both the churches and the Labour movement were divided over the war; Pelling's comment that it caused 'a remarkable re-alignment of friendships and hostilities among the British Socialists' can be applied almost equally to the situation in the churches.[73] By a small minority the Fabian Society decided to make no official pronouncement on issues raised by the war. It was anxious on the one hand to avoid, as G. B. Shaw said, any commitment to 'a non-Socialist point of policy', and on the other, crippling the Society by going against the tide of popular Imperialism. Blatchford, an ex-sergeant in the 103rd Fusiliers, was strongly patriotic, although his view was not shared by other members of the *Clarion* staff. MacDonald resigned from the Fabian Society for its refusal to denounce the war, and Keir Hardie was thoroughly pro-Boer, believing that 'their Republican form of government bespeaks freedom.'[74] Although Hardie's support for the Boers was extreme, the ILP was opposed to the war, and after it was over remained strongly suspicious of the Imperialist tendencies which it had highlighted. In the churches, the anti-war faction, although not always small, had difficulty in keeping the issue before meetings because of the fear that it would be a cause of acrimonious division. At a meeting of the Manchester District Association of Unitarian and Free Christian Churches, an anti-war motion put by the Rev Francis Wood was discussed after an unsuccessful attempt to prevent it by the moving of 'The Previous Question', but after a brief debate the meeting became so small that the proposer asked leave to withdraw it, and the matter was not again raised during 1900.[75]

The London Baptist Association avoided discussing the war in the autumn of 1901, for fear of revealing its divided counsels; but a leading Baptist minister, J. G. Greenhough, president of the National Council of the Evangelical Free Churches in 1901, and one of the men mentioned by MacDonald in his letter to Law, was a firm imperialist.[76] So also was the leading Methodist MP, Robert Perks, another subject of MacDonald's criticism, who was referred to as 'Imperial Perks' for his lead in organising the Liberal imperialists.[77] The prevailing Nonconformist response to the war is explained by a general growth of nationalism and racialism, which was intensified by British support for the Americans in the Spanish-American War of 1898, and a belief that the extension of British rule would benefit the human race. Three quarters of the Wesleyans are estimated to have supported the war, and in July 1901, only four of the 94 ministers serving Liverpool circuits opposed it.[78] In spite of some strong opposition, such as that of S. E. Keeble, the Methodist socialist, Nonconformity as a whole was seen to endorse the imperialism that fuelled the war. As a result, the ILP, which had so strongly opposed it, was unlikely to be very ready to take up suggestions from the churches for closer co-operation, at least at official level, and this was an important fact determining the nature of the rather cool relationship of the Labour movement to the churches in the early years of the twentieth century.

Nonetheless there is evidence which suggests that during 1905 an attempt was made to forge an alliance between the Labour movement and the Free Churches. It was resisted by members of the Social Democratic Federation, which had consistently opposed all co-operation with the churches, even in North-East Lancashire. For here, unlike the ILP, SDF branches developed in complete isolation from the local Nonconformist culture, though some branches were closely linked with the ILP. The London Trades' Council (Chairman: Harry Quelch; Secretary: James Macdonald) passed a resolution in November 1905 'dissociating itself from the effort being made to bring about an alliance between the Free Church and the Labour movements. It further expresses its disgust at the methods by which the promoters of such an alliance are seeking to attain their end, and refuses to believe that secret conferences between leaders of political nonconformity and carefully selected representatives of Labour can be a step towards the social and political emancipation of the workers'.[79]

Two years later, however, under attack from the Anti-Socialist Union, it became necessary for the Labour movement to reconsider its attitude to religion, and expedient to show that it was not opposed to the churches. The appearance in parliament of the 29 Labour MPs returned at the 1906 General Election and of the Labour Representation Committee as an identifiable and independent political party was a breakthrough for socialist advance. The success was quickly followed by two sensational by-elections in 1907. Pete Curran, a militant member of the ILP, was elected for Jarrow and Victor Grayson won Colne Valley, standing as a socialist with local ILP, if not LRC, help. As a result, by the autumn of 1907, there was disquiet amongst the more conservative sections of the Liberal Party about the growing influence of Labour in organized politics. Unreasonably, it was suggested that Labour's advance would erode the moral fibre of the nation by replacing individual with corporate responsibility, by attacking Christianity, private enterprise and the structure of the family. To combat it the Anti-Socialist Union was formed in 1907.[80]

The Anti-Socialist Union believed that Christianity and socialism were incompatible ideologies and viewed with concern the permeation of the Church by socialism. It also gave considerable help to the Nonconformist Anti-Socialist Union which was formed at Baptist Church House in 1909 'to protest against the use of the pulpit for political ends, and to withstand the encroachment of Socialism and Socialistic teaching amongst the members of the Free Churches.'[81] The Nonconformist Anti-Socialist Union campaigned to persuade local authorities to impose rates on churches where ministers openly declared their support for socialism, since they regarded them as political pulpits. Its council 'would be the last to discourage Social Reform. The socialism which they assail is the Socialism which would associate the Free Churches with the National Debt, would nationalise the means of production, distribution and exchange, would abolish indirect taxation, and destroy all forms of private property, which would mean revolution.'[82] It came into existence as a response to the formation by 65 Free Church ministers of the Free Church Socialist League in 1909, under the chairmanship of the Rev. Herbert Dunnico, a Liverpool Baptist minister. And, in turn, as a reaction,[83] it led to the formation of the Sigma Society (sometimes referred to as the Sigma Club) on 15 April 1909, in which socialist Methodist ministers grouped themselves under the leadership of S. E. Keeble, when they adopted the following creed-basis:

> Believing that our Lord's teaching concerning the Kingdom of God on earth necessitates both a regenerate individual life, and a new social order, we the undersigned – Ministers of the Wesleyan Methodist Church in full connexion – avow our conviction that the promotion of a Christian civilization requires the evolutionary socialisation of the chief means of production, distribution and exchange.

Forty-two ministers appended their signatures and the membership gradually increased to 93 by November 1913.[85] What then became of it is unknown. It was perhaps a victim of the 'resentment of the Sigma Club as being a secret society which is striving to sow Socialism in Methodism',[86] in addition to the Wesleyan Methodist Union for Social Service's approach that was less party political, the advent of World War I and a recognition of the real difficulties of the members that 'very few of us could carry out a propaganda to enforce the actual words and ideals of our constituting belief.'[87]

The Anti-Socialist Union and its Nonconformist counterpart accused Socialism of being atheistic and a threat to institutions and values upon which the British way of life had rested. It encouraged emotional responses which suggested that Socialists were all atheists. A candidate at Kirkdale found himself regarded 'not only as one who denied the bible but as an advocate of free love and the state ownership of children.'[88] Under the paid and trained speakers of the Anti-Socialist Union, the smear campaign gathered momentum, and the ILP, whose stronghold was in the Nonconformist districts, had to defend itself against the absurd charges. In October 1907 the National Administrative Council agreed and issued to the press a resolution on 'family and home' in which it rejected the attack upon Socialism on the ground that Socialism is opposed to religion, and declared that 'the Socialist movement embraces men and women of all religions and of all forms of belief, and offers the most complete freedom in this respect within its ranks.'[89] It further rejected the charge that Socialism was antagonistic to family organisation, and reminded the public that the disintegration of the family, which had been in progress for some generations, was due to the creation of slums, the employment of children in factories, the dragging of mothers into workshops and factories (through economic pressure created by the low wages of men), sweating, and other operations of capitalism which the Anti-Socialist Campaign was designed to support, and which it was the purpose of Socialism to supplant. At the same meeting it was agreed that there should be a reprint of a tract entitled 'Can a man be a Christian?' Further counter-measures were adopted in 1908 when the Council agreed that Margaret McMillan, the Rev. W. G. Moll and the Rev. J. E. Rattenbury should prepare pamphlets on the subject 'Is Socialism opposed to Religion?'[90]

From the defensive position into which it was forced by the advent of the Anti-Socialist campaign, the Labour movement once again found it advantageous to draw closer to its sympathizers within the churches, if only to show to the chapelgoers that it was not subverting moral and religious foundations. But the time had passed when Labour could expect much official response from Nonconformity, which was becoming disillusioned with politics and turning again to the business of evangelism. An anonymously written work, *Nonconformity and Politics*, published in 1909 was widely discussed in chapels.[91] Probably written by H. W. Clark, Congregational minister at Harpenden, it argued that Nonconformity was becoming too political. Whilst not questioning the responsibility of individual Nonconformists to participate in politics, it suggested that political activity was secularising the Free Churches. The Free Church Council too became less involved with political campaigns after its secretary, Thomas Law, had committed suicide and been succeeded by the Rev. F. B. Meyer, whose doctrinal position is indicated by the fact that each year he attended the Keswick Convention, the annual gathering of Evangelical Christians for prayer, Bible study and addresses.[92]

The emergence of the Labour movement also meant that many Nonconformists preferred not to discuss politics for fear of disrupting the harmony of local congregations. The Free Church Socialist League founded in 1909 was an ephemeral body, and politically it came to little. The Methodist Sigma Club, whose formation had been precipitated by objections to Socialist ministers from leading Wesleyan members of the Nonconformist Anti-Socialist Union, lost the reason for its existence after the death of Lord Wolverhampton (Henry Fowler) in 1911. After the lead given by the Wesleyans in 1905, several Nonconformist denominations formed Social Unions which effectively subverted the efforts of the socialists within them by making a broader appeal on social issues. And when the Congregational Union created its own Social Service Committee in 1910, the wind was taken out of the sails of Campbell's Progressive League. In such a climate, there was little point in the Labour movement making overtures of any kind to Nonconformity during the four years before World War I.

As the independent Labour movement emerged, there were Labour leaders and Nonconformist social reformers who believed that some sort of alliance might prove advantageous. On the one hand the Labour movement needed to win over middle-class Liberal voters, many of whom where loyally attached to the Nonconformist chapels, and, on the other, the declining Free Churches were desperate to re-establish contact with the working classes. It must be emphasized, however, that these efforts to establish closer links were always variable and never resulted in anything more than the weakest of associations. Both sides blew hot and cold in fairly rapid succession. The Nonconformist backgrounds of many Labour leaders and the form which the Labour cause took as the 'religion of socialism' provided many meeting points during the 1880s. By the early 1890s, however, Labour leaders had begun to believe that the churches had turned their backs on the Labour movement and this led to the formation of the Labour Church in 1891. Yet, if the intention was that Labour would go its own way, the opposite seems to have happened, for until about 1895 sympathetic Nonconformist ministers were frequent speakers at Labour Church meetings, and Labour pioneers seized every opportunity to address Nonconformist assemblies. Then, between the mid-1890s and the early years of the twentieth century, relationships were weakened by the fact that the Labour movement was preoccupied with building up the party machine after the disappointing 1895 General Election results.

This involved the abandonment of the ILP's largely teetotal stance in favour of gaining more support within the popular working-class culture of the public house and working-men's clubs, and thus losing an area of common ground which the Labour movement had shared with the chapels. The Labour movement's concern with securing electoral success also seems to have led to the decline of the 'religion of socialism', and less use of the terminology that appealed to those whose social hopes were expressed in religious language. And at the end of the nineteenth century a further wedge was driven between the two movements by the imperialistic attitudes of prominent Free Churchmen at the time of the Boer war. In 1903, the Labour movement was in two minds about its attitude towards the churches. Blatchford, now becoming isolated from the main stream of Labour advance, completely rejected religion, whilst Philip Snowden courted Nonconformist support with his lecture *The Christ that is to be*. From the churches' side, the popularization of theological modernism in R. J. Campbell's New Theology movement suggested closer links with the Labour movement in 1904, but this had little effect on the leaders of mainstream, Evangelical Nonconformity. Yet, in 1905 the National Council of Evangelical Free Churches did make an attempt to draw closer to Labour through the holding of a conference with leading representatives of workingmen.

But Labour leaders, whilst politely co-operating by attending the conference, were not optimistic that it would lead to anything, largely on the grounds of the attitudes that Free Churchmen had taken during the Boer war, and this attempt to form an alliance was strongly resisted by the doctrinaire members of the London Trades' Council and leading SDF members. In turn, as one side attempted to draw close, the other found reasons for retreating, until, soon after 1906, Nonconformity became less interested in politics and the Labour movement more confident in itself as a growing Parliamentary force. It no longer needed the somewhat compromising support of the largely middle-class churches. The question that remains is, what was the fundamental reason for the failure of closer associations between the Labour movement and Nonconformity? The historic association of Nonconformity with the Liberal Party was clearly an obstacle, particularly in the early years, and even as late as 1906 most Nonconformist Liberals still believed that capitalist society's ills could be remedied by New Liberalism's social policies. Nonconformist attachment to Liberalism had, however, been declining, largely because of the Liberal Party's failure to deliver on such matters as Disestablishment and Education. More fundamental was the individualistic spirit of the Nonconformist evangelical majority, which believed that personal and social salvation could only be a product of personal redemption. Significantly, it was from amongst those Nonconformists who broadened their views of redemptive processes to include collective as well as individual salvation that there came most support for close links with the Labour movement. The majority of Nonconformists, however, were Evangelicals, and their theology of personal salvation did not relate easily to the Labour movement seeking collectivist solutions.

Notes

1. *Congregational Year Book*, 1891, p.70.
2. Rev. Edward White in *British Weekly*, 31 October 1895, p.20.
3. Quoted by Philip Snowden in *The Christ that is to be* (Independent Labour Party, London, 1903), p.9.
4. Independent Labour Party, National Administrative Council Minutes, 28 May 1894.
5. P. d'A. Jones, *The Christian Socialist Revival 1877–1914* (Princeton University Press, Princeton, New Jersey, 1968), p.361.
6. J. Trevor, *My Quest for God* (Labour Prophet Office, London, 1897), p.241.
7. J. Trevor to J. K. Hardie, 20 April 1895, Archives of the ILP, Series III, *The Francis Johnson Correspondence*, 1888–1950, 1895/75 (Harvester Press Microfilm).
8. J. K. Hardie to J. Trevor, 23 April 1895, Archives of the ILP, Series III, *The Francis Johnson Correspondence*, 1888–1950, 1895/78 (Harvester Press Microfilm).
9. See L. Smith, 'John Trevor and the Labour Church Movement', Huddersfield Polytechnic MA dissertation, 1986.
10. Printed as Appendix I in E. P. Thompson, *William Morris, Romantic to Revolutionary* (Revised Edition, Merlin, London, 1977).
11. G. Lansbury, *My Life* (Constable and Co., London, 1928), p.78.
12. Eleanor Marx Aveling to Council, Socialist League, 5 October 1885, in Socialist League Papers, Amsterdam, quoted by S. Yeo in 'A New Life: The Religion of Socialism in Britain, 1883–1876', *History Workshop Journal*, 4–6, 1978–79, p.6.
13. Yeo, *op. cit.*, pp. 5–56.
14. W. T. Stead, 'The Labour Party and the books that helped to make it', *The Review of Reviews*, 1906, pp. 568–582.
15. *Ibid.*, p.570.
16. K. D. Brown, 'Nonconformity and the British Labour Movement: A Case Study', *Journal of Social History*, VIII, 1975, p.116.
17. *Ibid.*, pp.116–117.
18. D. E. Martin, '"The Instruments of the People'?: The Labour Parliamentary Party in 1906' in D. E. Martin and D. Rubinstein (eds.), *Ideology and the Labour Movement* (Croom Helm, London, 1979), p.133.
19. *Ibid.*, p.132.
20. *Ibid.*, p.133.
21. Independent Labour Party, National Administrative Council Minutes, 2 January 1896.

22. Hyde, Pleasant Sunday Afternoon, Minutes, 1894–1900. (Tameside Public Library).

23. Miss D. Price, Flat 15, Llys Pedr, Lampeter, Dyfed, to L. Smith.

24. Independent Labour Party, National Administrative Council Minutes, August 1898.

25. Charles Leach to Keir Hardie, 20 August 1894, Archives of the ILP, Series III, *The Francis Johnson Correspondence*, 1888–1950, 1894/184 (Harvester Press Microfilm).

26. Jones, *op. cit.*, pp.353–367.

27. Independent Labour Party, National Administrative Council Minutes, November 1898.

28. *Uses*, A Monthly New-Church Journal of Evolutionary Reform, Vol.III, No 31, October 1898.

29. *Clarion*, 23 January 1903.

30. *Ibid.*, 1 May 1903, 17 July 1903, 23 October 1903 and 11 December 1903.

31. A. Thompson, *Here I Lie* (George Routledge and Sons, London, 1937), p.109.

32. *Ibid.*

33. Quoted by F. Reid, 'Socialist Sunday Schools in Britain, 1892–1939, *International Review of Social History*, 1966.

34. Thompson, *op. cit.*, p.107.

35. D. Howell, *British Workers and the Independent Labour Party, 1888–1906* (Manchester University Press, Manchester, 1983), p.4; See also P. Viscount Snowden, *An Autobiography* (Ivor Nicholson and Watson, London, 1934), vol.1, pp.20, 25–29.

36. *Ibid.*, p.174.

37. Stead, *op.cit.*, p.580.

38. *The Labour Prophet*, April 1898, pp.169–170.

39. *Ibid.*

40. P. Firth, 'Socialism and the Origins of the Labour Party in Nelson and Colne', Unpublished MA Thesis, University of Manchester, 1975, p.33n.

41. P. Snowden, *The Christ that is to be* (Independent Labour Party, London, 1903).

42. *Ibid.*, p.3.

43. *Ibid.*, p.5.

44. *Ibid.*, p.5.

45. *Ibid.*, p.5.

46. *Ibid.*, p.7.

47. *Ibid.*, p.13.

48. Jones, *op. cit.*, p.353.

49. *Colne Valley Guardian*, 26 July 1907.

50. Independent Labour Party, National Administrative Council Minutes, 31 October and 1 November 1904.

51. Rev. Aubrey Martin, Garwen, Rhydowen, Llandysul, Dyfed, to L. Smith, 30th June 1986.

52. Brown, *op. cit.*, p.118.

53. Marsden Congregational Church, Minutes of Church and Congregation, 22 April 1903

54. *Marsden Congregational Church Messenger*, February 1907.

55. Interview with Mrs. Isobel Armitage, Crow Hill, Marsden, who was baptised by the Rev. F. R. Swan.
56. *Colne Valley Guardian*, 18 January 1907.
57. *Ibid.*, 1 February 1907.
58. Marsden Congregational Church, Deacons' Minutes, 23 January 1907.
59. Interview with Mrs. Armitage.
60. Marsden Congregational Church, Church and Sunday School Stewards' Minutes, 10 April 1907.
61. D. Clark, *Colne Valley: Radicalism to Socialism* (Longman, London, 1981), p.148.
62. R. MacDonald to J. H. Belcher, 29th December 1905, Archive of the LP, Series III, *General Correspondence and Political Records*, LRC28/13 (Harvester Press Microfilm).
63. Martin, *op. cit.*
64. I. Ap Nicholas, *Heretics at Large* (Gomer Press, Llandysul, 1977), pp.22–29.
65. For Grayson, see David Clark, *Victor Grayson, Labour's Lost Leader* (Quartet Books, London, 1985).
66. Martin, *op. cit.*
67. R. Holt to J. K. Hardie, 9 and 14 March 1905, Archives of the ILP, Series III, *The Francis Johnson Correspondence*, 1888–1950, 1909/100 and 106.
68. T. Law to J. R. MacDonald, 16 June 1905, Archives of the LP, Series III, *General Correspondence and Political Records*, LRC24/119 (Harvester Press Microfilm).
69. *Ibid.*
70. J. R. MacDonald to T. Law, 20 June 1905, Archives of the LP, Series III, *General Correspondence and Political Records*, LRC24/120 (Harvester Press Microfilm).
71. J. R. MacDonald to T. Law, 6 July 1905, Archives of the LP, Series III, *General Correspondence and Political Records*, LRC24/123 (Harvester Press Microfilm).
72. J. R. MacDonald to T. Law, 20 June 1905, Archives of the LP, Series III, *General Correspondence and Political Records*, LRC24/120 (Harvester Press Microfilm).
73. H. Pelling, *Origins of the Labour Party* (Oxford University Press, Oxford, 1965), p.187.
74. *Ibid.*, pp.188–189.
75. G. Head, 'Unitarians and the Peace Movement, 1899', *The Inquirer*, 7 January 1984.
76. D. W. Bebbington, *The Nonconformist Conscience* (George Allen and Unwin, London, 1982), p.122; J. R. MacDonald to T. Law, 20 June 1905, Archives of the LP, Series III, *General Correspondence and Political Records*, LRC24/120 (Harvester Press Microfilm).
77. Bebbington, *op. cit.*, p.122.
78. *Ibid.*, pp.122–123.
79. London Trades' Council, *Notice of Resolution Passed*, November 1905, Archives of the LP, Series III, *General Correspondence and Political Records*, LRC27/173 (Harvester Press Microfilm).
80. See K. D. Brown, 'The Anti Socialist Union, 1908–49' in K. D. Brown

(ed.), *Essays in Anti-Labour History* (Macmillan, London, 1974), pp.234–261.

81. Nonconformist Anti-Socialist Union, *Pamphlet*, 1909, S. E. Keeble archive (John Rylands University Library of Manchester).

82. *Ibid.*

83. J. E. Rattenbury to Carter, 14 February 1910, S. E. Keeble archive (John Rylands University Library of Manchester).

84. *Sigma Papers*, No.2, June 1909, S. E. Keeble archive (John Rylands University Library of Manchester).

85. *Ibid.*, No.2, June 1909, No.3, December 1909, No.4, July 1910 and No.5, November 1913, S. E. Keeble archive (John Rylands University Library of Manchester).

86. Rattenbury to Carter, 14 December 1910, S. E. Keeble archive (John Rylands University Library of Manchester).

87. W. F. Lofthouse to Carter, 21 May 1912, S. E. Keeble archive (John Rylands University Library of Manchester).

88. Brown, *op. cit.*, p.237.

89. Independent Labour Party, National Administrative Council Minutes, 4 and 5 October 1907.

90. *Ibid.*, 16, 17, 18 and 20 April 1908.

91. A Nonconformist Minister, *Nonconformity and Politics* (Sir Isaac Pitman and Sons, London, 1909).

92. Bebbington, *op. cit.*, p.80.

Chapter 5

The Reaction of the
Nonconformist Leadership:

The Debates on the 'Social Question' at Free Church Conferences

Although flimsy and fluctuating, the relationships between the Labour movement and its sympathizers within the Free Churches were at times sufficiently strong to prompt the Nonconformist leaders to table debates on the 'Social Question' into the programmes of their national and regional church assemblies. There could be no such thing as an official Nonconformist response to the Labour campaign, for Nonconformity was no more than a generic name for a diffuse variety of denominations, within several of which the independency of the local congregations made it virtually impossible for the assembly of churches to speak corporately. Nor is it possible to determine precisely how representative one denomination is of the rest. For example, although Unitarianism is historically a facet of Nonconformity, its exclusion from the National Council of Evangelical Free Churches is evidence that the mainstream Nonconformist churches did not regard it as having anything in common with their evangelical spirit. Nonetheless, a study of the annual reports of the various denominational assemblies at national and regional level does reveal the reaction of those who may be regarded as the leaders of their denominations by virtue of their election to chairmanship of national and county unions, district associations, home missionary societies and national conferences, or because they were sent as delegates to the annual or triennial meetings, which frequently occupied three or four days. Their opinions were not expressed representatively, and although they may be regarded as characteristic of Nonconformists generally, it must be borne in mind that those who had sufficient leisure to attend assemblies and conferences held over periods of three to four weekdays must have been from the middle-class sections of the churches, unless they happened to be ministers.

There is no straightforward way of studying the Nonconformist reaction to the Labour challenge by setting the denominational responses side by side, for each of the Free Churches had its own particular denominational polity. For example, at national level the Baptist and Congregational Unions and the Methodist Conference met annually, but the much smaller Unitarian body only held a triennial conference. There were differences too in the regions. Debates on social issues were confined to national conferences in the Unitarian body, and the regional associations did little more than give financial aid to weaker churches.

The far greater number of Congregational churches necessitated stronger regional organization. In Lancashire and Yorkshire the Congregational county unions were well organized by full-time secretaries and held conferences lasting three to four days. These were almost identical with the national conferences of the Congregational Union of England and Wales, and the Church's relationship with the poor and with Labour was debated frequently in the late-1880s and throughout the next two decades. It is fortunate, therefore, that, in respect of the Congregationalists, who provided the largest section of Nonconformist support for the emergent Labour movement, there is well documented evidence of reaction to Labour at the annual meetings of the Congregational Union of England and Wales, and at the annual meetings of the Congregational Unions of Lancashire and Yorkshire, where it was locally felt that the Congregational churches were less exclusively middle class.

It is clear that there is much more evidence of the attention that the Free Churches gave to the problems created by capitalism than has generally been credited by Labour historians. Nonetheless, the Free Churches appear only to have debated the 'Social Question' in so far as they were forced to do so in response to Labour pressure, and readily set the matter aside in favour of Disestablishment, Education and Evangelism when the challenge was weakest. Evangelical Nonconformity, in particular, was so preoccupied with individualism, both spiritually and economically, that it could not progress beyond a very moderate collectivism as a solution to problems of poverty and unemployment, and thus continued to put its faith in new Liberalism, rather than the Labour movement.

Wesleyan Methodism

Remarkably, the conservative Wesleyan Methodists were the first to debate the plight of the poor living in the centres of large towns, when the subject was discussed at their annual Conference in 1885. Dr. Edwards, the Methodist historian, has observed that 1885 is a convenient date to mark the decline of the movement's older conservatism and the 'beginnings of a dominant Liberalism within the Methodist Church'.[1] Under the leadership of the Hugh Price Hughes, the Forward Movement in Methodism was directing attention to the areas neglected by the comfortable, suburban middle classes in an attempt to evangelize the working classes. The Conference resolved 'that more practical interest should be shown' in their 'domestic and social' well-being.[2] It was probably taken by most delegates to mean that a measure of temporal aid was necessary if the poorest were to be elevated to a level where they could receive the spiritual salvation that evangelical religion offered them. But a bolder statement was addressed to the Methodist societies in 1887 when the Conference recommended sympathy towards the 'legitimate efforts' of the working classes 'to ameliorate their conditions'.[3] And, again, in 1891 and 1892 the Conference stressed the social responsibility of Methodism, which was given practical expression in the development of the Forward Movement, with its Central Halls ministering to the city centre working classes, long since out of touch with the middle-class customs of suburban chapel going.

But within Methodism this new-found concern about the poverty of the working classes was frequently qualified by an attempt to adopt a neutral position in respect of capital and labour, as when, in 1891, Conference declared: 'Let us protest ... against trade oppression, by master or by man.'[4] The general attitude of indifference within Wesleyan Methodism towards the social consequences of capitalism can be more correctly gauged from the fact that at the 1899 Conference, S. E. Keeble's motion 'that the study of social problems be included in the training of theological students' got no further than a committee.[5] Few Methodists still held the view of their great organizer in the first half of the nineteenth century, Jabez Bunting, who had said that 'Methodism was as much opposed to democracy as to sin',[6] but there were not many who positively favoured it, particular among the ministers. Stemming from the Evangelical Revival of the eighteenth century, with its emphasis on personal salvation, Methodism remained true to the purpose of its founder, John Wesley, to seek the redemption of the individual sinner, primarily for an eternal destiny, and only secondarily for the improvement of the human condition in this life. It was this individualism that determined Methodism's official reaction to the Labour movement's emergence, which was summed up at the Conference in 1894, only a year after the formation of the ILP: 'Our great work is to save the soul from sin, and if we can accomplish this, all other evils will naturally disappear. It is through the individual we must work on society.'[7]

Unitarians and Philip Wicksteed

A much more positive response was made at the Triennial National Conference of Unitarian, Liberal Christian, Free Christian, Presbyterian and other Non-Subscribing and Kindred Congregations in 1891, when the Rev. Philip Wicksteed, minister of Little Portland Street Chapel, London, addressed the assembly on 'The Church and Social Questions'. The way had been prepared at the previous conference in 1888 when, like the Methodists, concern was felt at the failure to attract working men, and the Rev. T. W. Freckleton read a paper on 'The Obstacles to the advancement of Free Christianity among the People' in which he drew attention to the interest which 'perhaps not less than two thirds of the whole number' of working people were taking in 'real or hypothetical alleviations of their lot, such as Co-operation, Socialism, the Management of Trades Unions, and Radical Politics' and to their indifference to the churches. He called for religion to be democratic, and suggested there would be no difficulty in attracting the poor to the churches if beds were put into the pews to lodge the homeless poor, or the buildings opened as play-houses for street children.[8]

Wicksteed, who had played a large part in the evolution of Fabian economic theory and had gained practical experience of industrial life when he was minister at Dukinfield, near Manchester, began where the earlier conference had left off, by recounting that he well remembered William Ellery Channing, the American minister, saying to an unsympathetic assembly, 'Not one of you here is living the Christian life. Not one of you *can* live it. You cannot live the Christian life save in a Christian Society. In a society reared upon or in league with the brothel and the sweating den no man can live the pure and loving life.'[9] He did not accept the saying without much qualification, but it led him to understand that there was an 'indirect responsibility for tyranny and misery'. But having dealt with the social aspects of personal life and the problems of personal morality suggested by changing social conditions, Wicksteed then turned to 'the social movements of the times', which he enumerated as: the 'eight hours' day', the 'new unionism', the 'international organisation of labour', 'State emigration', 'State regulation of shop hours', 'free education', and perhaps 'co-operation and 'consumers' leagues'; and their concrete manifestations in such phenomena as the dock and railway strikes, and the Trafalgar-square meetings. Answering the question, 'What should be the attitude of the Church towards them?', he declared 'It is as much a part of the function of Christianity to regenerate our collective as to regenerate our personal and individual life.'[10]

This was a much more balanced approach than that taken in the evangelical branches of Nonconformity, where collectivist solutions to social problems were ruled out because of the overwhelming emphasis on the regeneration of the individual. And, amongst Unitarians, Wicksteed was by no means alone in the views he expressed. Stopford Brooke, the former Anglican turned Unitarian who had been chaplain to the Queen, believed that 'the whole future of the Unitarian Body' lay 'in taking the side of the people as opposed to the privileged classes.' The Rev. A. Webster of Aberdeen, a member of the Christian Socialist Society, supported Labour Church meetings and was a leading figure in the formation of the Scottish ILP, which preceded its English counterpart. The Rev. Harold Rylett, minister at Flowery Field, Hyde, where he edited a local paper and was one-time editor of the *New Age*, was an Irish Nonconformist radical who had stood as a candidate in the Tyrone by-election of 1881, where he was fully supported by H. M. Hyndman's newly-formed Social Democratic Federation. He co-operated with Stewart Headlam of the Guild of St Matthew and was elected to the Committee of the English Land Restoration League in 1884. An advocate of Henry George's 'Single Tax' solution to the land question, Rylett supported John Trevor in the formation of the Labour Church, but was opposed to an independent political party and played no part in the formation of the ILP a year later. Herbert Vincent Mills, like Wicksteed, Trevor, Stopford Brooke and several influential laymen, was a member of the Fabian Society, and, in advance of the developments which led to the formation of the Labour Church and the ILP, he had taken steps to relieve the problem of unemployment by a communitarian experiment at Starnthwaite, Westmorland, which has already been referred to.[11] But Unitarian laymen took little part in the discussions which followed the papers on the 'Social Question' at the Unitarian assemblies. Unlike the ministers, they had too many interests vested in the capitalist system. The leading Unitarian laymen were still at this time members of the factory owning dynasties, such as the Gregs and the Ashtons, and even though they might agree with the premise that 'man is a child of God and we are all brethren', they were unlikely to accept as a practical solution Wicksteed's assertion that

> all questions of industrial organisation are to be regarded simply and without qualification from the point of view of the worker, that the employer, the professional man, the artist, the statesman, the man of science, the poet, all who do not in the strictest sense "make" their living must stand or fall by the simple test of whether they make life more truly worth living to the hewers of wood and the drawers of water.[12]

Yet, if Philip Wicksteed's speech produced a feeling that the Unitarian movement was advanced in its sympathy for Labour's aspirations, the conference was quickly disabused when Ben Tillett and Herbert Burrows, the Labour leaders, were invited to the platform to denounce the delegates' aloofness, misunderstanding, sleepiness and heartlessness. The churches had been disputing about doctrines of little or no importance and, meanwhile, they had allowed the workingman 'to be crushed by competition or starved through unfair distribution' and had said practically nothing about it.[13] The speakers left a reporter in no doubt that the movement was 'as yet out of harmony with the bulk of the working class', but with the hope that the advent of the typical 'working man' on the Liberal Christian platform was a prophecy of 'a closer relationship in a time not far off.'[14]

There was no fundamental theological reason why Unitarians should not support collectivist answers to society's economic problems. Under the influence of the Enlightenment they had abandoned the Biblical doctrine of the Fall of Man and the consequent necessity of personal Salvation, which was central to most other Nonconformist denominations. So there was not the same emphasis on the need to save individuals. When Unitarians did speak of salvation they meant a state achieved by the development of character through good works, and this had made them pioneers in the field of social service amongst the poor. But they were nonetheless committed to economic individualism. They had been the foremost supporters of the Manchester School and Free Trade and against any kind of protectionism or state interference, although in Birmingham they had supported Joseph Chamberlain's adoption of moderate collectivism for public services. The result was that although their theological liberalism permitted a much freer consideration of the 'Social Question' than was the case in other denominations, the practical outcome was little different. They were even more exclusively middle class than other Nonconformist denominations, inhibited by their concern for respectability and generally saw no reason to abandon the competitive system that had produced their wealth and given them an enviable status, particularly in municipal life. Their sense of brotherhood produced a generous philanthropy, but, except in the case of a few ministers and even fewer laymen, stopped well short of Socialism.

To many of those who supported the idea of an independent Labour movement the impossibility of securing Unitarian support was already evident as Wicksteed delivered his address. If anyone could have persuaded the conference it was someone of Wicksteed's calibre. But, in spite of the encouragement received from the address, after the Conference was over John Trevor returned home to Manchester to found the Labour Church. His first intention was that it should exist side by side with his ministry to the Upper Brook Street Free Church (Unitarian) and that he would carry his congregation with him in the formation of a working mens' church, but the hope had to be abandoned within a few months, partly because of opposition from leading members of the congregation and partly because of the rapid expansion of the Labour Church movement. Wicksteed himself accepted the need for a separate movement because reaction was so deeply rooted in the conventional churches that to make advance from within was impossible. Trevor always acknowledged that Wicksteed had prophesied the Labour Church and that 'it rested on his broad shoulders.'

Amongst the ministers who addressed Labour Church meetings, Unitarians appear to have been the most numerous, with the result that the progress and concerns of the Labour churches were well known in Unitarian circles. This proved a stimulus and the 'Social Question' continued to be a subject for addresses and discussion at denominational meetings up to 1894. At the end of October 1891, four weeks after the inaugural Labour Church service, Wicksteed preached the sermon at the annual meeting of the Provincial Assembly of Lancashire and Cheshire, taking 'The Battle with Materialism' as his subject, and suggesting that the most urgent task of religion was that of 'purifying the great labour movement.'[15] He believed that if working men were seeking to 'realise their lives simply by increasing the multitude of things which they possess', then 'the fruit of the promised land will turn to ashes in the mouths of those who pluck it'.[16] It was a view shared by many Labour supporters in the conventional churches and amongst the earliest members of the Labour Church, before Fred Brocklehurst succeeded Trevor and made the movement into little more than a branch of the electoral machine. They saw 'the labour movement as a religion, devout, earnest, self-sacrificing, lofty in its ideals, generous in its aspirations ... claiming the heritage of man for all mankind, as consecrating the body to the service of the soul, and respecting material conditions as the foundation of spiritual life,'[17] and as the party machinery was developed to achieve electoral success, they unsuccessfully struggled to preserve the Labour movement as a religious movement.

At the following Unitarian Conference in Liverpool, in 1894, the Rev. Charles Hargrove of Mill Hill Chapel, Leeds, spoke on 'The Churches and the Poor'. He argued that whilst the church could effectively work by the 'bettering of the individuals', it was a corporate body and had a duty to act as such on the social evils of the day, which he enumerated as unemployment, bad housing, and the impossibility of children growing up to be respectable citizens in conditions that bred vice. Charity was not an effective remedy and competition was denounced on the grounds that success in life does not consist in getting on above others. It was the churches' duty 'to assert and uphold and proclaim aloud the principles of the kingdom which Jesus came to announce and to found, principles diametrically opposed to those hitherto accepted by the world.' There could be 'a revolution of peaceful ideas if the Churches do their part and take the lead, and Christ heads the movement; but revolution violent and subversive if they uphold to the existing confusion and preach peace where there is no peace.'[18]

The speech was received with applause and those who took part in the discussion which followed were mainly the Unitarians who played an active role in supporting the emergent Labour movement: Charles Peach of Sheffield claimed it was not 'the Anarchist, the Socialist or the trade unionist who was dangerous to society, but those who are callous and indifferent in the recognition of the power of labour, and who fail to appreciate the real extent of the problem.'[19] John Trevor of the Labour Church described Unitarianism as 'one of the most backward of religious forces in our time. It takes the lead in religious freedom; why should it not take the lead in economic freedom?'[20] The Rev. Potter Hall of Trowbridge spoke of work he was doing amongst the weavers and agricultural workers and argued that 'the churches needed to be democratised, freed from the tyranny of the "big man". The existence of an employer of labour in the Church should not fetter the minister and the rest of the congregation in their ambition to raise the status of the workers'.[21]

Others taking part in the debate were P. H. Wicksteed and H. V. Mills. Only one speaker, the Rev. J. McGavin Sloan, of Liverpool, was hostile to the mildly collectivist sentiments expressed by Hargrove. In an impassioned speech 'he denounced, as an individualist, all movements towards State Socialism.' He also took an attitude hostile to the Labour Church, and said that more money and leisure for the workers would mean more drink and immorality. Further he protested against the claim that Unitarian ministers and churches were engaged in a propaganda of the principles of State Socialism.[22] But Mr. Sloan need have had little anxiety on the last count, for this was to be the last year that Unitarians, like all other denominations, were to consider Social Questions until the early years of the twentieth century. After 1895, they returned to consider more internal issues, and occasionally Disestablishment and Education, the reasons for which will be considered later.

The Congregational Union of England and Wales

The pattern of concern for problems of unemployment, poverty and slums was virtually the same amongst Congregationalists as amongst the Unitarians. Throughout the 1880s the annual reports of the Congregational Union of England and Wales reveal an increasing involvement in social and economic questions, stemming from a realization that something had to be done if the churches were to re-establish contact with the urban working classes. In 1883, the London Congregational Union published Andrew Mearns' *Bitter Cry of Outcast London* to advertise its missionary work in the slums. Amongst the older conservatives, who held that poverty was necessary in order that Christians might do good works of charity, it made little impression, but they could not altogether ignore it. One of them, Joseph Parker, who was chairman of the Union in 1884, expressed his lack of sympathy with it when he declared: 'I cannot but feel that the world would be poorer but for its poverty ...', a remark which was cited by Philip Snowden, when, in 1903, he attempted to win over Nonconformity for the Labour cause in his pamphlet *The Christ that is to be*.[23] The sometimes heated discussions between those like Parker and the few more socialistically-minded ministers generally led to compromise resolutions, such as that passed in 1885:

> That this Assembly, while deprecating all action that would lessen the sanctions of the rights of property, and recognising the conditions which at the present time control the markets both of labour and material, affirms it to be the duty of every Christian citizen to seek by all means in his power to diminish the inequalities which unjust laws and customs produce in the conditions of those who are common members of the State; and further, it calls upon every Christian man and woman to remember that the so-called laws of trade and economics are not the only rules which should direct the transactions of manufacturers, traders, labourers and purchasers.[24]

In 1886, however, a year of massive unemployment, labour demonstrations and street disturbances, the Congregational Union meeting in the autumn failed to acknowledge that the churches had any responsibility by declaring that:

> No great public question in which the interests of the Churches or of national morality were involved, has during the year called for the judgement of the Committee. Political issues of first rate importance have been before the nation, but these ... had no direct bearing on the position and work of the Churches, or on the interests which the Union is set to protect.[25]

Nonetheless, social questions were kept before the Union by a minority who were sympathetic to Labour's interests. For example, in 1887 the Rev. W. Whittley, a member of the Christian Socialist Society, preached a sermon in which he asked, 'What is the use of preaching patience to toiling and suffering ones? It is unnatural! It is brutal! Tell them to have patience only when you are busy trying to strike off the fetters.'[26] The Union heeded him sufficiently for a Social Questions Committee to be formed in 1890, and James Keir Hardie was invited to address a session of the assembly when it met in Bradford in 1892, when momentum was gathering for the formation of a national independent Labour party. Speaking on 'The Church and the Labour Problem', Hardie, much heckled, told the delegates that the Labour movement had turned its back on the churches because the churches had turned its back on them.[27] It was an assertion confirmed locally that year when F. W. Jowett was refused permission to speak in support of independent labour candidates at a meeting of the Bradford Nonconformist Association.

The fracas over Keir Hardie's speech to the Bradford conference highlighted the bitterness of relationships between the Labour movement and the Nonconformist churches, which were now regarded as having betrayed their traditional role of concern for the dispossessed, and it led to an attempt to redeem the situation. This took the form of a Labour Conference meeting in two sessions on 6 December 1892 and 8 February 1893, at which representatives in the House of Commons of the Labour party were invited to meet with the Committee of the Congregational Union and with the Congregational Members of Parliament. The Labour members present at the first session were J. Wilson of the Miners' Association, J. Keir Hardie and W. Randall Cremer. At the second meeting Mr. Cremer attended again, and with him was Mr. W. P. Byles.[28] The spirit of the Conference was one of mutual goodwill and the fact that the Nonconformist Churches had not been indifferent to 'the cries of necessity' was admitted by the Labour members.[29] They also recognized that, particularly in Wales, Lancashire and other industrial centres, the fact that a large part of the artisan population was included within the membership of the Free Churches was a direct consequence of the determination shown by the Churches in maintaining popular rights.[30]

The Evangelical backgrounds of the Labour delegates is no less evident than those of the Congregationalists in their agreement that 'the Gospel is primarily individualist, as requiring men to seek a personal salvation', but it was agreed that it nevertheless involves 'a distinct social responsibility' and 'cultivates individual character as the appointed instrument of social amelioration.'[31] Complaints were made that the social aspects of the Gospel had not received a sufficient proportion in the conscience of the Churches, nor in the teaching of their ministers. There was a need for direct support for those who were demonstrating to establish the relationship between overcrowding and immorality, to abolish insanitary dwellings, and reduce the number of public houses and beer shops in districts occupied by the poor.[32] In the latter case, there could be no doubt about the need for co-operation between the Nonconformist chapels and the ILP, whose leaders were committed to teetotalism, and still at that time shared the view that drunkenness was a cause of social problems, rather than a consequence.

The outcome of the Conference was a general agreement that it was neither necessary nor desirable for any Church to take up party politics, but it was contended that there were great social questions in which the Churches should show themselves to be on the side of the people and, through the Union, the Congregational churches were invited to consider the relation of the Gospel to the working population.[33] There is not much evidence to suggest they did so, or that there was any enthusiasm for the outcome of the Labour Conference. Many shared the view of the Chairman of the Union in 1890, that 'the undue obtrusion of the secular element threatens to hide Jesus Christ by confounding the Gospel with a comprehensive but material benevolence'.[34] They believed it was necessary to reassert the priority of Congregationalism's evangelical position, which the Chairman of the Union did in 1894, when he told delegates that 'they should assert the authority of Christ's law over the conscience of society', but reminded them that 'the church's first duty was to save the soul, not the body.'[35] Not surprisingly then, between 1894 and the end of the century, social issues ceased to occupy an important place on the agenda of the annual conferences of the Congregational Union, although in 1897 there was a minor resolution urging both parties in industrial disputes to go to arbitration, and in 1899 one in support of the national campaign for old-age pensions.

Lancashire and Yorkshire Congregationalism

The distinctive class structure – more artisan and less middle-class – of the Congregational churches of the industrial areas, particularly of Wales and Lancashire, had been remarked upon by those who attended the 1893

Labour Conference arranged by the Congregational Union.[36] It is a variant for which too little allowance may have been made in the evaluation of Congregational relations with the Labour movement, and it remains to be examined whether in the heartland of independent labour's advance there was any distinctive response not shared with Congregationalism generally.

Both Lancashire and Yorkshire had many Congregational chapels and strong county Unions, which held annual assemblies lasting three or four days, after the pattern of the national Conference of the Congregational Union of England and Wales. The records of these impressive gatherings suggest that consideration of social questions filtered down from national to regional level after two or three years, but that the county Unions continued to discuss them in the final years of the century in a way the national Conference did not. In other words, the cut-off point for denominational interest in Labour questions was later amongst the Congregationalists of Lancashire and Yorkshire, and less sharp.

For example, it was 1888 before the Rev. J. Todd Ferrier told the delegates to the Lancashire Congregational Union's assembly that they 'must pass from the inner circles of church life into the arenas of social and political conflict.'[37] And it was not until ten years later, in 1899, that the Rev. Dr. Charles Leach, one of Keir Hardie's converts to the ILP, who later returned to the Liberals, spoke on 'The New Century and the spirit in which to welcome it', somewhat unrealistically claiming that Congregationalists had 'passed beyond the foolish and unwise individualistic idea largely to the collective idea of the thinking of God's kingdom.'[38] His appeal for greater interest in the cause of crime, the abolition of slums and the removal of the unequal economic conditions that led to so much poverty, went largely unheeded and the following year the Chairman, the Rev. E. R. Barrett, speaking on 'The Revival of the Spiritual Life of our Churches', defended the churches against the charge of Christian Socialists that they were centres of organized selfishness, and the main obstacles to social reform. He argued that social reform was not the chief mission of the Church and that 'the world's great wrong can only be set right by those who are themselves right'.[39]

At the assemblies of the Yorkshire Congregational Union, debates similarly swung between the traditional concern for redeeming individuals and a moderately collectivist approach to social reform, but almost invariably the primary envangelical concern for the individual was expressed to qualify any standpoint that might appear too sympathetic to the Labour movement, thus satisfying Congregationalism's largely middle-class and Liberal membership. In 1887, the Chairman, the Rev. John P. James, after reviewing the social and spiritual condition of the masses, declared that the only remedy he knew was the evangelistic method.[40] Yet, two years later, in 1889, his successor, the Rev. Frederick Hall of Heckmondwike, saw the true solution of the social problems of the time in the Church's mission not to a segment of man's nature, but to the whole man – 'Man in his totality'. He told the delegates:

> We cannot then as Churches be indifferent to the social problems that crowd upon us in our time; problems which grow out of the contrast between the Haves and the Have-nots ...problems which grow out of the relations of landowner and tenant, of capital and labour, of the needs of the poor and the duties of the rich ...[41]

and went on to say:

> Our place is not in the rear, but in the van of the so-called Socialist, Social Reformer, Political Economist, and Statesman. The foremost in every forward movement should be those who have their inspiration direct from Christ. If the root principle of Socialism is doing unto others as we would that they should do unto us, then we should do our utmost to mould the Socialism of our time.[42]

The following year, 1890, a lay Chairman, Mr. Edward Sykes, stated that he did not take a dark view of strikes, unions and agitations for restricted hours, or regard all these things as signs of bad times. It would be a dark day for England if men were satisfied with things as they are. No one could rebuke as not righteous the demand for a day's work to be restricted to eight or ten hours in pits and perilous places. He did sometimes regard working-class movements with concern because the people were apt to be misled, but he did not decry all the leaders and he went on to quote Ben Tillett at length.

Nonetheless, Sykes rounded off his address by adopting the usual evangelical position: 'We welcome the efforts of Philanthropists to win back the outcast and fallen. But, after all, these efforts only touch the environment of the man, and very partially the man himself ... It is only the blessed Gospel of Jesus Christ that can remake the man.'[43] The importance of the relationship between personal regeneration and social reform was, however, discussed at a meeting entitled 'What can be done by us to reach and rescue the Submerged Tenth in our own County?', introduced by T. Rhondda Williams, at which he gave a graphic description of life in the Bradford slums.[44]

The following year, turning to the question of how far the Church should concern herself in such matters as land tenure, the Labour Movement, the social problems of the time and the true basis of international relationships, the chairman asked how the churches could fight shy of such questions without still further cutting themselves adrift from the main currents of the life of the people at large. The great and necessary thing was to let it be seen that the church was on the side of 'the right against the wrong, of liberty against oppression, of human birthrights against hoary privileges, of man against monopolies', but, and here again is the typical qualification, 'she may have, and may exhibit strong sympathies without declaring herself the partisan of any of their socialistic schemes.'[45]

With the exception of 1897, in the last few years of the century the Union's chairmen made no further references to social progress, and then it was to enunciate three conservative principles: it must be 'by slow and gradual changes', 'it is by a change in man, rather than in his circumstances, that the true secret of social regeneration lies' and 'the new man in Jesus Christ will create a new world for himself to dwell in.'[46] Such statements suggest that, although some prominent Congregational ministers expressed an interest, the Congregational movement as a whole was unsympathetic to the Labour campaign.

The Chronology of the Debates

The national assemblies of all the Nonconformist denominations vigorously addressed the 'Social Question' before 1895, but thereafter, until about 1906, it was neglected in favour of debates about education, disestablishment, spirituality and denominational policy. This is explained by the fact that up to 1894 widespread attention was drawn to the problems of poverty and slum conditions, sometimes by the unemployed themselves filing into prosperous churches during times of public worship.

The winter of 1894/5 was particularly bad and unemployment was high – up to a quarter of the population of cities like Bradford being affected. The churches could not ignore the problem without being accused of lacking any semblance of the compassion of Christ. Furthermore there were those, even amongst the Evangelicals, who felt it necessary to draw the attention of their co-religionists to the difficulties of Evangelical work amongst people so reduced in physical circumstances. Internal concern, but even more the fear of public recrimination by the leaders of the Labour movement if they neglected it, appears to have kept the 'Social Question' on the agenda of the Nonconformist assemblies until 1894.

In the 1895 General Election, however, the Labour movement suffered a crippling set-back. Twenty-eight ILP candidates had been fielded, with high hopes that Labour would be well represented in the new Parliament. In the event all were defeated, including Keir Hardie, Labour's lone voice in the Commons, who lost his seat at West Ham. In the aftermath, support for Labour fell-off as the vision of independent Labour representation receded several years into the future. In the ILP, fee-paying membership dropped from 10,720 in 1895 to 6,300 in 1896, and the total membership claimed by the national officers from 35,000 to 25,000. And if Hardie's optimistic estimation of 50,000 members in 1895 was correct, the decline of interest was even more dramatic. The Labour Church Movement also went into steady decline from 1895, until it was virtually moribund by 1902.[47]

At the movement's peak in 1895 there had been 54 congregations, but the number fell to 45 in 1895, 40 in 1897, 28 in 1898, 26 in 1899, and remained steady at about 22 or 23 between 1900 and 1902. From its formation in 1891 it was the most notable attempt to give institutional form to 'the Religion of Socialism' and as it declined, socialist propagandists less frequently used quasi-religious expressions to articulate their view of socialism, thus losing a link that had once suggested an affinity between the Labour movement and the Nonconformist churches. And after the election defeat some of the Labour leaders who had most of all goaded the Nonconformist churches to consider Labour questions went abroad on lecture tours. Thus, seeing the Labour campaign so severely depressed, the Nonconformist churches, by tradition still strongly attached to the Liberal Party, must have felt under no further pressure to respond to it. This was not, however, quite so true of the industrial areas, especially West Yorkshire, where the ILP had its base and claimed the interest of a few sympathetic Nonconformist ministers, who kept the issues before their county unions. David Clark has argued that the Labour Clubs, (a prominent feature of the independent Labour culture in strongly Nonconformist districts of the West Riding), with their permanent premises and peculiarly ethical brand of Socialism, were a crucial factor in preventing the collapse of the Labour campaign in the district after the 1895 General Election.[48] The fact that the Yorkshire Congregational Union, alone, continued to debate Labour questions in the last few years of the century can be explained by the impossibility of ignoring them altogether in towns and villages where the Labour club offered an alternative culture to that of the chapel – sometimes even a quasi-religious one if the club accommodated a Labour church meeting on Sundays.

In general, then, the Free Church assemblies tended to ignore Labour questions after the post-1895 collapse of the campaign for Labour representation, and they did not return to them until after the 1906 General Election, when, with Labour representatives now a significant force in the new parliament, the movement once again had to be reckoned with. In the intervening years, however, a number of developments kept the discussion of the churches' relationship to the Labour movement alive at an 'unofficial' level, sometimes driving a wedge between the movements, and at others drawing them closer together.

In 1903, Robert Blatchford's rejection of religion incensed many Nonconformist readers of the *Clarion* and, at first, alienated those who felt that if there had to be a choice between religious and political inclinations, their religion must take precedence. The ethically-minded readers, many of whom were members or ministers of Nonconformist chapels, were in no mind to allow that atheism was the only basis for Socialism. The overall result was probably just the opposite of what Blatchford intended, bringing Nonconformity and Labour closer together as a result of the lively correspondence that filled the pages of the *Clarion* throughout the following year.

Another factor was the religious revival which swept through Wales in 1904–5, the influence of which was felt even as far afield as West Yorkshire. A group of Colne Valley Baptists travelled to south Wales to hear the revivalist preacher, Evan Roberts, who sent a message back to Colne Valley which was read out at a local revivalist meeting.[49] Although it was essentially an evangelistic campaign, it contained an unusual social dimension and, remarkably, assimilated many of the attitudes of R. J. Campbell's 'New Theology' movement, which suggested a closer link between Christianity and the Labour movement.

Indeed, it was Campbell's espousal of Socialism and the development of Nonconformist modernism into the 'New Theology' movement that seems to have heralded the revival of interest in Labour questions at the denominational assemblies. Campbell first aroused interest amongst fellow Congregationalists by his appearance on Labour platforms from 1904 onwards, and only afterwards was he suspected of heretical views. The Lancashire Congregational Union had invited him to preach the Assembly Sermon in 1907, before they were aware of his theological position. When the theological storm broke early in 1907 there was some discussion as to whether the invitation should be withdrawn, but it was decided to let it stand. In the event Campbell preached a sermon which gave no offence to orthodoxy either theologically or politically.[50]

The ferment of the 'New Theology', however, was working, particularly in the development of the Social Gospel. In a speech marking the centenary of the Lancashire Congregational Union, the Rev. Dr. Goodrich spoke of the churches being 'avoided as the fortresses of the religious belief and social system which are the greatest barriers to the State socialism to which many people now look for social salvation',[51] and, attempting to lift the Assembly above the narrow concern for appointing a Temperance Committee, he moved, 'that it is desirable that a Congregational Social Service Committee be formed in which the temperance question, with other social questions, shall receive consideration.'[52] It was a prelude to a developing concern with issues of social amelioration which the churches could share with the Labour movement. The Assembly's Public Meeting that year was addressed by J. Crompton Rickett, MP, on the 'Congregational Churches and Labour Ideals'.[53]

Individualism versus Collectivism

In the years that followed, attitudes swung like a pendulum between mild support for collectivism and the reaction of the traditional Nonconformist individualism. In 1908, for example, the Rev. George Shillito of Park Chapel, Ramsbottom, defended the churches against Labour supporters charges that they were asleep and unaware of pauperism, the overcrowded haunts of the poor, the sordid details of the sweating systems, the ostentation of wealth, and the fact of the everlasting struggle of decent folk to keep their heads above the bare subsistence level. He was 'deeply sensible that to mention charity and the humanising of the system by voluntary individual reformation is to tap one of the few sources of humour that remain to the complete Socialist', but 'believed middle courses were not necessarily either cowardly or erroneous' and that they should not be diverted from the practice of sane and scientific charity. He also believed that 'Socialism without Christ would mean the return of the evicted devil of materialism'.[54] At the 'Public Meeting' of the same year, however, the Rev. Herbert Brook of Accrington spoke more encouragingly of the attitude of the Labour movement. Noticing the tendency in some quarters to regard it as 'already saturated with Atheism', he believed this was not the case in England, although it might be true of the Continental section of Socialism, which was a reaction against priestcraft. He was certain that 'the simple, manly Christianity of the Free Churches of this land will save the great party of Labour from Atheism.'[55] Brook also saw the possibility for closer links with the Labour movement because he did not accept that Charles Booth's declaration that 'Congregationalism is the church of the middle classes' was true for the textile regions of Lancashire and Yorkshire.[56]

The Nonconformist Anti-Socialist Union

In 1909, the formation of the Nonconformist Anti-Socialist Union at Baptist Church House and the publication of the anonymously written book, *Nonconformity and Politics*, probably by a Congregationalist, conflated to suppress the discussion of political questions at the denominational conferences. Social questions were still raised, but now with fewer references to socialism or the Labour movement. And, after the formation of several denominational Social Service unions in the wake of the Wesleyan Methodist Union for Social Service in 1905, the consideration of social issues tended to be diverted from the main debates to these sectional societies. This left the main meeting reasserting the traditional view that what the churches had to offer was the old solution, 'the regeneration of the individual, not simply the betterment of the outward environment, gladly as we help in this.' The Chairman of the Lancashire Congregational Union, the Rev. G. E. Cheesemen, admitted that 'it is not easy to purge the programme of our assemblies of political leaven' because 'some questions, apparently political, are really moral issues'. But we must put 'first things first ... A regenerated England can only result from regenerated individuals who constitute the nation.'[57] Nonetheless, that same year, a Labour leader, Will Crooks, MP, was invited to address the Public Meeting.[58]

Non-Political Social Unionism

When, in 1906, the Unitarian triennial conference again turned its attention to social issues, it was, once again, the Rev. Charles Hargrove of

Leeds who was chosen to address the delegates with a paper entitled 'The Church and the World – The Relation of Ministers and Congregations to Social and Political Questions of the Day.' Wicksteed, who might otherwise have been the appropriate choice, had, in 1897, in mid-life, retired from the ministry to devote himself to writing and lecturing. On this occasion, as in 1894, Hargrove insisted that it was the Church's duty to denounce social and moral evils, but recognizing that it was unlikely that a congregation would be of one mind about what remedy should be applied, he therefore concluded that, in his judgement, 'the office of the Church and its ministry, of each congregation and its minister' was 'not to take active part in the world's affairs, but to interfere perpetually on behalf of the Kingdom of God'.[59]

This was a very different view to the one he had expressed in 1894 when he had said that the Church was a corporate body and had a duty to act as such on the social evils of the day.[60] But it was perhaps no more than the accommodation of opinion to the reality of the situation. In the tradition of their forebears, who had been pioneers of domestic missions, public wash-houses and district nursing, Unitarians were not slow to recognize the social evils, but they risked deep divisions over whether the remedies were to be sought through collectivism or individualism, and their debates avoided this issue. The formation of their Union for Social Service in 1906 tended to subvert the intentions of ministers like Wicksteed, Stopford Brooke, John Trevor, H. V. Mills, H. Bodell Smith and Charles Peach, who would have liked to see more Unitarian support for the emergent Labour party. The union attempted to deal with social problems in a broader non-political way; but the failure to grasp the political nettle meant that its work was only on the margins of the great social issues of the day and a poor substitute for the earlier, mid-nineteenth century Unitarian social concern.

The National Free Church Council

Soon after 1906, however, the discussion of Labour questions in the denominational assemblies virtually ceased. The formation of the Anti-Socialist Union in 1907, the Nonconformist Anti-Socialist Union in 1909 and the publication of *Nonconformity and Politics* had all brought pressure on the churches to avoid political questions, although many individual church members congratulated the Labour Party on its success in 1906, just as did about 200 Anglican clergymen. The accusations that Socialism would undermine the moral fibre of the nation, although wildly untrue, made Nonconformists fearful of appearing to be identified with any aspect of Socialism. As a result, the debate about Nonconformist relations with the Labour movement moved to the broader forum of the National Free Church Council, a body which for some years had been gravely disturbed by the growing indifference of the working classes to the Free Churches and had supported several schemes of social amelioration on an inter-denominational basis.

At Blackheath in Staffordshire, free meals were provided for children by the local branch, and at Putney the Council organized a soup kitchen for the needy. At Pwllheli, where great numbers of navvies were engaged on harbour work, the Council acquired a large site and provided temporary dwellings for the migrant workers.[61] The Council's work in these fields naturally attracted the most socially progressive members of the evangelical Free Churches and it was, therefore, easier to discuss collective remedies at its conferences, than it was to raise them amongst the generally more conservative delegates at the assemblies of the separate denominations. For example, in 1906, the Council's Social Questions Committee put forward a Scheme of Social Reconstruction pleading for a number of necessary and urgent reforms, and the Birmingham meeting expressed 'the determination of Free Churchmen to support Labour in its efforts to secure better conditions for the poor and distressed.'[62] The chairman of the Labour Party, Arthur Henderson, a Wesleyan Methodist, was present at the Council's Southport conference in 1908 and made a statement of Labour ideals.[63] At the same conference, the Rev. J. Ernest Rattenbury, a Wesleyan Methodist minister, also delivered a defence of Socialism in response to the propaganda of the Anti-Socialist Union that had been formed the previous year.

He defined Socialism as a great human achievement with a passion for the masses worthy of the greatest religious zeal. He claimed that the churches should be one with Socialism in its abhorrence of modern conditions; in its view of individual life as more important than property; and in its effort to reconstruct society in terms at any rate nearer to the Kingdom of God than the prevailing ones.

Rattenbury went on to condemn the vulgar and furious attacks which accused Socialism of immoral and atheistic foundations, as worthy only of the gutter press.[64] Amongst those who associated themselves with the Free Church Council there was sufficient agreement with his views to ensure that addresses on social problems were included at conferences over the following few years, and in 1911, J. Ramsay MacDonald attended to deliver an address on the topical problem of industrial unrest.[65]

But the Free Church Council's positive attitude towards Labour was unusual. As the ecumenical body uniting the evangelical Free Churches, its support for the Labour movement did not reflect the position taken by its constituent members, and it cannot, therefore, be regarded as being representative of Nonconformity. The separate churches were not, however, as indifferent to the social problems of the capitalist system as contemporary Labour leaders tended to suggest. Labour historians have, perhaps, too readily accepted the view that the churches were unconcerned about unemployment and poverty. On the contrary, there is abundant evidence that the Churches repeatedly dealt with the 'Social

Question' in their national and regional meetings, particularly between 1880 and 1895, and again during the revival of interest in independent Labour representation which surrounded the 1906 General Election. But there were historic and contemporary reasons why Nonconformity, as expressed in its Church assemblies, did not adopt a more supportive view of the emergent Labour party.

First, its predominantly evangelical ethos made it view religious and socially redemptive processes entirely in individualistic terms, thus blinkering it from collectivist remedies; and the Unitarians, who did not share the general evangelical outlook, were nonetheless deeply rooted in the economic individualism of the capitalist system. Secondly, the assemblies were attended entirely by Nonconformists from the upper echelons of the middle classes, the employers, people with wealth and leisure, who were least likely to recognize any need to change the competitive system, and who believed its victims could be suitably helped out of their misery by charity. Thirdly, the frequent association of Socialism with immorality and atheism made Nonconformists, who were preoccupied with respectability, wary of becoming too closely identified with it. Fourthly, the historic loyalty of Nonconformity to the Liberal Party, which had relieved so many of the dissenting disabilities, made most members of the Free Churches believe that a New Liberalism, with social policies, was capable of remedying the distress without any need of a new party, and they tended to be confirmed in this view after the 1906 General Election.

In 1906, an Education Act permitted local authorities to make free school meals available for poor children; in 1907 a school medical service was begun and every rate-aided secondary school was required to keep a quarter of its places open, or free, to pupils from State elementary schools. In 1908, the eight-hour day was introduced for miners and the same year the government set up a system of old-age pensions, payable at the age of seventy. Whether such reforms were a genuine development of Liberal social policy, which took the wind out of the sails of the Labour Party, or a response to Labour pressure, is an issue on which historians are divided. Most Nonconformists, however, saw them as meeting the immediate collectivist needs of society and they, at least temporarily, revived the credibility of the Liberal Party.

Concern for social questions amongst the Nonconformist leadership was limited before 1906 and thereafter practically non-existent. It was partly a continuation of earlier mid-nineteenth century social reforming traditions, but, more importantly, it was a response to Labour accusations that the Churches were doing nothing for the poor and unemployed. The Churches debated the 'Social Question' only as the strength of the Labour challenge forced them to do so. From 1884 to 1894, social questions were raised annually at the denominational assemblies, but after Labour's failure to win any seats at the 1895 General Election, social

126

questions were not debated again until the early years of the twentieth century, when they were revived by pressures from the New Theology and Social Gospel movements. By 1906, however, most denominations had formed unions for social service, and, whilst these gave the impression of greater social concern, the effect was in fact to subordinate the 'Social Question' and remove it from the main debates. Thereafter, social questions became matters for optional and sectional interest and therefore of less concern to the leadership.

Notes

1. Maldwyn Hughes, *Methodism and England* (Epworth Press, London, 1943), p.168.
2. *Wesleyan Methodist Conference Minutes*, 1885, p.256.
3. *Ibid.*, 1887, p.304.
4. *Ibid.*, 1891, p.378.
5. S. E. Keeble, Note Book, 1909.
6. T. P. Bunting, *The Life of Jabez Bunting* (Longman, Brown, Green, Longmans and Roberts, London, 1859), II, p.112.
7. *Wesleyan Methodist Conference Minutes*, 1885, p.256.
8. *Report of the National Conference of the members and friends of Unitarian, Liberal Christian, Free Christian, Presbyterian, and other Non-Subscribing and Kindred Congregations*, 1888, p.93.
9. *The Inquirer*, 25 April 1891, p.275.
10. *Ibid.*
11. P. d'A. Jones, *The Christian Socialist Revival, 1877–1914* (Princeton University Press, Princeton, New Jersey, 1968), pp.397, 398.
12. *The Inquirer*, 25 April 1891, p.275.
13. *Ibid.*, 2 May 1891, p.283.
14. *Ibid.*
15. *Ibid.*, 31 October 1891, p.703.
16. *Ibid.*
17. *Ibid.*, pp.703, 704.
18. *Ibid.*, 14 April 1894, pp.229, 230.
19. *Ibid.*, p.231.
20. *Ibid.*
21. *Ibid.*
22. *Ibid.*
23. *Congregational Year Book*, 1885, p.63.
24. *Ibid.*, 1886, p.17.
25. Cited by Jones, *op. cit.*, p.416.
26. *Congregational Year Book*, 1887, pp.2, 25f.
27. *British Weekly*, 13 October 1892, p.401.
28. *Congregational Year Book*, 1894, p.59.
29. *Ibid.*, p.59.
30. *Ibid.*, p.60.
31. *Ibid.*
32. *Ibid.*

33. *Ibid.*
34. *Ibid.*, 1891, p.70.
35. *Ibid.*, 1895, pp.23, 40.
36. *Ibid.*, 1894, p.60.
37. *Lancashire Congregational Calendar*, 1889, p.27.
38. *Lancashire Congregational Year Book*, 1899, p.47.
39. *Ibid.*, 1900, pp.7, 8.
40. *Yorkshire Congregational Year Book*, 1887, p.19.
41. *Ibid.*, 1890, p.19.
42. *Ibid.*, 1890, p.20.
43. *Ibid.*, 1892, p.24.
44. *Ibid.*, 1892, p.26.
45. *Ibid.*, 1892, p.33.
46. *Ibid.*, 1898, pp.20–23.
47. H. Pelling, *The Origins of the Labour Party* (Macmillan, London, 1954), Appendix A, p.229.
48. D. Clark, *Colne Valley: Radicalism to Socialism* (Longman, London, 1981), pp. 117, 182, 183.
49. *Ibid.*, pp.147, 148.
50. W. G. Robinson, *A History of the Lancashire Congregational Union, 1806–1956* (Lancashire Congregational Union, Manchester, 1955), p.72.
51. *Lancashire Congregational Year Book*, 1907, p.19.
52. Robinson, *op. cit.*, p.74.
53. *Lancashire Congregational Year Book*, 1907, pp.36, 37.
54. *Ibid.*, 1908, pp.26–33.
55. *Ibid.*, p.40.
56. *Ibid.*, p.39.
57. *Ibid.*, 1909, p.34.
58. *Ibid.*, p. 59.
59. *The Inquirer*, 21 April 1906, p.253.
60. *Ibid.*, 14 April 1894, p.230.
61. E. K. Jordan, *Free Church Unity: A History of the Free Church Council Movement, 1896–1941* (Lutterworth, London, 1956), p.154.
62. *Ibid.*
63. *Ibid.*
64. *Ibid.*, p.155.
65. *Ibid.*

Chapter 6

Local Church and the Labour Movement: Four Case Studies

It was one thing for the 'Social Question' to be discussed by the almost exclusively middle-class delegates to the national and regional Free Church assemblies, where, as was said of the Unitarian triennial conference, 'working men were as rare as nightingales in Piccadilly.'[1] There, apart from the occasional harangue by an invited Labour leader, such as Ben Tillett or Will Crooks, the suggested solutions were rarely, if ever, more than what might be described as an advanced Liberalism. However, it was quite a different matter when these questions came to the fore in the more intimate context of relationships within local congregations, particularly in the Nonconformity of industrial districts which was less exclusively middle class. Here, the emergence of aspirations for independent Labour representation to pursue collectivist solutions threatened the traditional unity which was based not only on a commonly held Evangelical faith but also on a commitment to the Liberal Party. For example, when the Rev. Basil Martin, the father of Kingsley Martin, preached a sermon based on the parable which suggests that men should be paid a living wage, whether they had worked enough hours to earn it or not (Matt. 20, vss.1–16.), he illustrated it with a story of Will Crooks', about a man with a wooden leg who could only earn ten shillings a week: 'It doesn't matter that he has a wooden leg. The point is that he hasn't a wooden stomach.' When Martin said this, a 'Mr. Taylor, the coal merchant, a fat man who drove in a smart gig with his wife and children squeezed in against his broad backside, noisily walked out of the church and slammed the door in the middle of the sermon. He never came back.'[2]

Taylor accused Martin of stirring up trouble with his workmen, but there was probably also resentment of the parson's support for the newly formed Hereford branch of the ILP,[3] which, in contesting local School Board elections, threatened the influential social status of respectable Nonconformist tradesmen. Unlike the occasional meetings of the national assemblies and the district unions, in the cheek by jowl, day by day close relationships of the local churches it was more difficult to avoid acrimony when the emergence of the new democratic political force was being discussed. With employer set against employee, father against son, it is not surprising than there were resignations from chapel membership rolls. But if a local tradesman stormed out because of the pulpit utterance of a socialistic parson, it was even more likely that working men would leave the chapels because of Nonconformity's entrenched Liberalism.

If more light is to be thrown on the nature of the relationships between the Nonconformist chapels and the early independent Labour movement it must be achieved by supplementing the work of Mayor and Jones with local studies on the lines of that of Moore for the Methodism of the Deerness valley, but with respect to the branches of Nonconformity that appear to have played a greater role than Methodism, (particularly the case in the West Riding of Yorkshire and Lancashire), where the main thrust of independent Labour advance took place during the 1890s. Although there are isolated hints in the literature about the part played by local congregations in helping labour and socialist organizations to get started in particular localities, the subject has not so far been systematically investigated. In attempting to remedy this situation the focus of this chapter will be on four case studies of local churches belonging to the Independent Methodist, Unitarian, Baptist and Congregationalist denominations, situated in or close to the ILP industrial heartland.

Salem Independent Methodist Chapel, Nelson

The Clitheroe parliamentary constituency, which consisted of the industrial towns of Clitheroe, Nelson, Colne and Padiham, and the surrounding agricultural districts, was unusual in being a Liberal stronghold in an overwhelmingly Conservative Lancashire. Since the creation of the constituency by the Redistribution Act of 1885, the seat had been held by Sir Ughtred Kay-Shuttleworth, the son of Sir James Kay-Shuttleworth, the educational administrator and reformer. If popular working-class Conservatism is correctly explained by resentment of Irish immigration, the remoteness of this part of North East Lancashire from Liverpool, the port of entry, may be a reason why Clitheroe did not share the general political outlook of Lancashire. But, although within Lancashire, the constituency bordered the West Riding; unlike the cotton spinning towns to the south, its textile industry was mainly concerned with weaving and its firms were relatively small, sharing much in common with the neighbouring West Riding woollen industry.

With the rapid growth of the principal industrial towns, Nelson and Colne, immigrants had come to work in factories from the neighbouring West Riding, and from as far away as Cornwall, bringing with them radical political and Nonconformist religious traditions that reinforced a strong local radicalism.

In matters of religion the district was a stronghold of Nonconformity. In Nelson, in the 1890s, there were only two Anglican and one Roman Catholic churches, but sixteen Nonconformist chapels, representing the Wesleyans, Baptists, Congregationalists, Independent Free Gospel Methodists, United Methodists, New Connexion Methodists and the Primitive Methodists.[4] More importantly, within this broad spectrum of

Nonconformity, there were two denominations in the district which had been involved in the Chartist agitations of the 1840s – the Methodist Unitarians, whose centre was Padiham, and the United Free Gospel Methodists,[5] later to become known as Independent Methodists, with their centre at Nelson. Both were working-class churches with lay ministers, although the Methodist Unitarians were a stream of the wider Unitarian movement and might occasionally take inspiration from professional ministers who had been active Chartists. In particular there was Goodwyn Barmby, minister at Lancaster, 1853–1858, and Wakefield, 1858–1888, who was pontifarch of the Communist Church, London, between 1841 and 1847, and was said to have been responsible for the introduction of the designation 'communist' into the English language;[6] and Henry Solly, minister at Lancaster, who founded the Workingmen's Club and Institute Union, to appeal to those beyond the reach of the purely educational programmes provided by the Mechanics' Institutes.[7]

It is this particular kind of radical, working-class, democratic Nonconformity, which shared the more general Nonconformist concern for temperance, that is the key to the development of the ILP kind of socialism that was to appeal to the disenchanted Liberals of the Clitheroe constituency, enabling David Shackleton to be returned unopposed as the third Labour Representation Committee MP, in August 1902.

Salem Independent Methodist Church, Nelson, had been founded in 1852 as a United Free Gospel Church, a breakaway from the Primitive Methodist Connexion because of resentment of the authority exercised by the ministers and the circuit. Like all Methodist secessions, its formation resulted from a desire for more democratic control, rather than from any deviation from traditional Evangelical doctrines. By 1905 it was the largest church in the Independent Methodist Connexion and one of the 17 churches of the Colne and Nelson District Circuit. At that time the circuit had 1,276 members, 46 lay ministers, a Sunday School scholars roll of 4,700 and 400 people acting as teachers and officers.[8] In the 1890s the Salem Church, itself, had a membership of over 500. Its Sunday School had 600 scholars divided up into thirty or forty classes, most of whose teachers were factory workers.[9]

During the 1880s the church had met with rapid success in meeting the needs of the expanding population of the growing town. It had not narrowly confined itself to spiritual provision but had sheltered the inaugural meetings of the first Local Board, followed by the School, Water and Gas Boards, and in 1860 its members had been founders of the Local Co-operative Society. It was deeply committed to the temperance cause and peace movement, although it was not pacifist. So great was the part played in local life, that in 1893 an impressive new church was erected to accommodate the wide range of auxiliary societies connected with the church. In addition to the Sunday worship and Sunday School classes, there was a church choir needing a room for rehearsal, a glee union, a quartet party of singers, an orchestra, a minstrel group, a team of hand-bell ringers, many vocal and instrumental soloists, elocutionists, humourists and a dramatic group. There was also a weekly discussion class called The Young Men's Mutual Improvement Society, to which one must look for evidence of the role the Salem church played in the development of the local ILP group.[10]

Salem's relationship to the emergent Labour movement has to be traced from somewhat fragmentary sources, as neither the church records for the period nor those of the Nelson branch of the ILP, with the exception of the first account book, have survived. Amongst the present day members of the Salem congregation, now merged with another to form the Nelson Independent Methodist Church, there survives an oral tradition about a group of young men who broke away in the 1890s to join the local ILP. A brief reference to this fact was made in a centenary booklet published in 1952, which states that 'Salem people were Liberals and left wing Liberals at that; in the 1890s half a dozen young men, all teachers in the Sunday School, four of them showing promise as acceptable preachers, found the position too uncomfortable',[11] which may be taken to mean that even an advanced Liberalism was too constraining for them to remain in membership. It does not, however, explain that some who supported independent Labour's advance remained in membership, notwithstanding their professed difficulties.

Oral history assists with the reconstruction of the list of Mutual Improvement Society members who quit the church, even if it does not account for them all. Attracted to the Mutual Improvement Society were young men who at the turn of the century would lead Nelson's growing socialist groups. Stan Iveson, a local man active in the Labour movement (born 1912) recalled the egalitarian instincts of three brothers, Dan, William and Harrison Carradice, typical Salem members. They were immigrants from Kirkby Malham, a Dales village, where they had worked in the lime quarries:

> They were Liberals in those days .... They went to the Methodist church, and the squire was Tory and High Church. But they didn't conform. Not only did they not conform in religion, they didn't conform in many ways. Dan used to tell me a story about how they used to come down the lane, and they were expected to touch their cap t'squire. And they wouldn't. But if the road sweeper ... if he was about and the squire was there, they used to touch their hat to the road sweeper, bid him "good morning" and call him "sir".[12]

With attitudes like this it seemed only natural that the Carradice brothers and other like-minded people would be attracted to the newly-formed socialist group, even to an extent that they would throw off their allegiance to the chapel if they met resistance within it. To refer to the defection of six or so men from a congregation of over five hundred as a secession implies a greater change than actually took place, but with regard to another of the half dozen seceders, if we may call them that, the friend of the Carradice brothers continued:

> The ILP sprang out of Salem Chapel ... Jack Robinson ... originally, as a young man, was Secretary of the Young Men's Class at Salem. And they were getting that many socialist speakers coming, and listening to them, and out of the ILP, that Jack thought he might as well be in the ILP. So he dropped the Salem side. It wasn't what they required. It wasn't supplying the needs what they wanted, wasn't religion. And they thought the ILP and socialism were – or would do – and they left. And Dan Carradice were brought up Methodist – came over into ILP.[13]

It is impossible to say at what point the Salem people went over to the ILP, or whether they were responsible for its foundation. It is difficult to give a precise date to the formation of the Nelson branch, beyond the fact that the first entry of a surviving account book is dated 1st January, 1893,[14] which implies at least informal meetings were being held at the end of 1892, in advance of the inaugural conference of the national ILP at Bradford. The impetus for the formation of the branch may have come from members of the earlier Social Democratic Federation, founded in 1881 by H. M. Hyndman, which had met with considerable success in the Burnley area under the leadership of Dan Irving. Indeed, the ILP *Annual Report* 1893 notes the Nelson delegate as Ernest Johnson, who was the first socialist on the Nelson School Board in 1894, and was selected the same year as the SDF parliamentary candidate for Clitheroe, though he later withdrew. Other sources note that C. W. Parratt, a long-standing SDF supporter also attended, along with S. R. Lowe, JP for the Nelson ILP.[15] None of these were members of Salem, which suggests that Salem members responded to an SDF initiative.

There was, of course, much closer cooperation in the north of England between SDF and ILP than is suggested by the relations between the two bodies at national level. In the Nelson district the SDF may have seen the emergence of a national ILP linked closely with Temperance as a means of making a socialist breakthrough amongst Nonconformists. Here they had previously gained no ground because of their ambivalence over the drink question, (expressed in the fact that SDF clubs sold alcohol). There is no doubt that the ideological rift on the issue of 'drink' shaped the struggle between the contending socialisms of the SDF and the ILP and determined the chronology of its emergence as a political force.[16] Committed as they were to Temperance, Nonconformists in Nelson were not prepared to commit themselves to Socialism until it recognized their existing principles and moulded itself to their teetotal culture.

The half-dozen young men who left Salem found themselves becoming increasingly isolated on account of their political views because although Salem people were radicals, they were deeply entrenched in the Liberal political tradition. The Mutual Improvement Society was a young men's group, open as the young are to new ideas not so easily assimilated by older people. The differences over the emergence of a new political party were to a great extent a product of the conflict of the established life patterns of older people with the quest of the young for new solutions. Surrounded as they were by rock solid Conservative Lancashire constituencies, it would have been surprising if in Nelson the Nonconformist Liberals had not been particularly fearful of how an emergent party might divide the radical vote. Wilfred Wellock, a member of Salem who was elected as the Labour member for Stourbridge at the General Election 1929, was in his mid-teens when the church passed through this rather traumatic period. He has recalled an incident of family life which illustrates how the movement leftwards away from the Liberal Party caused friction between members and within families, particularly between parents and children, as the young began to be attracted to the Labour Party.

Already attending public political meetings, at about the age of 14, Wellock was excited at the prospect of a visit to the district by Keir Hardie. About a week before the meeting, during the family's evening meal, he stated that he and his cousin were thinking of attending. After a brief silence his father referred to Keir Hardie's reputation as a "wild man", irresponsible and socially dangerous. When the day came and he announced that he was going to the meeting, there was no reply. On returning home he gave his father a descriptive account of the meeting, which again was received without response. Many years later, Wellock wrote that 'What my father thought I can only guess, but I imagine he was most concerned about my enthusiasm over the meeting's success!'[17] Had Wellock been a few years older he might well have been amongst the small group that left Salem for the ILP branch. As it was, he remained a life-long member of the church, but not without difficulties.

Even from an early age something in his spirit revolted against the two Evangelical concepts that dominated Salem's religious witness, 'first, that human nature is sinful, whence man's primary need is to purge himself of sin, and second, that Christ, as the Divine and only begotten Son of God had been sent into the world for the specific purpose of saving men from sin and so fitting them for eternal life'.[18] His view of Jesus as 'a lone, deep thinker who in years of quiet meditation had plumbed the depths of living Truth, the Truth, which, if followed would lead men by their own clear insight, understanding and volition into the ways of love and self-giving, and so enable mankind to move towards human and social health and wholeness',[19] caused consternation amongst Salem's elders as his preaching and Sunday school teaching increasingly dealt with the social consequences of capitalism. Attempts were made to silence him, but in the end he was tolerated because he 'had the support of the younger generation.'[20] Nonetheless, the church leaders must have been relieved when he left the district to attend Edinburgh University, after which he returned to Nelson and engaged in writing and lecturing, occasionally preaching at Salem, but having little direct contact with the church.[21]

The theological modernism reflected in Wellock's difficulties probably permeated the conservative Evangelicalism of Salem through the visits of a few socialist speakers who, as ministers or members of Nonconformist chapels, addressed Mutual Improvement societies. Prominent amongst these was the Rev. T. A. Leonard of Colne Independent Chapel, a member of Colne SDF and a popular speaker at Labour Church meetings, often speaking on 'Darkest England: the way in and the way out.' Before coming to Colne in May 1890, he had encountered problems over doctrinal points, when charges of 'Unitarianism' had been brought against him by some of the deacons and members of the Barrow-in-Furness Congregational Church.[22] Throughout his four years at Colne, Leonard was tireless in championing causes for the improvement of the mill workers. The National Home Reading Union, formed in 1889, which offered opportunities for adult education as 'the People's University', was particularly strong in Lancashire, and with Leonard's encouragement 'home reading circles' grew up in the Nelson and Colne district. Commending it, he wrote in the local paper: 'Individual members can join and read the course indicated by the Union, but by far the better way is to gather a circle of either the members of one's own household, neighbours, or those connected with any society or church to which one may happen to belong.'[23]

From these groups developed schemes to arrange inexpensive holidays in the countryside and later the Nelson Working Men's Holiday Association. In 1893, Leonard formed the Co-operative Holiday Association under the auspices of the National Home Reading Union to put this aspect of his work on a national and permanent footing.[24] It was an offer to manage one of the association's houses, at Keld, Swaledale, that provided the opportunity for Selina Cooper, the suffragist, to leave mill work in Nelson and begin her agitations demanding votes for women and decent maternity provisions; she was described as Mr. Leonard's 'right hand man'. Although absolutely forthright in the profession of his political views, the Rev. T. A. Leonard seems to have achieved the almost unique distinction amongst socialist ministers of retaining the confidence and support of a large majority of his congregation. When he resigned the pastorate on being appointed as Organizing Secretary of the London Social Institute, he was urged to reconsider; and when he confirmed his decision to go his congregation wrote of 'its sense of the deep loss it feels at the removal of a minister who has become so much entwined in the tender affections of the young men and women connected with the church' and 'whose denunciation of wrong in whatever form it has been presented to him has won him the sympathies of all true hearted men and women.'[25] Again one can detect the appeal of the new political views to the young, but it was unusual for them to be tolerated by almost an entire congregation.

The Independent Chapel in Dockeray Square, Colne, was no more typical of North East Lancashire Nonconformity than Salem Independent Methodist Church, Nelson. Events at Cannon Street Baptist Chapel, Accrington, a few miles to the south, in the 1920s, were more typical of the general attitudes of the churches and the way they lingered on. Whilst taking the study a few years beyond the period 1880–1914, an examination of them is necessary to emphasize the rarity of the situation at Salem. They brought to an end the ministry of the Rev. Ingli James, who went on to outstandingly successful pastorates at Swansea and Queen's Road Baptist Church, Coventry.[26] Cannon Street was one of the great churches of the Baptist movement, a cathedral-like building erected in 1871. In 1919 it had 750 members, 907 Sunday School scholars and 116 teachers.[27] The church stood opposite the impressive Conservative Club and round the corner from the even more impressive Liberal Club. In social composition the significant difference between Cannon Street, Accrington, and Salem, Nelson, was that Cannon Street had a 'big' family, the Macalpines, headed by Sir George, a past president of the Baptist Union and chairman of the local Liberal Association.[28]

Further north, in the Clitheroe constituency, the custom of small manufacturers renting space in large mills had meant that there were few industrial magnates on the scale of those who dominated the chapels to the south. Under Macalpine leadership the chapel was rock solid and aggressively Liberal. Problems arose when Ingli James, who settled at the church in 1920, took steps, in 1922, to enlarge his congregation by allowing open membership, while restricting church office and attendance at meetings to immersed members.[29] The minister was also criticised for not visiting members of the church and congregation as he should and of paying too much attention to the young people and neglecting the older members. Exception appears to have been taken to some of his sermons,[30] particularly those of a social or political nature, such as when, in September 1921, he preached about the state of affairs in Russia.[31] There 'were murmurings about unusual looking people who appeared at services – working men wearing mufflers …. Then came a parliamentary election and Ingli spoke for the Labour candidate. Previous ministers had always spoken on Liberal platforms, but Ingli's "meddling in politics" struck them as something quite different.'[32] It was, in fact, the General Election in November 1922 that brought conflicts to a climax, when James was criticised for making public his sympathy with the victorious Labour candidate, Charles Roden Buxton. As a result practically the entire Diaconate, led by James Langham, a staunch Liberal who had been elected to the Accrington aldermanic bench on 21 May 1921, waited upon the minister regretting 'the public propagation both in and out of the Church of so-called Socialistic doctrines which were quite unacceptable to the great majority of our Congregation.' They asked 'whether he could conscientiously abstain from advocating these socialistic views'. If that were not possible, they were aware that he had received invitations from another church and 'we should not part without feeling that we were losing one whom we had learned to love'.[33] The minister stood his ground, arguing that he had not preached socialism in the Church, but only the teaching of the New Testament and expressed his intention to speak for the Labour candidate on the following Friday evening.[34] Similarly to events at Park Lane Chapel (Unitarian), Ashton in Makerfield, following the dismissal of the Rev. J. Bellamy Highham, a deputation of young people took a letter of protest to the deacons, whereupon a half-hearted attempt was made to find a formula that would permit Ingli James to remain: 'That we put no restrictions on Mr. James going on political platforms and trust to his good sense to profit from his experiences of the past few weeks ...'[35] The ministry came to an end in March 1923.

Church members were inclined to put it about that the Rev. Ingli James's departure was a case of him pleasing himself; that no body of opinion was responsible. Local Labour supporters apparently took a different view of events. Amongst the Cannon Street archives is a cutting of the first part of an article from the Accrington *Labour News*, 23 January 1923, which proposes to tell the true facts. Unfortunately, however, extensive attempts to trace the complete article have proved unfruitful, but there is enough evidence to suggest that they believed he wished to remain in the district and was forced out by opponents of the local Labour campaign. Cannon Street Baptist Chapel's determination not to compromise its proud support of the Liberal Party, even at this relatively late date, can be taken as an indication of what would have been the attitude to Labour's emergence in most Nonconformist chapels prior to 1914.

If Cannon Street Baptist Chapel, Accrington, was typical of Evangelical Nonconformity's negative response to the Labour movement, what was distinctive about Salem Independent Methodist Chapel that led some of its young men to join the ILP? Salem shared the Evangelical doctrinal position of the Methodist movement, but Independent Methodism had originated as a reaction to the authority exercised by the circuit and its superintendent ministers. Salem members were therefore accustomed to deciding their own affairs. Independent Methodism had no professional ministers and, although the church had its deacons, the small firms of Nelson did not produce magnates who also tried to control the church. Leadership was less autocratic or oligarchical than in mainstream Methodism. The church had by tradition sheltered the inaugural meetings of radical and progressive causes, so that the emergence of a new democratic party was not dismissed out of hand, although the older Liberal members were worried by it. The large membership necessitated the sub-division of the church into a number of auxiliary societies, each controlling its own affairs. One of these, the Young Men's Mutual

Improvement Society, attracted people who were interested in hearing speakers with new ideas from whatever quarter. Amongst those who addressed the group were some already associated with the SDF, and others who held Modernist theological opinions. As they adopted socialist views and became influenced by the Modernist theological outlook of speakers like the Rev. T. A. Leonard, the members of the Mutual Improvement Society began to feel the tensions between their collectivist political viewpoint and the narrowly individualistic theology of their Chapel. When these eventually led to difficulties within the congregation, some left to join the newly-formed Nelson ILP, which was congenial to their new politics and their traditional Nonconformist teetotalism. Others, who did not leave, were tolerated by the overwhelmingly left-wing Liberal majority, although their contacts with Salem gradually became less direct.

Moore has shown that a group similar to the Salem Mutual Improvement Society was connected with the Primitive Methodist Chapel at Quebec in the Deerness Valley. It was, however, much less likely that such developments could occur in Wesleyan Methodism or even Primitive Methodism, because they would have been stifled by the more authoritarian regime. The more democratic traditions of Independent Methodism were clearly a factor in the events at Nelson. Nonetheless, all branches of Methodism placed their emphasis on the salvation of individuals, which itself precluded any close affinity with a political party having a collectivist programme. Such could not be said of the liberal theological position of the Unitarians, to whom we now turn.

The Free Christian Church (Unitarian), Beech Street, Crewe

Situated forty miles to the south of what is generally regarded as the crucible of early ILP activity and without a textile industry, Crewe was in many respects very different from the locations of the other churches surveyed in this study. Yet called into being by the Grand Junction Railway Company in 1843,[36] by virtue of its railway engineering industry it had good communications with Lancashire and the West Riding, and its workers had more in common with the textile operatives than the agricultural labourers of the surrounding South Cheshire farms. Like Nelson, its population had grown dramatically from 8,159 in 1861 to 17,810 in 1871.[37]

The fortunes of the small Unitarian congregation at Crewe, however, bore no relation to the successful well-attended Nonconformist chapels of North-East Lancashire, like Salem Independent Methodist Church, Nelson and Cannon Street Baptist Church, Accrington. The church, which was pioneered by the Liverpool District Missionary Association in 1861, made little headway and never became financially independent. Its weakness can be gauged from the attendances. Services in 1862 only occasionally reached double figures and only 17 attended the annual church meeting in 1883. Three ministers served the church between 1866 and 1871, and from 1872 until 1876, when the Rev William Mellor arrived, the church had no minister at all.[38] Nonetheless, despite its precarious existence, with Victorian optimism, the help of the missionary association and local benefactors, (including the railway engineer Richard Trevithick, one-time Superintendent of the London and North Western Railway Company's works at Crewe, John Ramsbottom, the company's Chief Mechanical Engineer at Crewe and Mrs. J. Locke, widow of the Chief Engineer of the Grand Junction Railway Company), the congregation eventually secured a permanent church building in Beech Street.[39]

Here, under William Mellor's devoted care, the congregation neither grew large nor financially independent, but it did achieve a reputation for the impact it made upon Crewe's political and social scene. Mellor, as president of the Crewe and District Liberal Association from about 1880 until 1886, played a leading role in the struggle against the Tory-orientated Railway Company, which at elections in the early 1880s intimidated workers into voting for so-called Independent candidates, who aligned with the Conservatives. In 1885, 150 workers were dismissed for political reasons, many of them being members of 'The Blue Ribbon Gang', the militant temperance movement, which attracted many Non-conformist Liberals.[40] The support given to the political emancipation of railway employees by Mellor and leading members of the Beech Street Free Christian Church brought the small Unitarian cause to the public attention with the result that there was a moderate growth of membership to around three hundred, making it necessary to consider the enlargement of the church premises in 1886. Mellor had resigned before the scheme materialised, but it was to provide his successor with the space to accommodate lectures by the leading Labour propagandists, Keir Hardie, Philip Snowden and Tom Mann.

The Rev. Harry Bodell Smith settled at Beech Street in 1889 and remained there until 1895. He had previously ministered at Darwen (1881–83), Droylsden (1884–85) and Pudsey (1886–90), and had been educated at the Unitarian Home Missionary College (1878–1881), where his fellow students included H. V. Mills, of Starnthwaite Home Colony, Joseph Harrison, who died at Starnthwaite in 1902, and Samuel Thompson, a member of the Bolton Whitmanites.[41] Bodell Smith was a teetotaller, vegetarian and a socialist. His belief in democracy and a desire to help working men merged into his attempt to extend the membership of the church. He did not go as far as Brooke Herford, who, at Strangeways Unitarian Church, in the 1860s, removed the pew doors from their hinges as a symbol of open membership,[42] but when he abolished pew rents it was an act unlikely to endear him to the treasurer of a church with the financial instability of Beech Street.

The situation was not made any easier because the treasurer happened to be James Briggs, a leading member of the town's Liberal Party, who bitterly opposed Smith's support of the emergent independent Labour movement and the Crewe branch of the ILP. Briggs had been trained for the Unitarian ministry at the Unitarian Home Missionary College, but left the ministry after only two years at Mossley and settled at Crewe as a pawnbroker and stockbroker. He became a member of the Local Board of Health (which governed the town until 1877, when it was incorporated), then a member of the town Council, on which he served with John Teasdale and John Bland, two other members of the small church. Briggs, a justice of the peace, became mayor, as did another Unitarian, Henry Wallwork.[43] In 1920, as leader of the Liberals, he founded the Crewe Progressive Union, an alliance of Tories and Liberals who aimed to combat the rise of Labour. And when he died, aged 87, he was a freeman of the borough, who for sixty years had exercised 'a powerful, if occasionally jaundiced, influence in the church and town.'[44] In his youth Briggs was a progressive Liberal and in political matters followed the example set by the Beech Street minister; but whereas Mellor's political development was to the left – one of his sons William Mellor (1888–1942) was an active socialist who in the inter-war years edited the *Daily Herald* and *Tribune*[45] – with the advent of a independent Labour movement Briggs entrenched himself in the Liberal cause. Relationships at Beech Street, which had been smooth and agreeable while his political and religious views were unitedly preached from the Beech Street pulpit, became acrimonious after Bodell Smith's arrival in the town.

In 1894, Bodell Smith was responsible for founding the Crewe branch of the Independent Labour Party. It drew support from the Amalgamated Society of Railway Servants, the National Union of Gasworkers and General Labourers, and the General Railway Workers' Union, whose branches had been established in the town between 1888 and 1894. The early years of its existence were occupied in converting an older body, the Crewe Trades Council, to a policy of direct Labour representation, and because the town Council and its Committees held only morning and afternoon meetings, one of its first campaigns was for evening meetings to encourage would be working-men town councillors.[46] The branch was inspired by the news of the inaugural conference of the national ILP at Bradford the previous year, but there were also local factors which prompted its formation in 1894. Crewe was normally a safe Liberal seat, secured by the strong attachment of railway employees to the Liberal Party. But the Party became unpopular in 1894 when the Liberals' Employers' Liability Bill threatened the pension scheme operated by the railway company, and because unemployment at the works was blamed upon the Government. With regard to the Employer's Liability Bill, the railway workers strongly approved of the Earl of Dudley's attempt to secure contracting-out by a Lords' amendment, and when the Liberal Government rejected this proposal, the Crewe Conservatives found it advantageous to appoint the Earl's brother, the Hon. R. A. Ward, as their candidate for the General Election in 1895. Unusually, the seat suddenly became unsafe for the Liberals, and this was bound to fuel the animosity over the formation of an ILP branch, which threatened Liberal solidarity. Matters were made even worse when, in the event, much to his surprise, Ward was elected with a swing of over 10 per cent. Ward did not find parliamentary life congenial and ceased to attend the Commons after a few months; in 1900 the seat was retaken by the Liberals.[47]

The critical position of the Crewe Liberals in 1894–95 made the strained relationship between Briggs and Bodell Smith even worse. In January 1894, Smith tendered his resignation with the intention of leaving in March. On being asked to reconsider his decision, he stipulated the following terms for the withdrawal of his resignation: better attendances at Morning Service, appointment of visitors to look up absentees, the congregation to try to secure singers for the choir, help in the Sunday School and the appointment of a small committee to improve the financial situation. The congregation resolved to accept them by 16 votes to 4.[48] Bitterly disappointed at the lost chance to rid the church of Bodell Smith's leadership, Briggs sent a letter to the next meeting of the committee resigning from the treasurership and membership of the Beech Street Free Church, and withdrawing his substantial and essential financial support. The extent to which the committee relied upon him is suggested by the secretary asking if there was any hope of him staying should a strong feeling of the members be expressed, and 'how would he like us to settle up, at once or would he grant us a little time?'[49] The small cause was devastated. Without Briggs's capital the church was virtually bankrupt.

After Briggs had gone, Bodell Smith developed the Evening Services along Pleasant Sunday Evening lines and it was to these that Labour leaders were invited as preachers. He proposed to make Beech Street 'a thorough Labour church' as it was 'the only church catering for the working class.'[50] John Trevor, the founder of the Labour Church movement and former Unitarian minister, was contacted but as he was unable to promise an early date for a visit, Fred Bocklehurst, Trevor's successor was invited instead.[51]

For a few months Bodell Smith struggled on, concentrating his efforts on building up the Pleasant Sunday Evenings and a programme of Labour Church type services. But the financial problems were intractable and within a a few months, with the church unable to pay more than £50 to his stipend and the Liverpool District Missionary Association unwilling to increase the grant, his departure became inevitable. Despite the deep respect of Unitarians for the freedom of the pulpit, Briggs' decision not to pay the piper if he could not call the political tune had finally rid the congregation of its turbulent minister. After Bodell Smith's departure, the congregation struggled on deeply divided, until the church was forced to close in the early years of the twentieth century.

Beech Street Church had given birth to the local ILP branch, but at the high cost of its own life, at least temporarily. Bodell Smith, too, was also a victim of his five-year political ministry, for although he continued as a Unitarian minister, particularly as an evangelist on the Unitarian Van Mission, there is no evidence of further political involvement. He was not alone in finding the tensions between ministry and political activism too great; whereas laymen could abandon the churches for the Labour movement when the strains became intolerable, ministers, whose livelihoods depended on the churches, had usually no option but to give up politics, unless they were very exceptional men. Such experiences suggest that the churches made life very uncomfortable for anyone who publicly supported the Labour cause. At the end the politics of the prominent laymen in the chapel determined what was acceptable.

In October 1903, two years after Beech Street Free Christian Church had closed, probably in part because the Labour Church movement had become moribund, a few local Unitarians and the East Cheshire Union made attempts to revive their cause in Crewe. James Briggs renewed his interest and took a leading part as the congregation's chairman. In 1904, the Rev. H. Fisher Short removed from Aberdare to commence a ministry. The bitter experience under Bodell Smith meant that the leaders of the revived congregation were unlikely to choose a minister who had shown any signs of sympathy with socialism or the ILP, and Fisher Short must have been very carefully vetted before being invited. He did not disappoint, for, in conjunction with Briggs, he brought the church back to its former pro-Liberal stance, and in doing so managed to alleviate some of the financial difficulties.[52] Soon after his arrival, Robert Blatchford's onslaught on religion provided Short with an opportunity to arrange a series of lectures to refute socialist doctrines and policies.[53] He also re-introduced the practice of pew-rents, which, whilst it does not appear to have been a deterrent, for membership increased, could not have been conducive to attracting the kind of working men who had attended the Pleasant Sunday Evenings during Bodell Smith's ministry.

It may not entirely do justice to describe Henry Fisher Short as 'the Liberals' man'. Eventually, when he was minister at Bootle, he was sufficiently sympathetic towards socialists to provide the bail for J. Vint Laughland. The minister of Pembroke Chapel, Liverpool, and former Unitarian, was arrested for his part in a violent demonstration of the Liverpool Unemployed Committee on 12 September 1921, at St. George's Hall and the Walker Art Gallery. But, arguably, the act was more religious than political in intent. Short's reputation as a 'trouble shooter' whenever socialism raised its head in Unitarian congregations seems to have gone before him. When, in 1912, Park Lane Chapel, Ashton in Makerfield, dismissed the Rev. J. Bellamy Higham for being a socialist, it was to Crewe that a deputation was sent to enquire about Short's work there, before he was invited from Mossley, where he had settled in 1909.[54] It may simply have been that Short was regarded as a minister who could effectively reunite divided congregations, but it seems there was more to it than that; anti-socialist Unitarians could have confidence that under his leadership a church would not become identified with the Labour party.

The exact reasons for Bellamy Higham's dismissal from Park Lane Chapel are difficult to determine. The church minutes make no reference to socialism, but such a statement would have been unlikely because to have done so would have been a denial of the liberty of opinion which Nonconformists, particularly Unitarians, professed. If a congregation disapproved of a minister's support for the Labour movement, there had to be other reasons for removing him. These were found in December 1911, when the main accusation brought against Bellamy Higham was that he did not provide adequate leadership; the congregation was 'like a ship without a captain'.[55] 'He had not attended a Teachers' meeting for three years, neither had he attended the Lantern lectures; his Preaching was not satisfactory, his sermons were not suitable for Park Lane, the average attendance had dropped from 50 to 30.' It was not unusual for socialist ministers to be criticised for their preaching. Their opponents suggested that their sermons were not sufficiently 'spiritual' because they occupied time dealing with questions of social concern.

At Park Lane Chapel, Mr. Thomas Martland said, 'we heard very little of Jesus from the pulpit'. Seconding the resolution for Bellamy Higham's dismissal, Miss Alice Leyland referred to her dislike for his pulpit utterances and said that she had often thought when listening to him of the Old Testament quotation 'Put off thy shoes from off thy feet, the place whereon thou standest is holy ground.'[56] The real reasons, however, were that the minister's openly declared support for the Labour movement had proved particularly embarrassing during the industrial unrest in the Lancashire coalfield in 1911–12.

Park Lane Chapel drew much of its income from coalfield revenues, and its members were employed in positions of authority in the coal industry. The chapel was not totally opposed to the emergence of the Labour movement, for throughout 1909 and 1910 it had allowed the Servants of the Cooperative Society, the Labour Party and the Miners to hold meetings on its premises.[57] But in the context of the strikes attitudes changed. Resentment was directed against the minister, who was not only 'socialistic in opinion', but who identified so closely with the working class by spending 'the greater part of his time bringing the Parsonage Garden into good condition. Dressed like a navvy to be seen day after day, labouring as a day labourer.'[58] Higham's politics and manner were not, however, unpopular with all sections of the congregation. The resolution to terminate his ministry was passed, 40 votes for, 10 against, and 4 spoilt papers, but Miss Rothwell 'protested against the action of the seatholders and read a list of names who threatened to leave the School and Chapel if Mr. Higham were discharged, a good many of the names were those of people who never attend, or of very young persons.'[59]

Again, as in the cases of Salem Independent Methodist Church, Nelson, and Cannon Street Baptist Chapel, Accrington, it was the older people, with their power as seat holders, who were set to exclude socialist views from the churches, often against the wishes of the young. A deputation of young people, led by Mr. E. W. Deacon (later the Rev. E. W. Deacon), met the Park Lane Chapel committee to discuss Mr. Higham's resignation, only to be informed that the six months notice would not be withdrawn. That there was a large measure of popular support for Higham is also suggested by the fact that the Trustees obtained a letter from the Charity Commissioners to say that they were justified in their action. But the evidence suggests that Higham was 'quarrelsome and devoid of tact',[60] which makes it difficult to establish the precise reasons for the problems at Park Lane.

At national level the liberal ethos of the Unitarian movement permitted fuller consideration of the claims of the Labour movement than was the case in the Evangelical churches. This was helped by the fact that a minister of Wicksteed's intellectual calibre was sympathetic to the re-ordering of society to benefit the producers of wealth. John Trevor's initiative in forming the Labour Church also helped to keep the discussion of the new politics alive in Unitarian circles. The Unitarians had rejected the doctrine of the Fall and were not preoccupied with saving individual souls. Their social service was not so closely linked with evangelism. They had supported the Whigs and Liberals, and, because of their commercial interests, generally remained committed to the competitive system, albeit tempered by a broad humanitarianism. Many of them were ready for an advanced-Liberalism, and a very few ministers for socialism. But the events at Crewe illustrate the conflicts which the emergence of an independent Labour movement caused in localities where leading church members had played a prominent part in the Liberal Party. At Crewe they occurred in a relatively weak church that had been founded by a missionary society, and were the result of a socialist minister attracting members of the working class, with a programme of activity similar to that of a Labour church. When this led to the formation of the Crewe ILP at a critical period for the Crewe Liberal Association, the Liberal members withdrew their active and financial support, leading to the temporary closure of the church. Eventually it was re-opened and the staunch tradition of support for the Liberal Party re-established. However sympathetic the denominational debates may have appeared towards Labour, at local level few were prepared to see Liberalism threatened by a new party and this was particularly the case at Crewe, where the threat to railway company pensions and local unemployment made the Liberal Party particularly vulnerable in 1894–95. If the weakness of the Beech Street Free Church had permitted its significant but temporary associations with the ILP, a similar weakness in a Baptist church in Liverpool was to lead to more enduring support for the Labour movement.

144

Pembroke Chapel (Baptist), Liverpool

Unlike the Unitarians, whose liberal theology did not itself create any obstacle to the espousal of collectivist solutions to social problems, (even if, with few exceptions, their commercial interests and a desire for respectability prevented fuller participation in the emergence of the Labour movement), the Baptists were deeply entrenched in the Evangelical tradition. And what is more, their Evangelical principles had been very forcefully reasserted, as late as 1877–78, by the so-called Down Grade controversy,[61] which argued that the Arminian theology of the General Baptists (of which John Clifford was the leading minister) was spreading and tending to down-grade the evangelical truth. This led to the Rev. C. H. Spurgeon's separation from the Baptist Union, but not before he had fired warning shots against the tendencies of some younger ministers to dilute evangelical religion with a concern for social change. Against such a background, it was not surprising that Baptists remained among the most socially and politically conservative of all Nonconformists.

The formation of the Nonconformist Anti-Socialist Union at the Baptist Church House in 1909 to 'discountenance politics in the pulpit' and to 'exterminate socialism from Church and State' was a late attempt by the denomination's right-wing pressure group. This was led by the Rev. J. G. Greenhough, who, as president of the Baptist Union in 1895, had delivered a violent denunciation of all socialism. Most Baptist leaders shared Greenhough's viewpoint, which merely confirmed the Rev. James Owen's presidential address of 1890, arguing that their main aim was not to help the poor but to save individual souls. The Baptist Union was not however totally impervious to social change. Even Owen admitted the influence of environment on character, and in 1892 the president, the Rev. R. H. Roberts, (speaking about 'The Kingdom of God on Earth') quoted the prophet Isaiah with reference to the land question, and denounced monopolists who 'join house to house, lay field to field, till there be no room and ye be made alone to dwell in the midst of the land'.

But Baptist expressions of social concern were little more than aberrations. The movement, as a whole, had been conditioned to be non-political by the instruction of its greatest preacher, C. H. Spurgeon, to 'serve the Lord Christ by quiet acquiescence in the arrangement of Providence'.[62] The most evangelical of all denominations was therefore unlikely to take much interest in the questions engaging the Labour movement, and only Baptists of exceptional ability and rugged independence could afford to resist the pressures of the movement to remain narrowly concerned with doctrinal questions.

This was done most successfully by Dr. John Clifford of Westbourne Park Chapel, London, who was exceptional in achieving prominence as a Baptist minister and a Socialist leader. It was all the more remarkable that, during the 1890s, the foremost Nonconformist socialist, (who led the Christian Socialist League), should have been a minister of the most politically conservative denomination. The reason is partly explained by the fact that, as a boy in Leicestershire, Clifford had been strongly influenced by moral-force Chartists and never lost his concern for the emancipation of working people. His chapel at Westbourne Park was organized on open-membership and institutional church lines, providing a wide range of educational and social activities. But so unusual was this approach amongst Baptists during the 1890s, that Baptist relations with the early Labour movement have generally been explained solely in terms of the role played by Clifford, which does not tell the whole story. There were a few other Baptists who supported Labour's advance, although most of them did so by breaking off relations with other churches and distancing themselves from the Baptist Union, as happened at Pembroke Chapel, Liverpool.

Pembroke Chapel is an example of a Baptist congregation which moved progressively towards the political left from 1890 onwards. Founded in 1836, it had prospered under the long ministry of the Rev. C. M. Birrell, father of Augustine Birrell, education minister in the Liberal government of 1906. During his thirty-four years at Pembroke, Birrell's restrained and cautious theology and political liberalism attracted large congregations and new members were constantly being received. Alongside the cultured preaching, in common with other chapels, Pembroke gradually became 'institutional', with the formation of a Benevolent and Friendly Society, a Penny Bank for workingmen and children, a Dorcas Society, Clothing and Book Clubs. Although the chapel did not officially engage in social endeavour, members with a social conscience found an outlet by assisting the social work of John Cropper of Diggle Bank, an influential member who had inherited a concern for philanthropic activity from his Quaker past. However, in the end Birrell stayed too long (1838–72) and as his immediate successors failed to establish themselves, the membership fell off and the church became moribund. However illustrious its past, in such a condition it could not be particularly choosy when it became necessary to appoint a new minister in 1890.[63]

The Rev. Charles Frederick Aked, who is the key figure in the development of a radical political tradition at Pembroke, came to the pulpit after differences with his congregation at Earlstown Baptist Church. These had culminated when he said that certain members of the congregation should be taken out into the nearest field and shot.[64] Born in Nottingham in 1864, he had worked as a junior clerk in a coal merchant's office, and later as an auctioneer's assistant and bailiff to the Sheriff of Derbyshire, a position which provided experience of the plight of the poor and unemployed. He was about to emigrate to New Zealand when he suddenly decided to enter the Baptist ministry. Three years at the Midland Baptist College, Nottingham, were followed by a pastorate amongst colliers at Ilkeston.

146

Thence in 1886 he removed to Syston, Leicestershire, and two years later to the joint pastorate of St Helens and Earlstown.

Aked had always ministered to working men, but it was only when he settled in the Lancashire coalfield that he saw the kind of distress which prompted him to go about 'with fever in the blood, and passion in the heart.'[65] Under Aked's leadership the recovery of the Pembroke Chapel congregation was phenomenal. His popularity can be judged from attendances at services. On the first Sunday of 1890 the congregation totalled 35 in the morning and 60 in the evening: in 1893 the respective figures averaged 700 and 1,400 and in 1902, 1,375 and 1,973. As early as 1891 it was necessary to have two new doors cut in the front of the chapel. At the same time the pews were removed and replaced with drop seats, and intending hearers could purchase tickets to avoid up to an hour's queueing.[66] A large proportion of the new members were young people, drawn mainly from the middle classes, who through the chapel found opportunities for social concern which were denied them by the atrophied nature of local politics. In the space of ten years a struggling cause became one of the most powerful churches in the city.

The success has been partly explained by Aked's striking appearance,[67] as was later the case with R. J. Campbell, but one might suspect that this has its origins amongst those who were opposed to the speaker's radical message and would not admit the attractiveness of the message itself. The fact is that Aked had espoused the Social Gospel and was expounding it as vigorously as his friend and mentor, Dr. John Clifford, was doing at Westbourne Park Chapel, London. His popular preaching, which rested a concern for social justice on religious foundations, touched a chord in a city where poverty, slums, and the social consequences of the Capitalist system were so evident.

Aked's theology was far from orthodox. In 1892 he published a series of addresses under the title *Changing Creeds and Social Struggles* in which he violently attacked religion based too narrowly on the Bible, referring to the 'disease of Bible worship... The book whose authority has been evoked to support the foulest crimes committed by the vilest men... its phrases the shibboleths of pietistic sectarians'.[68] His somewhat muddled position is illustrated by the fact that at one time he would use the conventional trinitarian formulae, and at another announce complete agreement with Unitarian thought. Profoundly affected by the Higher Criticism, he had a broad view of religious inspiration: 'The Word came to Abraham, Moses, Isaiah, to the Buddha, to Zoroaster, to Socrates, and to prophets everywhere'. On the nature of God, he shared the immanental view that was later to become the central belief of the New Theology movement led by R. J. Campbell: 'In all of us there is divinity, and divinity of the same nature as was in Christ'.[69] Such views inevitably set him and Pembroke Chapel apart from the general life of the Baptist churches. However, after 1892, Aked concerned himself less with

147

polemical theology and sermons were only occasionally biblical. Instead books, plays, personalities and politics increasingly became the subjects of his pulpit addresses.[70] Co-operation with other Free Churches virtually ceased with the chapel's withdrawal from the Boys and Girls Religious Service and Ragged School Union in 1893.[71] The church became anti-missionary and no further contributions were made to the Baptist Missionary Society after 1900.

As Aked and Pembroke Chapel became isolated from the Baptist movement there was more time for building up the internal organization of the church. Many of the fifty or more societies connected with the chapel were socially relevant to the condition of the poor. In the winter months, a strong Dorcas society, in conjunction with the Salvation Army, provided hot-pot suppers for poor children in the area. There were sporting clubs for swimming, cycling, football and tennis, and Aked played an important part in the work of the Liverpool Sunday Society, an organization formed by liberal ministers to relieve Sabbath gloom with innocent recreation.[72] Yet, whilst accepting the broadening outlook of the decade with regard to popular amusements, the chapel did not depart from the traditional Nonconformist advocacy of Temperance, and every member of the chapel was expected to belong to one of its Bands of Hope or Temperance Societies. As the self-styled 'minister of social righteousness', Aked conducted a personal Temperance campaign which did not lay the blame for social evils at the feet of the intemperate poor. The drink Trade had a great deal to answer for. 'Democracy' could not be born while 'the river of Death flowed black as Hell from the open flood-gates of the brewery, distillery and public house.'[73] And, second only to drink, he attacked the sheer poverty which contributed to the degradation of the slums. Solutions must be found in Land Nationalization, 'for the land belongs to the people', the substitution of collectivism for competition, 'for our whole competitive system is wrong in economics and morals';[74] at local level he called for public works during periods of distress, a municipal farm colony, and gradual municipalization, particu-larly of the tramways.[75] In the strike crisis of 1893, Aked cooperated with the Rev. R. A. Armstrong of Hope Street Church (Unitarian) and with the Rev. C. W. Stubbs, the Socialist rector of Wavertree, in the establish-ment of the *Liverpool Pulpit* fund for relief of distress in the Lancashire coalfield, and Pembroke Chapel itself organized special collections for the wives and children of 'our industrial serfs'.[76]

It is not easy to determine the precise political position of Charles Aked. He referred to his 'Socialistic dreams' and, as a member of the Liverpool Fabian Society, was in favour of municipalization of public services. His advocacy of temperance must have disposed him more to the ILP brand of socialism. A friendship with Philip and Ethel Snowden had begun when Ethel was a student at Edge Hill Training College and had become one of his 'disciples' in temperance work at Liverpool. But he was

148

bitterly opposed to Robert Blatchford and the Clarion movement, particularly after Blatchford's rejection of religion. Neither could Blatchford's liking for fine wine have pleased such a doughty temperance fighter. Much of Aked's energy was devoted to preventing the Labour movement selling out to what he regarded as the godless demagogy of popular leaders, such as Hyndman, Mann, 'whose rowdyism does more harm to the cause than all the capitalist press of Europe',[77] and Tillett, 'a demagogue drunk with place and power'.[78] They were, however, simply adopting a good old Nonconformist oratorical style of presentation to their audiences, and the criticisms had little weight coming from one who was himself inclined to be a demagogue. He was not uncritical too of local Labour leaders, but for opposite reasons, because they were far too tender in the interests of employers. As with his theology, he often appears to be propounding the progressive view without actually coming down on its side, and, not surprisingly, some have doubted whether he was more than an advanced Liberal.[79] This view is perhaps supported by the fact that his most fruitful involvement in civic affairs began when revived Liberalism made inroads on the entrenched Tory majority of the City Council, and ended when the Liberals were driven from power in 1895. For Aked the last years of the nineteenth century passed in comparative quiet. He left Pembroke Chapel in 1906 to become minister to the millionaires of Fifth Avenue Baptist Church, New York, at a salary of $10,000, (much to the disgust of many at Pembroke Chapel, who regarded it as the equivalent of 30 pieces of silver). Nonetheless, he left behind him a radical tradition that paved the way for the congregation to move further to the left under his more outspokenly socialist successors,[80] particularly the Rev. Harry Youlden.

Just how much Pembroke's success had depended on Aked's personal magnetism was evident the Sunday after his departure, when the chapel was almost empty. Only 164 members attended the meeting to elect his successor.[81] Unanimously they invited the Rev. Harry Youlden of Unthank Road Baptist Chapel, Norwich, an active socialist and a man of advanced theological views. At the time of his appointment his theism was suspect and whilst at Pembroke he advanced still further, so that by 1911 he was definitely agnostic. He frequently supplied the pulpits of Ethical Societies and one of his sermons at Pembroke Chapel was entitled 'Glory to Man in the Highest'. His preaching dealt with the drink question, sweating, prisons, capital punishment and war - all the topics that were of concern to the politically progressive. Illustrations were drawn from the latest play or political event, rather than from the Bible. On the accession of George V he published a 6d. pamphlet which began with advice about how to deal with the House of Lords and ended with an attack on monarchy itself.

But Youlden's radicalism was intellectual, rather than practical. In the strike crisis of August 1911, he contented himself with an evasive address on the moral lessons to be learnt from the disturbances. Amongst his followers there were those whose support for the Labour movement took more active forms. Whilst Aked had been at Pembroke Chapel, local Clarionites had been subjected to mild persecution and finally driven from the church.[82] Under Youlden's leadership they received encouragement, and one of the first events of the new ministry was the provision, on the chapel forecourt, of stands for the bicycles that symbolized the Clarion movement.[83] Spearheaded by the Clarion fellowship connected with the church, a revolution took place causing the withdrawal of the wealthier and more influential deacons, who were replaced by people of more pronounced left-wing sympathies. A Social Reform League, which made the chapel the local suffragette headquarters,[84] became the vehicle of the chapel's active witness to progressive principles, whilst Youlden's pulpit addresses provided the intellectual stimulus. His ministry came to an end in January 1912, as a result of an affair with a lady member of the congregation. After this he established himself as lecturer to a local ethical church, and died in poverty and obscurity in 1917.[85]

Youlden's successor was the Rev. Donald Frazer, a Congregational minister who had come from the David Thomas Memorial Church, Bristol. Immediately after the nominal closing date for this study, Pembroke chapel became the rallying point of local pacifist endeavour, and the target of patriotic sentiment. At the outbreak of hostilities the congregation included seventy to eighty men who were conscientious objectors. On 5 August 1914 a local peace meeting was broken up by police and the *Liverpool Forward*, the newspaper of progressive forces in the city, forced to close down, whereupon the left-wing organizations quickly formed the Joint Committee of Liverpool Socialist, Pacifist and Democratic Organizations, with Pembroke Chapel as its headquarters. Frazer, who saw the Russian Revolution of 1917 as 'the full flood of the river of ordinary God-warranted humanity', suggested that 'the pulpits of England ought to ring out with commendation'. They did not, and Frazer, dubbed 'the crazy crank of Liverpool' and subjected to ugly threats, felt himself helpless and isolated, especially after the passing of the Defence of the Realm Act. His health impaired by the strain, in 1918 he accepted an invitation to Exeter Unitarian Church. Like several other ministers who adopted the New Theology, denominational ties seem to have meant little to him; he moved freely between socially and politically progressive Congregationalist, Baptist and Unitarian churches.[86]

The full significance of Pembroke Chapel's movement to the left and the support it gave to the emergent Labour movement can, however, only be fully appreciated by going well beyond our period and reviewing the ministry of the Rev. J. Vint Laughland. Laughland became minister of Pembroke Chapel in 1920, after the congregation of Crookesmoor Unitarian Chapel, Sheffield had stubbornly opposed his political activities. This had led him to conclude his valedictory address by saying: 'I would advise you to take a course of lessons on how to treat your minister when you get one. I do not want a minister to stand in a corner with his hands folded to heaven, nor do I want him to be a kind of errand boy.' When Laughland arrived in Liverpool, the city's Labour movement was hopelessly divided by the formation of the Communist Party in 1920, and the position worsened after the break down of the traditional pact between the Irish and Labour, when, with the connivance of the Tories, Irish candidates began to oppose Labour candidates in local elections. As a result of these rifts and the failure of the Right of the Labour movement, led by Sir James Sexton, to do anything about the city's unemployment, (which increased from 6,700 in October 1920 to 28,000 in July 1921), Labour representation on the City Council declined from 22 in 1919 to 4 in 1924. Immediately, Laughland joined a group of Progressives pledged to organize the unemployed. In this they were not at first very successful because they failed to induce demoralized workmen to rally openly in sufficient strength. But the opportunity came almost spontaneously when, in response to a rumour that the City Council was going to debate a project to introduce public works, a large crowd gathered on 7 September 1921. Led by Laughland and Tissyman, the leader of the police strike of 1919, a series of demonstrations followed over the next few days. On 10 September, a mass meeting elected the Liverpool Unemployed Workers' Committee as a branch of the Communist Unemployed Workers' Association, with Laughland as its secretary and Mrs. Bessie Braddock as treasurer. On the following day the notice-board at Pembroke Chapel announced the title of the evening address: 'A word to the unemployed – come as you are.'

The agitations reached a climax on 12 September, when a crowd estimated at 25,000 assembled in front of St. George's Hall, with the intention of persuading the authorities to let them hold a meeting inside the Hall. When this was denied the crowd surged across the road and up the steps of the Walker Art Gallery. Laughland, Tissyman and a handful of others found themselves inside the building with the rest shut out. Attempting to escape, they were subjected to considerable police violence, which resulted in Tissyman's arm being broken and Laughland being badly cut about the head. The following day they were charged with disturbing the peace and granted bail for seven days. When the case came before the City Sessions on 29 September more serious charges of riotous and unlawful assembly were brought, and there was an additional charge against Laughland for incitement to steal. The verdict could not have pleased the authorities, for the sentence was a nominal one of one day's imprisonment and the Recorder, suspecting perjured evidence, referred to the 'definitely disquieting features of the case' and the 'unnecessary violence, cruel and improper punishment' suffered by the accused.[87] Subsequently the authorities made further attempts to suppress the activities of the Unemployed Committee by depriving them of the use of Liberty Hall, whereupon Pembroke Chapel became increasingly a venue for the meetings of the Labour Left.

It must not be thought that Laughland's rabble-rousing activities met with the approval of those who had called him to be minister of Pembroke Chapel. Differences between minister and congregation reached a crisis two days before the great unemployment rally, when two secretaries, deacons, treasurer, organist and Sunday School staff resigned.[88] A month later 71 members also resigned.[89] Laughland's activities had, in fact, proved too much for the class of intellectual socialists who had been attracted by Youlden. Between May and October 1921 the church received 263 new members, more than the number that had elected Laughland as minister, many of them from amongst the unemployed. Under their control the choir vestry was used for the Unemployed Committee meetings, the gym for the juvenile workless, the upper hall for the distribution of bread and, when necessary, for the homeless to sleep in, and the lower hall for medical aid voluntarily provided by a doctor member.[90]

The Minister's vestry became the headquarters of *Justice for All*, a new journal to conduct propaganda of behalf of the unemployed.[91] In 1922 a scheme was launched to commence several Socialist Sunday Schools throughout the city[92] and in the general elections of 1922 and 1923 the minister stood unsuccessfully as the official Labour candidate for the Wavertree division. Not surprisingly, there were many who thought that a church which was so involved with politics had no right to exemption from the payment of rates, and threats to impose them led to the curtailment of Russian relief activities and other, more extreme aspects of Pembroke's political programme.[93] When the church decided to terminate its affiliation to the Baptist Union, with the intention of becoming a non-denominational Community Church, the Union and the Charity Commissioners also began to show interest in Pembroke on the grounds that the trust deed had been violated by the appointment of Unitarian to the pastorate.[94] Confronted by these threats, and with his salary in arrears, Laughland resigned and sailed for New York in July 1924, where until very recently it was assumed he sought obscurity. New information, however, has revealed that he settled in Rochester, NY, becoming a popular lecturer and radio broadcaster on Labour topics. He died in November 1957.[95]

Baptist relations with the Labour movement in Liverpool are not entirely exhausted by a study of Pembroke Chapel, where the leadership was highly critical of the timidity of the city's Labour Party. The leftward movement and the identification of the Chapel with the more extreme forms of Socialism proved too much for many of the members who left and probably joined other Baptist causes. Some may have transferred to Kensington Chapel, where the Rev. Herbert Dunnico settled in 1906 and stayed until 1916, becoming involved with the main stream of the Liverpool Labour movement of which Laughland was intensely critical. Dunnico came to Kensington Chapel, Liverpool, from Warrington where he had been active in the Liberal Party. Influenced by the theology of R. J. Campbell, Dunnico threw off his Liberal allegiance and joined the Labour Party when he arrived in Liverpool, quickly becoming chairman of both the Labour Party and the Liverpool Fabians. Under his leadership the Fabians fostered relationships between the Labour movement and the city's churches; in 1912 they published a leaflet entitled *What the Churches say of Socialism*,[96] a series of statements by leaders of various denominations; and in Liverpool, unusually, the Fabian Society was responsible for the formation of a late Labour Church at that time. Dunnico's outspoken support for Socialism lost him many church members, but others quickly came to take their places and the open-membership never fell below 500. For many church-attending Labour supporters, only gradually being transformed from Liberals, the message they heard from Dunnico must have been acceptable, whereas that of Aked, Youlden and Laughland was too extreme. Dunnico's subsequent career was as secretary of the International Peace Society and as Member of Parliament for Consett, 1922–31.[97]

It was unusual for Baptist churches to become involved in politics because the denomination was firmly Evangelical. Furthermore the Down Grade controversy of 1887–88 had been a warning that any divergence into social and political spheres would incur the disfavour of the Baptist Union. How was it possible for Pembroke Chapel to break away from this apolitical stance? It had been a large and important church, with an overwhelmingly Liberal membership, but its activities were atrophied and failing following an over-long ministry. The chapel's straitened circumstances resulted in a succession of socialist ministers, each a little further to the left of his predecessor, all of whom had abandoned Evangelicalism for theological modernism.

The 'New Theology' at Pembroke Chapel led to isolation from other Baptist churches and energies that might otherwise have gone into evangelism were transferred to the social and political sphere. Responding to poverty and unemployment, which were particularly severe in the cities, Aked, Youlden, Fraser and Laughland conducted socially relevant ministries and associated themselves with the Labour struggle. However, the timidity of the city's mainstream Labour movement did not satisfy and by the 1920s the church was used as a headquarters for the movement's most left-wing groups. This was finally brought to an end by the Baptist Union threatening legal action for the violation of the Trust Deed. The fragmentary developments at Pembroke Chapel were, however, very different from those at Greenfield Congregational Church, Bradford, where support for the Labour movement developed more gradually and was less direct.

Greenfield Congregational Church, Bradford

At Bradford in the West Riding of Yorkshire, where the dominant form of Nonconformity rested upon a tradition of Independency reaching back to the seventeenth century, relationships between the churches and the Labour movement found fullest expression amongst Congregationalists, and particularly through the ministry of the Rev. T. Rhondda Williams at Greenfield Congregational Church.

It is not surprising that in Bradford, where the inaugural conference of the ILP had taken place in 1893, relations between the Nonconformist chapels and the emergent Labour movement should have been particularly difficult and bitter. The chapels had been the backbone of support for the Liberal Party and the emergence of an independent Labour party threatened the entrenched Liberalism of West Yorkshire. It was seen by some as an affront to the moral stance taken by the chapels in supporting the party which, by comparison with the Tories, had been concerned for working people. Compared with the few but growing number of people who had lost faith in the Liberal Party, there were many Liberal Nonconformists who believed that, given time, a new kind of Liberalism could eradicate the worst evils of the capitalist system. Naturally they resented the emergence of an independent Labour movement and resisted it. Writing in 1937, Rhondda Williams recalled that 'in Bradford we had a very troubled time owing to the bitterness of resentment in the old parties at the emergence of the new, a bitterness returned by the latter in full measure, and so far as the churches were concerned, owing to the great blunder they made.'[98]

The 'blunder' was the decision of the Nonconformists to oppose Ben Tillett's candidature in West Bradford at the general election of 1892, and to oppose it not only as individual citizens, but collectively in the Bradford Nonconformist Association. Further offence was given when the town's Nonconformist ministers appeared together on the platform in support of Tillett's successful Liberal opponent, Alfred Illingworth.[99] As a result, the supporters of the independent Labour movement, (several of whom where members of Nonconformist congregations), came to the conclusion that the churches were against them. They left in a body to form the Bradford Labour Church, with Jowett as the first president and Edwin Halford as secretary. 'From that time on things were very bitter for years', wrote Williams. The refusal of all but four Bradford churches to provide relief for the Manningham Mill strikers had certainly not helped.

The Nonconformist ministers were not, however, unanimous in opposing the new Labour movement. During his General Election campaign in April 1892 Ben Tillett was invited to speak in Listerhills Congregational Church, and Keir Hardie preached at Brownroyd Congregational Church.[100] The Rev. Robert Roberts, minister of Frizinghall Congregational Church, became one of only two of the town's ministers to join the ILP (the other was the Rev. W. B. Graham, rector of St. Aidan's, who was later active in the Labour cause at Colne Valley. Blatchford described him as 'six foot a Socialist and five inch a parson'). Roberts represented the ILP on the School Board and Town Council.[101] In 1898, he acted as lecturer to the newly-formed Bradford Ethical Society, whose object was 'to promote by every means possible the moralisation of society in all the great concerns of personal, family, national and international affairs.' The Ethical Society reported its purpose and progress in the year book of the Bradford and District Trades and Labour Council, from which it attracted members.[102]

Roberts believed that 'Socialists should pursue a moderate policy and co-operate wherever possible with the Liberals so as not to split the progressive vote'. He resigned from the ILP in 1902 after being rebuked for appearing on a Liberal platform in opposition to a Socialist extremist, C. A. Glyde, in the Tong election, accusing his opponents 'of estranging men who ought to work together for the common good.'[103] But even such a moderate supporter of independent Labour's advance could not persuade his largely Liberal congregation to throw off their old political allegiance, and, having displeased them, he removed to Brownroyd Congregational Church in 1895, with a drop of £30 in salary. As was frequently the case when there were political differences between a minister and his congregation, no reference was made to them and other reasons were found for dissatisfaction. As a local reporter remarked,

> Private discussion turns almost wholly on the very point of which least was said during the formal debate on Mr. Roberts' letter of resignation. What was described as "the lack of spirituality" in his discourses resolves itself clearly enough into dissatisfaction with what were regarded as Mr. Roberts' too pronounced and insistent Independent Labour sympathies.[104]

At Greenfield Congregational Church, Rhondda Williams met with unusual success in retaining the confidence of his congregation while lending his support to the Labour movement. Throughout a long ministry he led the Greenfield congregation to adopt a thoroughly liberal New Theology and espouse the Social Gospel, but this did not necessarily lead to the adoption of Socialism, and many of those who flocked to hear him were satisfied that a progressive Liberalism could be the vehicle for an applied Christianity. The key to Williams's success, where other Socialist ministers often ran into trouble, appears to lie in the fact that he never became a member of the local ILP. He was advised, he said by F. W. Jowett, not to join the party, 'because we shall sometimes say and do things which you would not approve. If you protested from within, and were out-voted, the public would still hold you responsible.'[105] By standing aside from Liberal opposition and remaining outside the party, Williams was able to do a good deal to assuage the 'war' between the Nonconformist churches and the Labour movement. He also cultivated the personal acquaintance of the Labour men, believing that 'one cannot understand men from reports of them ... Nor can the spirit of a movement be understood from reading only – the men in it must be known.'[106]

In the end, however, even Greenfield was not exempt from the internal conflict and bitterness that the emergence of Labour caused in many Nonconformist chapels. The congregation contained some notable Liberals, including W. H. Boothroyd and W. E. B. Priestley (later Sir William Priestley, MP). They had stood all the minister's Social teaching and would probably have gone on standing it, and all the pressure from a circle of friends who asked why they regularly listened to a New Theologian and Socialist parson[107] Boothroyd was a deacon, a stalwart church worker and a good personal friend of the minister. He was so relieved when, in 1904, Williams decided to remain at Greenfield instead of accepting a call to another church, that he said 'he felt constrained to give Mr. Williams a blank cheque for his future preaching.'[108] There is no evidence that advantage of this liberal gesture was immediately taken – Williams continued to preach about social issues but without reference to parties. However, in the autumn of 1907 he became more outspoken in his support for Labour representation and introduced the topic into his preaching.

The subject for his sermon at Greenfield Church on 15 September was 'What Attitude should the Church Assume Towards Socialism?'. He argued that a great change had taken place since the general election in 1906. With the return of so many Labour members of Parliament 'there had been a considerable change in the tone and language of many prominent Labour men. It was more moderate and respectful, though not one whit less earnest or thorough.' This was explained by the fact that all young movements for reform, even religious ones, were accompanied by some measure of violence and vituperation. The growth of the Labour movement was a phenomenon of great importance and 'it was time for the Church to settle what her attitude was to be'. The church as such was above partisanship, and that should mean it 'should not favour the Liberal Party any more than the Socialist or the Tory party.' It should also mean that 'the Socialist should be as welcome in the Christian Church as a member of any other body. This had not always been the case.' However, 'this did not mean that ministers and church members as citizens should be neutral'. The first attitude towards Socialism he would urge upon every Christian man was that of the fair-minded student, because 'in its ethical principle it was identical with Christianity.'[109] Almost a month later, on 7 October – a week after R. J. Campbell had spoken at Greenfield Church on 'Socialism and Christianity: the failure of the Churches'[110] – Rhondda Williams appeared on a platform in support of William Leach's adoption as the Socialist and Labour candidate for the Great Horton Ward in forthcoming elections for the City Council, declaring 'I am here to-night to advocate Socialism'. And referring to the position of the Churches, he went on to say

it was not enough to play the Good Samaritan; they must try to catch the robbers or else there would be more wounded men than they could help. It was not for religion to go out as an ambulance brigade in the evening; what was wanted was a religion that would stop the war in which men were falling (applause). The splendid spirit of care for the poor that went out in charity and mission work should be enlisted for the social reconstruction which alone was adequate to deal with the magnitude of the problem (applause).[111]

Whether or not, in the light of his previous address, Williams intended these remarks to be an expression of his position as a citizen rather than as minister of Greenfield Congregational Church, in the eyes of his congregation and the public at large it was impossible to separate the man from his office. Neither Boothroyd nor Priestley could stand it any longer and both resigned their membership.[112] They were the richest members of the congregation and their departure was a great loss both financially and because they had been regular worshippers and influential in local affairs.

The resignation of the two Liberal stalwarts from the Greenfield Congregational Church was not only unsettling for the congregation but also for the minister. A month later, in a sermon entitled 'My Ideal Church', Williams felt it necessary to defend his appearance on the Labour platform by saying, 'Nonconformists generally had always welcomed their ministers on the political platform, and they still did so as long as it was the platform they themselves occupied. To appear on another platform was a somewhat unusual thing and created surprise. That was only a passing phase ... and in a few years the appearance of a minister on a Labour platform would occasion no more surprise than his appearance on a Liberal one did now.'[113]

The conflict had, however, weakened the pastoral relationship and within a year of the resignations Williams accepted an invitation to follow R. J. Campbell at Brighton. And, in 1911, after an interregnum of almost three years, he was succeeded by the Rev. Vivian P. Pomeroy, who shared the same theological convictions and led the church in an active programme of social action,[114] until he left for a Unitarian pulpit in America, in 1923. Pomeroy was also a supporter of the independent Labour movement, and his wife became a Labour member of the Bradford City Council. At that time a ministry of twenty years duration was not unusually long, but it certainly was amongst ministers who had so outspokenly supported the Labour movement, for the risk of dividing congregations was very great indeed. It was all the more remarkable that Williams succeeded in Bradford, where the opposition of the Noncon-formist Association to Tillett's independent Labour candidature had, in the early years, produced so much resentment amongst Labour's supporters. Yet, if relations between the Labour movement and the Non-conformist chapels in Bradford were poor, the ministry of T. Rhondda Williams, followed by that of Vivian Pomeroy, and the social programme of Greenfield Church helped to improve them. As William Leach said, when he was adopted as a local candidate, 'Only one pulpit he knew anything about had had anything to say about the horrors of slum dwellings, and the occupant of that pulpit, Mr. Rhondda Williams, got himself into grievous trouble with slum landlords as a consequence. That was a distinct feather in Mr. Rhondda Williams's cap (applause)'.[115] Local Labour leaders valued the attention drawn to their cause by Williams's preaching and writing, and candidates were glad to have his support on their platforms.

Conclusion

The four chapels examined in this chapter were unusual in the closeness of their relations with the emerging independent Labour movement. In no sense can they be regarded as representative of Nonconformity as a whole, which, whilst it continued to support the Liberal Party, resisted independent Labour representation. Even in Lancashire and the West Riding of Yorkshire, the 'cradle of the ILP', where Nonconformity was traditionally strong, the four examples almost exhaust the evidence of congregations supporting Labour's advance, and the paucity of examples has necessitated one being taken from Crewe, Cheshire.

Why were such congregations atypical? The answer would appear to be that most Nonconformist chapels were predominantly middle class and too far removed from social questions to be interested in a working-class movement. Many of them were also geographically remote from the worst effects of unemployment and wage cutting, although this was less likely to be true of chapels in the industrial areas. Of the congregations reviewed in this book, only Greenfield Congregational Church had and retained this almost exclusively middle-class membership. The others, for one reason or another attracted working-class members, which made them unusual. Salem Independent Methodist Chapel belonged to a denomination more traditionally working class, whilst at Beech Street Free Christian Church (Unitarian), Crewe, the influx of working-class people came with attempts to enlarge a very small membership, and at Pembroke Chapel it occurred when a formerly very strong congregation had lost its social status and been deserted by the middle classes.

It is also necessary to ask whether these unusual congregations were simply the products of strong leadership by socialist ministers. The influence of the ministry was clearly an important factor in most cases, but it does not apply to Salem Independent Methodist Chapel, which had no professional minister and a less hierarchical form of chapel leadership. Although the influence of the New Theology was fairly widespread in the early years of the new century, it was resisted by the Nonconformist leadership and therefore rejected by most congregations. In their openness to it, the ministers and congregations of these case studies were certainly unusual. In Lancashire and the West Riding of Yorkshire, and possibly in the whole of England and Wales, no denomination provides more than one example of a church which supported Labour, with the possible exception of the Baptists in Liverpool, which is all the more remarkable because they have generally been regarded as the most apolitical branch of Nonconformity.

Moreover, in addition to differences of denominational affiliation, these four churches bore little resemblance with regard to organization, strength and type of leadership. Greenfield, Pembroke and Salem's connexional associations were with avowedly Evangelical bodies, whilst Crewe's were with the more liberal Unitarian movement. Connexional links remained close in the case of Salem and Crewe, whilst Greenfield's ties with the Congregational Union were weak and Pembroke completely broke off relations with the Baptist Union. Although all four chapels were in industrial towns, Greenfield and Pembroke, set in the cities of Bradford and Liverpool, were surrounded by problems of unemployment and slums more extreme than those of Salem and Crewe.

Only one feature appears to have been common to the four chapels that have been examined: they all embraced or were infiltrated by the spirit of theological Modernism, which, in its popular form, eventually became known as 'The New Theology'. It is this, with its emphasis on the immanence of God, the Social Gospel, the establishment of the Kingdom of God on earth, and the need of a corporate, rather than an individual salvation, that is the key to understanding why these churches developed such close relations with local branches of the Labour movement. Their views, of course, were not shared by the vast majority of Nonconformist congregations.

Notes

1. *Church Reformer*, X, No.5, May 1891, quoted by P. d'A. Jones, *The Christian Socialist Revival* (Princeton University Press, Princeton, New Jersey, 1968), p.396.
2. K. Martin, *Father Figures, a first volume of autobiography, 1897–1931* (Hutchinson, London, 1966), p.14.
3. *Ibid.*, p.24.
4. P. Firth, 'Socialism and the Origins of the Labour Party in Nelson and District', unpublished University of Manchester MA Dissertation (Method 1), Manchester, 1975, p.29.
5. See H. McLachlan, *The Methodist Unitarian Movement* (Manchester University Press, Manchester, 1919).
6. W. Hewitson, *Lancaster Unitarian Chapel* (T. Bell, Lancaster, 1893), pp.59f.
7. *Ibid.*, pp.62f.
8. A. Mounfield, *A Short History of Independent Methodism, Souvenir of the 100th Annual Meeting of the Independent Methodist Churches* (Independent Methodist Book Room, Wigan, 1905), p.175.

9. W. Wellock, *Off the beaten track* (Sarvodaya Prachuralaya, Tanjore, India, 1961), p.13.
10. *Ibid.*, p.13.
11. Joseph Robinson, *Salem Independent Methodist Church, Nelson, A Short History* (Elliot and Elliot, Nelson, 1952), pp.39, 40.
12. Tape recording by J. Liddington of interview with Stan Iveson, Tape 898, p.11 (Manchester Studies, Manchester Polytechnic); J. Liddington, *The Life and Times of a Respectable Rebel, Selina Cooper (1864–1946)* (Virago, London, 1984).
13. *Ibid.*, Tape 889, p.4; Liddington, *op. cit.*, p.38.
14. Liddington, *op. cit.*, p.465.
15. *ILP Annual Report*, 1893; *Colne and Nelson Times*, 13 January 1893.
16. F. Bealey and H. Pelling, *Labour and Politics, 1900–1906* (Macmillan, London, 1958), p.103.
17. Wellock, *op. cit.*, p.15.
18. *Ibid.*, p.16.
19. *Ibid.*, p.20.
20. *Ibid.*, p.19.
21. Letter, Mr. G. F. Kay (nephew of W. Wellock) to L. Smith, 27 June 1987.
22. Colne Congregational Church, Minutes, 19 May 1890.
23. Liddington, *op. cit.*, p.81.
24. *Ibid.*
25. Colne Congregational Church, Minutes, 29 November 1894.
26. Clyde Binfield, *Pastors and People* (Queen's Road Baptist Church, Coventry, 1984), pp.227–231.
27. Cannon Street Baptist Chapel, Minutes of Church and Congregation Annual General Meeting, 10 February 1920.
28. Binfield, *op. cit.*, p.227.
29. Cannon Street Baptist Chapel, Minutes of Church and Congregation, 16 May 1922, 22 June 1922.
30. *Ibid.*, 19 December 1922.
31. *Ibid.*, Deacons' Minutes, 5 September 1921.
32. Binfield, *op. cit.*, p.229.
33. Cannon Street Baptist Chapel, Deacons' Minutes, 7 November 1922; Minutes of Church Committee, 21 November 1922.
34. *Ibid.*, Deacons' Minutes, 7 November 1922.
35. *Ibid.*, Deacons' Minutes, 4 January 1923; Minutes of Church Committee, 9 January 1923.
36. P. Ollerhead, 'Unitarianism in Crewe, 1860–1940', *Transactions of the Unitarian Historical Society*, Vol. 17, No.1., September 1979, p.29.
37. *Ibid.*, p.30.
38. Beech Street Free Church, Crewe, Minutes, 28 February 1883
39. Ollerhead, *op. cit.*, p.30.
40. W. H. Chaloner, *The Social and Economic Development of Crewe, 1780–1923* (Manchester University Press, Manchester, 1950), p.156.
41. Unitarian College, Manchester, *Register of Students, 1854–1929*, pp.31–35.
42. C. S. Grundy, *Reminiscences of Strangeways Unitarian Free Church, 1838–1888* (Abel Heywood, Manchester, 1888), p.51.
43. Ollerhead, *op. cit.*, p.34.

44. *Ibid.*, p.33.
45. *Ibid.*, p.35.
46. Chaloner, *op. cit.*, pp.166–167.
47. *Ibid.*, p.169.
48. Beech Street Free Church, Crewe, Minutes, 11 February 1894.
49. *Ibid.*, 20 February 1894.
50. *Ibid.*, 19 August 1894.
51. *Ibid.*, 10 September 1894.
52. Ollerhead, *op. cit.*, p.32.
53. *Christian Life and Unitarian Herald*, Vol.31, 1905, p.117.
54. Park Lane Chapel, Ashton in Makerfield, Minutes, 1 December 1912.
55. *Ibid.*, 3 September 1911, 5 November 1911, 9 November 1911, 20 November 1911, 3 December 1911 and 11 December 1911.
56. *Ibid.*, 20 March 1912.
57. *Ibid.*, 17 October 1909, 12 January 1910 and 19 June 1910.
58. MSS Historical Notes of Park Lane Chapel, 1891–1914 (handwriting appears to be that of Peter Gorton, the Chapel Secretary), Wigan Record Office, D/NU1/1/3.
59. Park Lane Chapel Minutes, 7 January 1912.
60. Historical Notes, *op. cit.*
61. E. A. Payne, *The Baptist Union, A Short History* (Carey Kingsgate Press, London, 1959), pp.127–143.
62. Jones, *op. cit.*, pp.392, 393.
63. Ian Sellers, *Salute to Pembroke, Pembroke Chapel, Liverpool, 1838–1891* (Alsager, 1960), pp.6–9.
64. *Ibid.*, p.12.
65. C. F. Aked, *Changing Creeds and Social Struggles* (J. Clarke, London, 1893).
66. Pembroke Chapel, Minutes, 6 March 1891.
67. Sellers, *op. cit.*, p.14.
68. *Ibid.*, p.14.
69. *Ibid.*, p.12.
70. *Ibid.*, p.14.
71. *Ibid.*, p.12.
72. *Ibid.*, p.16.
73. *Ibid.*, p.16.
74. *Liverpool Pulpit*, 1893, p.46.
75. Sellers, *op. cit.*, p.18.
76. *Liverpool Pulpit*, 1895, p.69.
77. *Ibid.*, 1894, p.111.
78. *Ibid.*
79. Letter, I. Sellers to L. Smith, 28 June 1987.
80. Pembroke Chapel, Minutes, 25 November 1906; Deacons' Minutes, 2 December 1906.
81. *Ibid.*, Minutes, 9 September 1907; Deacons' Minutes, 16 September 1907.
83. *Ibid.*, Deacons' Minutes, 23 September 1908.
84. *Ibid.*, Deacons' Minutes, 26 October 1910.
85. *Ibid.*, Minutes, 10 January 1912; Deacons' Minutes, 2 January 1912.
86. Sellers, *op. cit.*, pp.27–29.
87. *The Times*, 1 October 1921.

88. Pembroke Chapel, Minutes, 7 September 1921.

89. *Ibid.*, Deacons' Minutes, 24 October 1921.

90. *Ibid.*, Minutes, 5 October 1921, 7 November 1921; Deacons' Minutes, 2 October 1921.

91. *Ibid.*, Minutes, 5 December 1921; Deacons' Minutes, 1 October 1921.

92. *Ibid.*, Deacons' Minutes, 28 August 1922.

93. *Ibid.*, Deacons' Minutes, 1 April 1923.

94. *Ibid.*, Deacons' Minutes, 25 September 1922, 27 November 1922.

95. Sellers, *op. cit.*, pp.30–36; D. Steers, "'The Bare-Headed Minister' – The Radical Career of James Vint Laughland", *Transactions of the Unitarian Historical Society*, Vol. XX, No.2, April 1992.

96. *What the Churches say of Socialism* (Liverpool Fabian Leaflet No. 11, Liverpool, May 1912).

97. Ian Sellers, 'An Edwardian Whirlwind: the Rev. Herbert Dunnico in Warrington (1902–1906), unpublished essay; for Dunnico's later career, see Jones, *op. cit.*, pp.350, 351.

98. Cuttings of articles by T. Rhondda Williams, *Bradford Telegraph and Argus*, 1937.

99. *Ibid.*

100. Rosemary E. Chadwick, 'Church and People in Bradford and District, 1880–1914.' Unpublished DPhil Thesis, University of Oxford, 1986, p.313.

101. *Ibid.*, p.315.

102. Bradford and District Trades and Labour Council, *Year Book*, 1899, p.166.

103. Bradford ILP Minutes, 22 October 1902.

104. *Bradford Observer*, 31 December 1894.

105. Cuttings, *op. cit.*

106. *Ibid.*

107. *Ibid.*

108. Greenfield Congregational Church, Minutes, 20 June 1904.

109. *Yorkshire Daily Observer*, 16 September 1907.

110. *Ibid.*, 2 October 1907.

111. *Ibid.*, 8 October 1907.

112. *Ibid.*, 29 November 1907.

113. *Ibid.*, 16 December 1907.

114. Our Special Commissioner, 'The Free Churches of Bradford', *Christian Globe*, n.d. (Bradford Public Library)

115. *Yorkshire Daily Observer*, 8 October 1907.

Chapter 7

Conclusion

With the advent of the Socialist Revival of the 1880s, when aspirations for independent Labour representation began to develop, intellectual impulses and a growing concern for social reform provided a number of meeting points between Nonconformity and the Labour movement. Intellectual revolutions in the biological, natural and social sciences caused widespread questioning of the established order. The churches, too, underwent their own upheaval as historical principles were applied to the study of theology. The general tendency of thought was to suggest a more evolutionary and social view of man, and liberal theology reinforced this with a new view of Jesus as one who had been concerned with the establishment of the Kingdom of God as a just social order in this life, not only as an eschatological event.

Such views, however, were slow to effect any change in political affiliations. They did not by themselves make socialists and most radicals were content to pursue their political aspirations by supporting the Liberal Party. This was particularly true of Nonconformists, who, over a century and a half, in the agitations for the removal of the Dissenting disabilities, had formed a powerful alliance with the Liberal Party. If any alterations were necessary to remove the worst economic consequences of the capitalist system, Nonconformists continued to believe that they could be made by the Liberal Party, which was traditionally regarded as the party of conscience and the friend of the dispossessed. This view only began to change as Nonconformists came into direct contact with the problems of unemployment and urban poverty as they engaged with the working classes in schemes of social amelioration.

There were different motivations for going to live in urban slums and work amongst the poor. For some it was part of the process by which the churches tried to attract the working classes after the scale of their absence was revealed by the 1851 Religious Census. In many cases, such as those of the Salvation Army and the more Evangelical branches of Nonconformity, the intention was primarily evangelical – to raise the physical condition of the poor in order to make them receptive to the spiritual message. For others, such as those who worked in the Settlement movement, the intention was humanitarian. From a variety of motives, small-scale charitable attempts were made to find solutions to the problems caused by enforced idleness, poverty and urban slums. Nonconformists, particularly those with a liberal theology, were prominent in support of the land nationalization societies, which have been widely

163

recognized as a route by which Liberal radicals progressed to Socialism. Communitarian experiments to provide work for the unemployed, such as the Rev. H. V. Mills' Starnthwaite Home Colony, obviously attracted the Labour movement, and although they failed, they were part of a process by which Liberal radicals came to realize that nothing short of independent Labour representation and a political programme, including legislation to limit the working day to eight hours, could provide a remedy on the necessary scale.

Indeed, the Independent Labour Party came into being only when it was eventually recognized that strikes and small-scale ameliorative schemes could achieve little and that parliamentary solutions were necessary. This gradual process of discovery included the trouble at Starnthwaite and culminated with the failure of the strike at Manningham Mills, Bradford, in 1891, which helped lead to the formation of the ILP. Naturally, with this background of Nonconformist concern for social reform, there were those in the Labour movement who recognized allies within the Churches. Many of the Labour leaders also had active or nominal associations with Nonconformist chapels. Their socialism was of a peculiarly ethical kind and owed little to Marxist theory. Its spirit of brotherhood and fellowship was identified with Christianity, often expressed in the terminology of the Sermon on the Mount. Even the older quasi-Marxist socialist bodies – the SDF and Socialist League – shared the characteristics of the 'religion of socialism', but they were based in London. The SDF did meet with success in Burnley, but its anti-religious dogmatism and its ambivalence over the 'Drink' question prevented it from making any impression on the strictly teetotal Nonconformist culture.

It was only when Labour leaders emerged who shared the strong Temperance stance taken by Nonconformity that closer relationships became possible. The formation of several Nonconformist socialist societies also suggested to Labour leaders that they had some support within the Free Churches. The cultivation of Nonconformist interest was also to become a necessity, especially if there was to be an electoral breakthrough, and this was particularly the case in the West Riding of Yorkshire and north-east Lancashire where both Nonconformity and the Liberal Party were entrenched. Liberal radicals had to be won over to Labour and their strong religious and temperance affiliations could not be discounted. These areas of overlapping concern meant that there were those in the Labour movement and the Nonconformist churches who would have liked to have seen closer relations. However, attempts to forge them never came to much. As one side found it expedient to draw close, the other had reasons for backing off. Relationships were never more than flimsy and fluctuating.

Although it is possible to find considerable evidence of Nonconformists who supported Labour's advance, they were never more than a small minority, and their support was often indirect and tangential. But, given this interest, common background and mutual fascination, why were relationships not closer? This can be answered in terms of issues on which the Labour movement disagreed with Nonconformist attitudes and *vice versa*, for example the Boer War; but fundamentally the obstacle was the middle-class social structure of Nonconformity and the Evangelical theology of all but the Unitarians, Quakers and Swedenborgians. The middle-class character of the Nonconformist churches is evident in the attempts that they made to re-establish contact with the working class. In areas such as Lancashire and the West Riding, where the Nonconformist culture deeply penetrated local life, the chapels did attract working-class members, but they tended to be from amongst the labour aristocrats. Except in the industrial areas and large cities, most Nonconformists were geographically and socially remote from the worst effects of unemployment and slum dwellings, and whilst they might have to tighten their belts in economic depressions, they remained comparatively affluent. Their incomes and social status rested upon the capitalist system, with its sweating dens, wage cutting and lock-outs, so that, whilst the more humane amongst them might have deplored poverty and relieved it with charity, few were disposed to favour any fundamental alterations in the way society was organized.

It was a society based upon economic freedom. Nonconformists had been the most ardent supporters of the free trade. They had agitated for the repeal of the Corn Laws and remained opponents of any government protectionist policies and State interference. Their religious history had involved a struggle for freedom of belief and to worship according to conscience. They had been forced into a particular way of life as a result of their Dissent. The disabilities curtailed their freedom to seek education in the ancient universities or to hold public office. Temperamentally they had been conditioned to react against anything that curtailed individualism. Some advanced Liberals did begin to see the need for limited State controls and municipalization, but generally Nonconformists opposed them. Equally, they feared the consequences which collectivism and the industrial policies of an independent Labour party might have upon their economic freedom. Moreover, the emphasis on economic individualism was powerfully reinforced by the Evangelical theology of mainstream Nonconformity.

Methodism had originated with the Wesleyan Revival in the eighteenth century, and, despite fragmentation into its Primitive, New Connexion, Independent and Bible Christian branches, no secession had ceased to stress the sinfulness of human nature and the need for personal redemption. Amongst the churches of the Old Dissent, the largest of the denominations, the Congregationalists and the Baptists, had also absorbed the Evangelical spirit of the 'New Dissent'. Only the Unitarians, who had retained the rational spirit of the Enlightenment, stood entirely apart from this depressing view of human nature. The Society of Friends for a time became evangelical, but eventually adopted a quietist approach coupled with social concern and became more middle class in the process. The New Church (Swedenborgian), whose origins were distinctive in being neither of the 'New' or 'Old' dissenting traditions, also had an unusually optimistic view of human nature. But the Unitarians, Quakers and Swedenborgians were tiny Churches, compared with the Methodists, Baptists and Congregationalists, and their theologies anything but representative of Nonconformity as a whole, which was overwhelmingly Evangelical.

With their emphasis on the need to redeem individuals for the benefits of an other-worldly salvation, the Evangelical Churches were essentially individualistic. Their concern was not with the conditions of life on earth, except insofar as they might be a hindrance to acceptance of the spiritual salvation the churches offered. They regarded collectivist attempts to improve human conditions in this life as being none of their business and a diversion from the true purpose of saving souls. Although social questions were raised in the denominational assemblies, any suggestions that solutions might be found through Nonconformity's closer association with the Labour movement were resisted by the Nonconformist leadership, and eventually diverted to the sidelines of Free Church concern by the formation of unions for social service. The Evangelical theology of Methodism meant that, contrary to the received view, Methodists, with one or two exceptions, played a minimal role in the emergence of the Labour movement. It is true that when the early Socialist strands of the Labour movement merged with the trades union movement, eventually to be submerged by it, Methodists were more prominent, and by the time of the 1906 General Election were well represented amongst the LRC Members of Parliament. But it is quite incorrect to project this later history back to the early years of the Socialist societies and the ILP.

With regard to the aphorism 'there is more of Methodism than Marxism in the British Labour movement', this study reveals that if the quasi-Marxism of the Hyndman's Social Democratic Party played only a small part, Methodism played even less. However, the personal intellectual influence of the Rev. S. E. Keeble, a Methodist who understood Socialist theory better than most Nonconformist socialists, should not be underestimated. Nonconformists were most easily able to identify with the Labour movement where the traditional Evangelical theology was rejected in favour of theological Modernism and, eventually, the New Theology. This occurred partly as a result of the spread of liberal ideas from continental centres of learning, mainly in Germany.

There is also some evidence that, quite apart from these academic developments, several of those who later became associated with the emergent Labour movement experienced personal spiritual crises which led to the rejection of the orthodox Christian view of sinful human nature as the root cause of social problems, and to the reconstruction of their theologies on Modernist lines. This certainly happened to John Trevor, the founder of the Labour Church movement. Eventually, the Modernist trend was popularized in R. J. Campbell's New Theology movement and the Social Gospel movement, which suggested that Socialism was applied Christianity. The New Theology's emphasis on the immanence of God, the religion of Jesus rather than the religion about him and the establishment of the Kingdom of God as a this-worldly just social order provided a religious framework that, unlike orthodoxy, presented no obstacles to supporting the Labour movement. Although the minority of Nonconformists who supported independent Labour's advance belonged to a wide variety of religious denominations, almost without exception they were those who embraced theological Modernism and the New Theology. Even the Rev. S. E. Keeble, the Methodist socialist, who professed to reject Campbell's theology, in later life declared that his 'sympathies had ever been modern'.

However, although Modernism and the New Theology were widely known, their influence was confined to the fringe of the Nonconformist movement – to its more scholarly, independent thinkers, its theological students and auxiliary groups. In the process of reconstructing their theologies those who adopted it often moved from denomination to denomination, usually but not invariably towards Unitarianism, and as a result, with the exception of Dr. John Clifford, the Baptist, they rarely occupied positions of leadership in their Churches.

The adoption of the Modernist theology within an Evangelical denomination tended to lead ministers and congregations into isolation from other churches. Modernism was only attractive to a few and it did not shift Nonconformity from its traditional Evangelical position. Yet, where its influence was felt and adopted, when it coincided with local industrial, social and economic problems, it usually led to greater participation in the Labour movement's emergence, as the four case studies of local churches have demonstrated. This was particularly the case in Bradford, where a small coterie of New Theologians, standing over against the general opposition of the Bradford Nonconformist Association, exercised an influence in support of independent Labour representation.

More practically, relations between the Churches and the emergent Labour movement got off to a bad start by the failure of the churches to recognize the political aspirations of working men, whilst trying to minister to their spiritual needs. This led John Trevor to found his Labour Church in Manchester in 1891, to overcome the problem of working men having to deny their political hopes whilst they worshipped in chapels led by middle-class Liberals. Two years later, in 1892, the problem which Trevor had identified was highlighted in Bradford, when the newly-formed Bradford Nonconformist Association marshalled most of the town's ministers and congregations to oppose Ben Tillett, the independent Labour candidate, by suggesting that Nonconformists should vote for Alfred Illingworth, the Liberal candidate. As a result, Fred Jowett, a Congregationalist, and several other Nonconformist independent Labour supporters left their chapels to form the Bradford Labour Church.

The entrenched Liberalism of the chapels and the impossibility of making headway from within led to the rapid expansion of the Labour Church movement in the textile districts of the Lancashire and the West Riding of Yorkshire, where the major thrust for independent Labour representation was being made by the ILP. Not surprisingly this made relationships bitter for some years. Yet the Socialism of the textile regions was of a non-doctrinaire variety and deeply rooted in the religious idealism of Nonconformity. Communities were too close-knit for political opponents never to speak to each other again, whatever their differences. Instead of creating a gulf between Labour and the Churches, the Labour Church in many ways provided a meeting point. It readily received sympathetic, socialistically-minded Nonconformist ministers to lecture at its services. Thus, the churches, especially those in Lancashire and Yorkshire, were kept in touch with Labour affairs and from time to time would invite Labour leaders to address their annual assemblies. This frequently seems to have resulted from charges that the Churches had turned their backs on the Labour movement and were indifferent to the plight of the unemployed and the poor.

Whilst the Labour movement was thrusting ahead with the formation of the Labour Church, then the ILP, the Churches were forced to meet the challenge by discussing the 'Social Question', but after the 1895 General Election, when the campaign of the ILP was severely demoralized by the failure to return any of the 28 candidates, the pressure was off and the Churches returned to their traditional evangelical interests. The Labour movement also became more concerned with its own internal affairs, as it engaged in building up a Party machine to secure electoral success. The overall result was that the Churches and the Labour movement made few contacts between 1895 and 1903.

One event during that period, however, proved to be an insurmountable obstacle in all future attempts to bring Nonconformity and the Labour movement closer together. The Anglo-South African war deeply divided the Labour movement, as it did the Churches. The problem for future relations between Labour and the Nonconformity was that the leaders of the sections most likely to seek some kind of alliance took opposite views. The ILP was pro-Boer. There were Boer supporters in the Churches, but several prominent Free Church leaders took a strong Imperialist stance and this was never forgotten by Labour leaders. After the Boer War, Labour leaders were usually sceptical whenever the

Churches made overtures about closer relationships. Nonetheless, the possibility of closer relations continued to be a matter of controversy amongst Labour leaders in the early years of the twentieth century. In 1903, when the LRC was making a secret pact with the Liberal chief whip, Herbert Gladstone, allowing a number of Labour candidates to stand unopposed by Liberals, two opposite tendencies arose, one repelling the Churches, the other attracting them.

Robert Blatchford's rejection of religion did much to alienate the largely northern, Nonconformist readership of the *Clarion*, whilst Philip Snowden's pamphlet, *The Christ that is to be*, suggested that Socialism was the practical application of the Christian hope for a just society. Overall the tendency was for the Labour movement to attract Nonconformist support, since Blatchford's onslaught provoked a backlash from Nonconformists who argued that Socialism could rest on Christian principles. The pamphlet, with its special appeal to northern workers in districts where the Chapel culture was deeply rooted, together with the decisions of the LRC to publish several religious pieces of propaganda and a hymn book, suggests that a deliberate attempt was made to win Nonconformist votes, or to make Labour candidates acceptable to Liberal voters in constituencies where the pact applied. In 1905, in the wake of the unofficial pact between the LRC and the Liberal Party, the National Council of Free Churches made attempts to forge an alliance between the Free Churches and the Labour Party, but by this time, with growing confidence that it would be well-represented in Parliament after the next election, the LRC leaders had less to gain from closer relationships, and preferred not to be compromised by associating with Church leaders who had shown strong Imperialist tendencies during the Boer War. As it prepared for the breakthrough that would, at last, return a body of representative working men to Parliament, the LRC leaders had also to foster Socialist unity with the more doctrinaire sections of the Labour movement, particularly in the London area, which bitterly opposed any negotiations for closer co-operation with the Churches.

After the 1906 General Election, when so many of the new Labour Members of Parliament acknowledged their actual or nominal links with Nonconformity, there was no advantage to be gained by the Labour Party doing anything to foster closer relations with the Churches. This retreat by the Labour movement was accompanied in the Churches by a reaction against involvement in politics, and against Socialism in particular. *Nonconformity and Politics*, published in 1909, argued that the churches had been too involved with political issues at the expense of their primary concern with spirituality. At the same time, the Nonconformist Anti-Socialist Union began a campaign to eradicate Socialism from the churches. The general result was that Nonconformists returned to their traditional concern for the saving of individual souls, which was the fundamental reason why they did not play a greater role in the emergence of the Labour movement, with its doctrine of social salvation and collectivist solutions.

Another factor which tended to draw the curtain on efforts to bring the Labour movement and the Churches closer together was the spread of Syndicalist views in the Labour and Trades Union movements in the few years before the commencement of World War I. There were those in the Labour movement who were turning away from parliamentary representation to find a solution to working-class emancipation through the establishment of government by large general unions. The widespread industrial unrest of 1911 and 1912 did little to endear the Nonconformist employers to the Labour cause, and made them fearful of the abandonment of parliamentary democracy. The fact that the Syndicalists were outside the mainstream of the Labour movement did not remove the employers' dread of strikes. It was only where Nonconformists adopted Modernist views culminating in the New Theology that they had doctrines compatible with the independent Labour movement's quest for emancipation through collectivist remedies. This led them to give support to local campaigns for Labour's advance, particularly in north-east Lancashire, the West Riding of Yorkshire, and other industrial areas, whereas, in general, Nonconformists opposed all attempts to have Labour represented by working men, other than through the Liberal Party.

Closer relations, where they existed, were usually at the expense of congregational harmony and by churches divorcing themselves from the life of their denominations. By 1906, however, the limited influence of R. J. Campbell's movement had already begun to decline with the advent of the broader based unions for social service established by most Nonconformist denominations. The same year, at the hands of one of its own theologians, liberal Modernism's intellectual foundations were shaken by the publication of Albert Schweitzer's *Von Reimarus zu Wrede* (English translation, *The Quest for the Historical Jesus*, 1910), in which he argued that Jesus had shared with his contemporaries a thoroughgoing eschatological view of the Kingdom of God, and not the earthly Utopian view that had been suggested by Modernism and the New Theologians, and to which they had looked to Socialism to help inaugurate. Many rank and file adherents to the New Theology became Unitarians, but the leaders, with the exception of T. Rhondda Williams, returned to the folds of orthodoxy. The movement had been short-lived and whilst it had provided a theological framework that enabled a few Nonconformists to relate more closely to the Labour movement, it made little impression on Nonconformity as a whole, which continued and reaffirmed its traditional Evangelical concern for individual souls.

The Free Churches found it advantageous to show some interest in the aspirations of the Labour movement as they attempted to re-establish lost contact with the working class, but not to the extent of alienating their middle-class Liberal membership by denying the alliance with the

170

Liberal Party. On their side, the less doctrinaire Labour leaders were prepared to court Nonconformity insofar as they believed it would assist them to achieve an electoral breakthrough, which it did not. Fundamentally, however, the middle-class membership of the churches and the individualist doctrines of orthodox Nonconformity made it impossible to establish closer relationships with the emergent independent Labour movement seeking collectivist solutions to the condition of the working class, in spite of the considerable efforts to achieve such relationships by some on both sides.

Bibliography

Manuscripts

Ashton under Lyne Pleasant Sunday Afternoon, Minutes (Tameside Public Library).

Beech Street Free Church, Crewe, Minutes (Cheshire County Record Office, Chester).

Bolton and District Ministers' Fraternal, Minutes (Lancashire County Record Office, Preston).

Bradford ILP Minutes.

Cannon Street Baptist Chapel, Accrington, Minutes, 1901–1927 (At the Church).

Cannon Street Baptist Chapel, Accrington, Deacons' Minutes, 1906–1923 (At the Church).

Colne Congregational Church, Minutes (Lancashire County Record Office, Preston).

Greenfield Congregational Church, Minutes (West Yorkshire Archives, Bradford).

Hyde Pleasant Sunday Afternoon, Minutes (Tameside Public Library).

Independent Labour Party, Minutes, 1893–1909.

Independent Labour Party, National Administrative Council, Minutes.

Independent Labour Party Pamphlet Collection, c.1890–1950.

Francis Johnson Collection, 1888–1950.

S. E. Keeble, Note Book, 1909. Seven in number. Held by G. W. Keeble, Handford, Cheshire.

Labour Party Pamphlet Collection, c.1900–1950.

Labour Representation Committee Correspondence, 1900–1907.

Labour Party National Executive Committee, Minutes, 1906–50s.

London Unitarian Ministers' Meeting, Minutes (Dr. Williams's Library).

Marsden Congregational Church, Minutes (West Yorkshire Archives, Huddersfield).

Marsden Congregational Church, Deacons' Minutes (West Yorkshire Archives, Huddersfield).

Historical Notes of Park Lane Chapel, 1891–1914 (Wigan Record Office).

Park Lane Chapel, Ashton in Makerfield, Minutes (Wigan Record Office).

Pembroke Chapel, Liverpool, Minutes, 1890–1922 (Regent's Park College, Oxford).

Pembroke Chapel, Liverpool, Deacons' Minutes, 1897–1928 (Regent's Park College, Oxford).

Pioneer Preachers, Minutes, 1912–1934 (Dr. Williams's Library, London).
Social Democratic Federation and British Socialist Party collection of
    pamphlets.
G. H. Wood Collection (Huddersfield University Library).

Printed Primary Sources

Bradford and District Trades and Labour Council, *Year Book*, 1899.
Ashton-under-Lyne Pleasant Sunday Afternoon, *Notice of Meeting*,
    (Tameside Public Library).
Ashton under Lyne Pleasant Sunday Afternoon, *Annual Report*, 1892.
    (Tameside Public Library).
Bradford Unemployed Emergency Committee, *Manifesto*, 1894.
    (Bradford Public Library).
R. J. Campbell, *Primitive Christianity and Modern Socialism*, Progress
    League Series No. 1, London, n.d.
Congregational Year Book, 1880–1914. Cuttings of articles by T. Rhondda
    Williams for *Bradford Telegraph and Argus*, 1937. (Bradford Public
    Library).
Patricroft Congregational Magazine and P.S.A. Record, Prize List, 1904.
    (Salford City Archive Department).
Lancashire Congregational Calendar, 1880–1897.
Lancashire Congregational Year Book, 1898–1914.
Lancashire Independent College, *Annual Report*, 1899.
Land Nationalisation Society, *Letterhead*, 1899.
Liverpool Fabian Leaflet No. 11, Liverpool, May 1912. *What the
    Churches say of Socialism*.
London Trades' Council, *Notice of Resolution Passed*, November 1905.
Queens Park Congregational Church, *Letterhead*.
Salvation Army, *Letterhead*.
Philip Snowden, *The Christ that is to be* (Independent Labour Party,
    London, 1903).
*Report of the National Conference of the members and friends of Unitarian,
    Liberal Christian, Free Christian, Presbyterian, and other Non-Subscribing
    and Kindred Congregations*, 1888.
Unitarian College, Manchester, *Register of Students 1854–1929*
    (Manchester, 1929).
J. Trevor, *Theology and the Slums* (Labour Church Tract No.1, Labour
    Prophet, London, n.d.).
Wesleyan Methodist Conference Minutes, 1880–1914.
Yorkshire Congregational Year Book, 1880–1914.
Yorkshire United Independent College, *Annual Report*, 1893–94.

Newspapers

Bradford Observer.
The British Weekly.

Christian Globe.
Christian Life and Unitarian Herald.
The Christian World.
The Clarion.
Colne Valley Guardian.
Halifax Evening Courier.
Halifax Guardian.
The Inquirer.
Labour Leader.
Labour Prophet.
Liverpool Pulpit.
Marsden Congregational Church Messenger.
The Methodist Recorder.
The Methodist Times.
The Methodist Weekly.
The Times.
Uses.
Yorkshire Daily Observer.

Books – Primary

C. F. Aked, *Changing Creeds and Social Struggles* (J.Clarke, London, Liverpool, 1893).

William Booth, *In Darkest England and the Way Out* (International Headquarters of the Salvation Army, London, 1890).

R. J. Campbell, *The New Theology* (Chapman and Hall, London, 1907).

R. J. Campbell, *New Theology Sermons* (Williams and Norgate, London, 1907).

R. J. Campbell, *Christianity and the Social Order* (Chapman and Hall, London, 1907).

J. Clifford, *The Ultimate Problem of Christianity* (Kingsgate Press, London, 1906).

J. Clifford, *The Gospel of World Brotherhood according to Jesus Christ* (Hodder and Stoughton, London, 1920).

H. George, *Progress and Poverty* (The Henry George Foundation of Great Britain, London, 1931; First edition, 1879).

A. Harnack, *Das Wesen des Christentums* (Berlin, 1900); English translation, T. B. Saunders, *What is Christianity?* (Benn, London, Fifth Edition, 1958).

M. Hindle and A. D. Fletcher, *Little Lane and Greenfield* (Girlington Congregational Church, Bradford).

C. S. Horne, *The Institutional Church* (James Clarke and Co., London, n.d. [1907]).

S. E. Keeble, *Industrial Daydreams* (Elliot Stock, London, 1896; Second Edition, 1907).

G. Lansbury, *My Life* (Constable and Co., London, 1928).

174

H. V. Mills, *Poverty and the State* (Kegan Paul, London, 2nd edition, 1889).

A Nonconformist Minister, *Nonconformity and Politics* (Sir Isaac Pitman and Sons, London, 1909).

A. Schweitzer, *Von Reimarus zu Wrede* (Mohr, Tubingen, 1906); English translation, *The Quest for the Historical Jesus* (A. & C. Black, 1910).

J. Trevor, *My Quest for God* (Labour Prophet Office, London, 1897).

Alex. Thompson, *Here I Lie* (George Routledge and Sons, London, 1937).

Mrs. Humphry Ward, *Robert Elsmere* (Smith, Elder, London, 1888).

W. Wellock, *Off the beaten track* (Sarvodaya Prachuralaya, Tanjore, India, 1961).

W. H. White (Mark Rutherford), *The Autobiography of Mark Rutherford* (T. Fisher Unwin, London, n.d. [1881]).

W. H. White (Mark Rutherford), *The Deliverance* (T. Fisher Unwin, London, n.d. [1887]).

P. H. Wicksteed, *Our Prayers and Politics* (Swan, Sonnenschein, Le Bas, and Lowrey, London, 1885).

P. H. Wicksteed, *The Social Ideals and the Economic Doctrines of Socialism* (National Conference Union for Social Service and Unwin Brothers, 1908).

T. Rhondda Williams, *The New Theology – An Exposition* (Peter Lund, Humphries and Co. Ltd., London, 1907).

T. Rhondda Williams, *How I found my Faith* (Cassell and Co., London, 1938).

Books – Secondary

F. Bealey and H. Pelling, *Labour and Politics, 1900–1906* (Macmillan, London, 1958).

D. W. Bebbington, *The Nonconformist Conscience* (George Allen and Unwin, London, 1982).

H. Begbie, *The Life of General William Booth*, 2 Vols. (Macmillan, London, 1920).

J. M. Bellamy and J. Saville, *Dictionary of Labour Biography*, Vols. 1–5 (Macmillan, London, 1972–1984).

C. Binfield, *So Down to Prayers: Studies in English Nonconformity, 1780–1920* (J. M. Dent and Son, London, 1977).

C. Binfield, *Pastors and People: The Biography of a Baptist Church, Queen's Road, Coventry* (Queen's Road Baptist Church, Coventry, 1984).

I. Bradley, *The Call to Seriousness* (Jonathan Cape, London, 1976).

A. Fenner Brockway, *Socialism over Sixty Years* (G.Allen and Unwin, London, 1946).

S. Bryher, *An Account of the Labour and Socialist Movement in Bristol* (Bristol Printers, Bristol, 1929).

T. P. Bunting, *The Life of Jabez Bunting* (Longman, Brown, Green, Longmans and Roberts, London, 1859).

T. Brennan, E. W. Cooney and H. Pollins, *Social Change in South West Wales* (Watts & Co., London, 1954).

K. D. Brown (ed.), *Essays in Anti-Labour History* (Macmillan, London, 1974).

K. D. Brown, *The First Labour Party, 1906–1924* (Croom Helm, London, 1979).

K. D. Brown, *A Social History of the Nonconformist Ministry in England and Wales, 1880–1930* (Clarendon Press, Oxford, 1988).

W. H. Chaloner, *The Social and Economic Development of Crewe, 1780–1923* (Manchester University Press, Manchester, 1950).

D. Clark, *Colne Valley: Radicalism to Socialism* (Longman, London, 1981).

D. Clark, *Victor Grayson, Labour's Lost Leader* (Quartet Books, London, 1985).

Horton Davies, *Worship and Theology in England*, vol. 4 and vol. 5, (Princeton University Press, Princeton, N.J., 1962, 1965).

W. T. Pennar Davis, *Mansfield College, Oxford* (Independent Press, London, 1947).

V. D. Davis, *A History of Manchester College, Oxford* (G. Allen and Unwin, London, 1932).

Michael S. Edwards, *S. E. Keeble* (Wesley Historical Society, Chester, 1977).

L. E. Elliott-Binns, *English Thought, 1860–1900: The Theological Aspect* (Longmans, Green and Co., London, 1956).

A. E. H. Gregory, *Romance and Revolution: The Story of the Brotherhood Movement 1875–1975* (The Brotherhood Movement, London, 1975).

C. S. Grundy, *Reminiscences of Strangeways Unitarian Free Church, 1838–1888* (Abel Heywood, Manchester, 1888).

J. W. Grant, *Free Churchmanship in England, 1870–1940* (Independent Press, 1955).

D. Hardy, *Alternative Communities in Nineteenth Century England* (Longman, London, 1979).

Royden Harrison (ed.), *Before the Socialists* (Routledge, London, 1965).

C. H. Herford, *Philip Henry Wicksteed* (Dent, London, 1931).

W. Hewitson, *Lancaster Unitarian Chapel* (T. Bell, Lancaster, 1893).

R. V. Holt, *The Unitarian Contribution to Social Progress in England* (George Allen and Unwin, London, 1938).

D. Howell, *British Workers and the Independent Labour Party, 1888–1906* (Manchester University Press, Manchester, 1983).

D. P. Hughes, *Life of Hugh Price Hughes* (Hodder and Stoughton, London, 1905).

Maldwyn Hughes, *Methodism and England* (Epworth Press, London, 1943)

E. Hobsbawm, *Primitive Rebels* (Manchester U.P., 1959).

K. S. Inglis, *Churches and the Working Classes in Victorian England* (Routledge and Kegan Paul, London, 1963).

P. d'A. Jones, *The Christian Socialist Revival* (Princeton U.P., N.J., 1968).

E. K. Jordan, *Free Church Unity: A History of the Free Church Council Movement, 1896–1941*(Lutterworth, London, 1956).

P. Joyce, *Work, Society and Politics* (Harvester, London, 1980).

S. Koss, *Nonconformity and Modern British Politics* (Batsford, London, 1976).

J. Liddington, *The Life and Times of a Respectable Rebel, Selina Cooper* (Virago, London, 1984).

H. McLachlan, *The Methodist Unitarian Movement* (Manchester University Press, Manchester, 1919).

S. H. Mayor, *The Churches and the Labour Movement* (Independent Press, London, 1967).

Sir James Marchant, *Dr. John Clifford, C.H.* (Cassell and Co., London, 1924).

D. E. Martin and D. Rubinstein (eds.), *Ideology and the Labour Movement* (Croom Helm, London, 1979).

K. Martin, *Father Figures* (Hutchinson, London, 1966).

T. Middleton, *The History of Hyde and its Neighbourhood* (Higham Press, Hyde, 1932).

R. Moore, *Pit-men, Preachers and Politics* (Cambridge U.P., London, 1974).

I. Ap Nicholas, *Heretics at Large* (Gomer Press, Llandysul, 1977).

E. A. Payne, *The Baptist Union, A Short History* (Carey Kingsgate Press, London, 1959).

H. Pelling, *The Origins of the Labour Party* (Macmillan, London, 1954).

H. Pelling, *Social Geography of British Elections, 1885–1910* (Macmillan, London, 1967).

S. Pierson, *Marxism and the Origins of British Socialism* (Cornell U.P., Ithaca, 1973).

Joseph Robinson, *Salem Independent Methodist Church, Nelson, A Short History* (Elliot and Elliot, Nelson, 1952).

W. G. Robinson, *A History of Lancashire Congregational Union, 1906–1956* (Lancashire Congregational Union, Manchester, 1955).

I. Sellers, *Nineteenth Century Nonconformity* (Edward Arnold, London, 1977).

I. Sellers, *Salute to Pembroke, Pembroke Chapel, Liverpool, 1838–1931* (The author, Alsager, 1960).

W. S. Smith, *The London Heretics, 1870–1914* (Constable, London, 1967).

G. Studdert-Kennedy, *Dog-collar Democracy* (Macmillan, London, 1982).

E. P. Thompson, *William Morris, Romantic to Revolutionary* (Revised Edition, Merlin, London, 1977).

J. W. Tuffley, *Grain from Galilee: The Romance of the Brotherhood Movement* (Headley, London, 1935).

K. W. Wadsworth, *Yorkshire United Independent College* (Independent Press, London, 1954).

I. H. Wallace, *The Brotherhood Movement at Patricroft* (The author, Eccles, 1971).

P. J. Waller, *Democracy and Sectarianism. A Political and Social History of Liverpool, 1868–1939* (Liverpool University Press, Liverpool, 1981).

R. F. Wearmouth, *Methodism and the Struggle of the Working Classes 1850–1900* (Backus, Leicester, 1954).

R. F. Wearmouth, *Methodism and the working-class movements of England* (London, 1937).

R. F. Wearmouth, *The Social and Political Influence of Methodism in the Twentieth Century* (Epworth, London, 1957).

E. R. Wickham, *Church and People in an Industrial City* (Lutterworth, London, 1957).

A. Mounfield, *A Short History of Independent Methodism, Souvenir of the 100th Annual Meeting of the Independent Methodist Churches* (Independent Methodist Book Room, Wigan, 1905).

Articles

A. J. Ainsworth, 'Religion in the Working Class Community, and the Evolution of Socialism in Late Nineteenth Century Lancashire: A Case of Working Class Consciousness', *Histoire Sociale*, Vol. 10, 1977.

K. D. Brown, 'Nonconformity and the British Labour Movement: A Case Study', *Journal of Social History*, VIII, 1975.

P. C. Gould, 'The Back to the Land Experiment at Starnthwaite, Westmorland (1892–1900)', *The Journal of Regional and Local Studies*, Vol.6, No.2, Autumn, 1986.

E. Halévy, 'La Naissance du Methodisme en Angleterre', *La Revue de Paris*, August 1906.

G. Head, 'Unitarians and the Peace Movement, 1899', *The Inquirer*, 7th January 1984.

K. S. Inglis, 'English Nonconformity and Social Reform', *Past and Present*, Vol. 13, April, 1958.

J. Kent, 'A late Nineteenth Century Nonconformist Renaissance', *Studies in Church History*, Vol.14, 1977.

S. H. Mayor, 'Some Congregational Relations with the Labour Movement', *Congregational Historical Society Transactions*, August 1956, 18(1).

H. McLeod, 'Religion in the British and German Labour Movements c.1890–1914: A Comparison', *Bulletin of the Society for the Study of Labour History*, Vol.51, No.1, 1986.

P. Ollerhead, 'Unitarianism in Crewe, 1860–1940', *Transactions of the Unitarian Historical Society*, Vol. 17, No.1., September 1979.

F. Reid, 'Socialist Sunday Schools in Britain 1892–1939', *International Review of Social History*, 1966.

W. T. Stead, 'The Labour Party and the Books that helped to make it', *The Review of Reviews*, 1906.

P. A. Whatmough,'The Origins of the SDF', *Bulletin of the Society for the Study of Labour History*, No. 34, 1977.

S. Yeo, 'A New Life: The Religion of Socialism, 1883–1886', *History Workshop Journal*, 4–6, 1978–79.

Unpublished Research Work

Rosemary E. Chadwick, 'Church and People in Bradford and District, 1880–1914', DPhil Thesis, University of Oxford, 1986.

P. Firth, 'Socialism and the Origins of the Labour Party in Nelson and District', University of Manchester MA Dissertation (Method 1), 1975.

C. E. Gwyther, 'Methodist Social and Political Theory and Practice, 1848–1914', University of Liverpool MA Thesis, 1961.

J. Hill, 'Working class politics in Lancashire, 1885–1906: a regional study in the origins of the Labour Party', University of Keele PhD Thesis, 1970.

M. E. Lloyd, 'The political attitudes and actions of the English Baptists, with special reference to the late nineteenth century', University of Leeds MPhil Thesis, 1973.

S. Mayor, 'Organised religion and English working-class movements, 1850–1914', University of Manchester PhD Thesis, 1960.

P. E. Ollerhead, 'Protestant nonconformity in Crewe, 1840–1940', University of Keele MA Thesis, 1975.

W. D. Ross, 'Bradford Politics, 1880–1906', University of Bradford PhD Thesis, 1977.

I. Sellers, 'Liverpool Nonconformity (1786–1914)', University of Keele PhD Thesis, 1968.

I. Sellers, 'An Edwardian Whirlwind: the Rev. Herbert Dunnico in Warrington (1902–1906), unpublished essay, n.d.

L. Smith, 'John Trevor and the Labour Church Movement', Huddersfield Polytechnic MA Dissertation, 1986.

Brief Biographies

Anderson, Rev. Dr. K. C. (1848–1923). Born Jedburgh, Scotland; educated at Edinburgh and Yale universities and Chicago Theological Seminary. Obtained doctorate of divinity in America. Held pastorates at Oshkosk, Wisconsin (1875) and Troy (American Episcopal Church, – 1885), before returning to England because of ill-health. Minister at Horton Lane Congregational Chapel, Bradford, 1885–1892. A theological Modernist, he later became associated with R. J. Campbell's New Theology movement. Sympathetic to the Labour campaign. He told his congregation, which included many prominent Liberal businessmen, that 'the socialist indictment against modern society is a true bill; we cannot answer the charge'. Left Bradford in 1892 and settled at Ward Chapel, Dundee, 1892–1919. Died 8 September 1923.

Belcher, Rev. J. H. Congregational minister at Erdington, Birmingham, 1887–1892, and St. Thomas Square, Hackney, 1892–. Secretary of the Christian Socialist League, 1894–1898. Became a Unitarian and was minister at Treville Street Unitarian Church, Plymouth, 1905–1910.

Blackham, J. R. Son of a Birmingham printer. An influential member of Ebenezer Congregational Church, West Bromwich, where he founded the PSA movement.

Blatchford, Robert (1851–1943). Born Maidstone, Kent, the son of an actor and actress. Began work at 13. Joined the army in 1871 and served for seven years. In 1878, he entered journalism and became a leader writer for the Sunday Chronicle, 1887–1891. Adopted as Labour candidate for East Bradford in 1891, but retired after six months to edit the *Clarion*. His paper and publications, including *Merrie England* (1894), were influential in persuading many northern working class Liberals to support an independent Labour movement.

Campbell, Rev. Dr. R. J. Of Ulster Nonconformist stock. Educated at University College, Nottingham and Christ Church Oxford (BA 1895, DD 1919) After a brief period as an Anglican at Oxford, he became Congregational minister at Union Street Congregational Church, Brighton, 1895–1903, and the City Temple, London, 1903–1915. Around 1904 Campbell became the leader of the New Theology movement, which combined a Modernist theology and Social Gospel with support for independent Labour representation. Denied access to many pulpits on account of his heresy, he was a frequent speaker on Labour platforms.

His publications included, *The New Theology* (1907), *Christianity and the Social Order* (1907) and *The New Theology and the Socialist Movement* (1907). However, in 1915, Campbell renounced his New Theology and joined the Church of England.

Clifford, Rev. Dr. John (1836–1923). A Baptist, of working class origins. At 11 years of age he worked a 16 hour day in a lace factory. Came under the influence of the East Midland moral-force Chartists. Educated at the Baptist College, Leicester, 1855–1858, and subsequently, as a part-time student, he graduated in three London University faculties (Arts, Science and Law). Clifford spent all his ministry in Paddington, London, and Westbourne Park Chapel, organized on institutional church principles, was his creation. President of the Ministers' Union, which became the Christian Socialist League, 1894–1898. Clifford was an active Fabian, and unusually, amongst Christian Socialists, occupied high office in his denomination, becoming President of the Baptist Union in 1888 and again in 1899, and of the Baptist World Alliance, 1905–1911.

Dunnico, Rev. Herbert (1876–1953). Son of North Wales miner. Worked in cotton mill at age of 10. Later, in the grocery trade, he rose to become a manager. By part-time study he won a scholarship to University College, Nottingham, 1898, and later proceeded to Rawdon and Midland Baptist Colleges for theological training. During his first ministry at Salem Baptist Chapel, Warrington, 1902–1906, he was active in the Liberal Party, but quit just before leaving for Liverpool, where, whilst minister of Kensington Baptist Chapel, 1906–1916, he joined the Labour Party, quickly becoming its Chairman, as well a President of the Liverpool Fabian Society. He was secretary of the International Peace Society, 1916–1953; Labour MP for Consett, 1922–1931; and a Deputy Speaker of the House of Commons, 1929–31. From 1932–1953, he was honorary warden of the Browning Settlement, Walworth. A knighthood was conferred upon him in 1938.

Foster, D. B. (1858–1948). A Wesleyan Methodist local preacher from the age of 17. A member of the Holbeck, Leeds, Board of Guardians, 1891–1892, and founder of the Holbeck ILP and Social Reform Union. He advocated total nationalization at an early date. Foster was Secretary of Leeds LRC in 1902, and of the Leeds Labour Party, 1912–1916. He was the member for Hunslet on Leeds City Council from 1911, and became Lord Mayor in 1928. In 1895 he joined the Labour Church and became President of the Labour Church Union, 1902–1903, but finding the organization too non-Christian he tried to start his own Socialist Christian Church in Bradford. Having worked himself up to a prosperous position in the drapery trade, at the age of 39, in 1897, Foster gave it up 'to live on the worker's economic level'. His publications include *Socialism and the Christ* (1921) and *Leeds Slumdom* (1897).

Goldsack, Rev. S. J. C. (1868–1957). Son of a New Church (Sweden-borgian) family. Post Office telegraphist, 1883–1889. Educated New Church College, Islington, 1889–1893. Minister of The New Church, Keighley, 1893–1897. Secretary of the New Church Socialist Society, 1895–. Served in India during World War I. Secretary of the New Church Conference, 1919–1929.

Hardie, James Keir (1885–1915). Son of a ship's carpenter. Started work at the age of seven and worked in the mines from the age of 10 until he was 20. Learned public speaking on Temperance platforms and as a member of the Evangelical Union. Moved into trade unionism and organized the Ayrshire miners. In 1886 he became the first secretary of the Scottish Miners' Federation, and in 1888 the first secretary of the Scottish Labour Party. Hardie was attracted to Socialism after the Liberals opposed his candidature in the Mid-Lanark by-election of 1888. Editor the *Labour Leader*. First secretary of the ILP. MP for West Ham, 1892–1895; unsuccessfully contested Bradford in 1896; MP for Merthyr Tydfil, 1900–1915. Leader of the parliamentary Labour Party, 1906–1908.

Henderson, Arthur (1863–1935). Wesleyan Methodist lay-preacher. MP for Barnard Castle, 1903–1918; Widnes, 1919–1922; Newcastle, 1923; Burnley, 1929–1931; Clay Cross, 1933–1935; Labour chief whip 1906–1914; president of Board of Education, 1915–1916; minister for labour as paymaster general, 1916; member of war cabinet, 1916–1917; home secretary, 1924; foreign secretary, 1929–1931. Trade union official. An architect of the 1918 Labour Party Constitution. President of the Brotherhood Movement.

Jowett, F. W. (1864–1944). Born Bradford, one of a family of eight children, three of whom died in infancy. Started work as a half-timer, became weaving overlooker at 21 and a joint manager of a small firm at 30. In his youth Jowett attended Listerhills Congregational Sunday School and then became a member of Horton Lane Congregational Church, which he left to become the first Chairman of the Bradford Labour Church, as a result of Nonconformist opposition to Ben Tillett's candidature in the 1892 General Election. He was the most prominent member of the independent Labour movement in Bradford. A director of the Bradford Co-operative Society; founder member of the Bradford branch of the Socialist League, Bradford Labour Electoral Association and Bradford ILP; Town Councillor 1892–1097; Poor Law Guardian 1901–1907; member of the National Administrative Council of the ILP in 1897; Labour MP for Bradford, 1906–1918, 1922–1924, and 1929–1931.

Keeble, Rev. Samuel Edward (1853–1946). Wesleyan Methodist minister and the leading Methodist socialist. Orphaned in infancy and brought up by elder brothers. Educated at Didsbury College, Manchester, 1876–1879. Read *Das Kapital*, October and November 1889. Contributed articles on socialism to Hugh Price Hughes' *Methodist Times*, 1889–1895, under the title 'Labour Lore'. Published *Industrial Daydreams*, 1895. Keeble broke with Hughes, who took an imperialist line on the Boer War, and commenced his own short-lived pro-Boer *Methodist Weekly* in November, 1900. Founded Wesleyan Methodist Union for Social Service in 1905. Executive member of the Sigma Club, 1909. Keeble's circuit ministries were: Ripley (1879–82), Reading (1882–84), Nottingham, Wesley (1884–87), Leeds, Chapel Allerton (1887–90), Chester (1890–93), Sheffield, Brunswick (1893–96), Bristol, King Street (1896–99), Manchester, Gravel Lane (1899–1902), Manchester, Pendleton (1902–05), Manchester, Gravel Lane (1905–08), Southport, Trinity (1908–11), Llandudno (1911–14), Southsea (1914–18) and Maidstone (1918–21).

Kirtlan, Rev. E. J. B. (1869–1937) BA, BD. Wesleyan Methodist minister at Kingley Park Chapel, Northampton. Preached two sermons at Regent Square Chapel on 21 May 1905 and announced that he would deliver a lecture the following evening, entitled 'Socialism for Christians'. The lecture had already been given in the Channel Islands, Leicester and Newcastle-on-Tyne. A member of the SDF, Kirtlan demanded total collective ownership of all national resources.

Laughland, Rev. J. Vint (1885–1957) Born at Southampton. Educated for the Unitarian ministry at Meadville Theological College and University of Chicago. After short pastorate in USA he returned to England in 1915 and became minister at Islington, before moving to Unity Church, Sheffield, where his political activities did not please his congregation. In 1920, he became minister of Pembroke Chapel (Baptist), Liverpool, which he made the headquarters of the Left wing of the Labour movement in Liverpool. Sailed for New York in July 1924, settled at Rochester, NY, and became a popular lecturer and broadcaster on Labour topics, promoting the idea of 'Universal Fellowship'.

Leonard, Rev. T. A. Educated at Paton College, Nottingham. Minister at Abbey Road Congregational Church, Barrow in Furness, 1887–1890, Colne Congregational Church, 1890–1894, and, again, 1896–1899. Labour Church lecturer. Organizing Secretary of the London Social Institute, 1894–. Founder of the Co-operative Holidays Association. Joined the Society of Friends.

Mills, Rev. H. V. (1856–1928) Born at Accrington. Educated at Owens College and Unitarian Home Missionary College, Manchester, 1876–1879. Unitarian minister at Temperance Hall, Bolton, 1879–80; Hamilton Road, Liverpool, 1884–87; Kendal, 1887–1916; Bridgewater, 1922–25;

Islington (Supply), 1925–27; St.Vincent Street, Glasgow, 1928. Member of Westmorland County Council and Kendal Board of Guardians. Published *Poverty and the State*, 1886. Founder of the Home Colonisation Society and the Starnthwaite Home Colony, 1892.

Roberts, Rev. Robert. Educated at Bala Theological College. Congregational minister at Guisborough, Yorkshire, 1876–82; Boston Spa, Yorkshire, 1886–88; Frizinghall, Bradford, 1888–95; and Brownroyd, Bradford, 1895–98. His support for the emergent Labour movement led to trouble with his Frizinghall congregation and his removal to Brownroyd. He was a Lib-Lab; started as a Liberal but joined the ILP in the late 1890s; later he rejoined the Liberals after failing to persuade F. W. Jowett to co-operate with the Liberals. Founded the Bradford Ethical Society in 1898.

Rylett, Rev. Harold (1851–). Born Horncastle, Lincolnshire. Educated at Owens College and the Unitarian Home Missionary College, Manchester, 1871; 1874–77. Unitarian minister at Reading, 1877–78; Moneyrea, Co.Down, 1879–84; Maidstone, 1884–87; Dudley, 1887–89; Flowery Field, Hyde, 1889–1896; Bermondsey, London, 1896–1900; Tenterden, Kent, 1904–. Member Maidstone School Board 1884–87; Manager under London School Board, 1896–1900. Editor *Hyde Telegraph*, *The New Age*, 1899–1907. Actively associated with political and social reform movements. Twice candidate for Parliament (Tyrone, 1888; Burton, 1910). At Tyrone, he was fully supported by H. M. Hyndman's newly formed Democratic Federation. Read lesson at John Trevor's first Labour Church service in 1891. Joined English Land Restoration League in 1884 and a member of its committee. Rylett opposed the idea of an independent political party for Labour and was unsympathetic towards the ILP.

Snowden, 1st Viscount, Philip (1864–1937). Born at Cowling, West Riding of Yorkshire. Wesleyan Methodist upbringing, but failed to have conversion experience and had no formal religious affiliation after the age of eight. Married Ethel Annakin of Colne, a Wesleyan Sunday School teacher. ILP propagandist and lecturer. Speaker at Labour Church meetings. Chairman of ILP, 1903–1906 and 1929–1931. Author of *The Christ that is to be*, 1903. Labour MP for Blackburn, 1906–1918, and for Colne Valley, 1922–1931. An expert on national finance, he became chancellor of the exchequer 1924 and 1929–1931, and lord privy seal, 1931–32. Strong temperance advocate.

Smith, Rev. Henry Bodell (1855–) Born at Leicester. Educated at Owens College and the Unitarian Home Missionary College, Manchester, 1878–81. Unitarian minister at Darwen, 1881–83; Droylsden, 1884–85; Pudsey, 1886–90; Crewe, 1890–95; Hamilton Road and North End

Mission, Liverpool, 1896–97; Darlington, 1899; South Shore, Blackpool, 1900; Mottram, 1902–10; South Shore (2nd time), 1912–15; Nelson, 1915–17; Mottram (2nd time), 1917–20. Founder of the Crewe branch of the ILP.

Swan, Rev. F. R. (1868–1938). Congregational Minister. Educated at Paton College, Nottingham. Minister at Marsden 1899–1906. Published *The Immanence of Christ in Modern Life*, 1907. Full time political work in Colne Valley, 1906–10. Minister of The Brotherhood Church, Southgate Road, London, 1910–38. On staff of the *Daily Herald*, 1912–38. Ardent New Theology and ILP man. Organizing secretary of the Progressive League.

Tillett, Ben (1860–1943). Born in Somerset. Mother died when he was 18 months and his father abandoned him when he was 8. Rescued from starvation in Bristol and apprenticed to the boot and shoe trade. After a period at sea and as a docker, he became a trade union leader. 1887, organized tea warehousemen in London. In 1889 he gained a national reputation, with Tom Mann and John Burns, as a result of the Dockers' Strike. Unsuccessfully contested West Bradford for the ILP at the general election of 1892 and 1895. Labour M.P., 1919–24; 1929–31.

Trevor, John (1855–1930). Born in Liverpool; the son of an unsuccessful linen-draper; father died when he was 4 and mother when he was 9. Brought up at Wisbech by relatives who were Johnsonian Baptists. Articled to a Norwich architect, 1871–76. Trevor underwent a crisis of faith, which led to the abandonment of Calvinist orthodoxy, and, during a voyage to Australia and the USA, the adoption of Free Religion. He was briefly a student at Meadville Theological College, Pennsylvania, 1878–79. Returning to England he preached in Unitarian pulpits, but unsuccessfully sought a settlement as a minister. After several years as an architect in Folkestone and Dover, he became a student at Manchester New College, London; then assistant minister to P. H. Wicksteed at Little Portland Street Chapel (Unitarian), London, 1888–90. In 1890, he became minister of Upper Brook Street Free Church (Unitarian), Manchester, from where he founded the Labour Church movement in 1891. He co-operated with Blatchford and others in the formation of the Manchester and Salford ILP in 1892, and the national ILP in 1893. *The Labour Prophet*, the organ of the Labour Church, was the main vehicle for his propaganda. Other publications include *Theology and the Slums* (n.d.) and *My Quest for God* (1897).

Wellock, Wilfred (1879–1972). Member of Salem Independent Methodist Church, Nelson. Sunday School teacher and lay preacher in his late teens. Educated at Edinburgh University, but did not take a degree.

Returned to Nelson and devoted half time to mill work and the other half to unpaid lecturing, propaganda work and occasional preaching. Contested Stourbridge for Labour in the 1923 and 1924 general elections; MP 1927–1931; unsuccessfully sought re-election in 1935. Publications include *Off the beaten track*, which explains the nature of the political crisis at the Salem Independent Methodist Church, Nelson.

Wicksteed, Rev. Philip Henry (1844–1925). Unitarian Minister, Mathematical Economist and Dante Scholar. Born at Leeds; the second son of the Rev. Charles Wicksteed of Mill Hill Chapel. Educated at University College, London, 1861–64, and Manchester New College, London, 1864–67. Minister at Taunton, Dukinfield and Little Portland Street, London. Warden of Mrs. Humphry Ward's University Hall Settlement. A member of the Economic Circle and the Fabian Society, he was responsible for converting G. B. Shaw from Marx's Labour theory of Value to the Jevonian theory of Marginal Utility. A keen supporter of the Labour Church movement.

Wilson, J. Stitt (1868–). American Congregationalist, Socialist evangelist. Born in Canada. Educated at Northwestern and Chicago Universities. Gave up the Methodist ministry to devote himself to full-time socialist agitation, moving to California c.1901. He made four crusades in Great Britain, using Brownroyd Congregational Church, Bradford (Rev. Robert Roberts), as his headquarters. In 1910 he was nominated as Socialist candidate for the Governorship of California, polling 50,000 votes, and in 1911 became Socialist mayor of Berkeley, California. Described as 'the most powerful figure that ever appeared in English Christian Socialism'.

Williams, Rev. T. Rhondda (1860–1945) Born Cowbridge, Glamorgan; the son of Calvinistic Methodist lay preacher. Educated at Carmarthen College, 1877–1880. Congregational Minister at Dowlais, 1880–84; Neath, 1884–88; Greenfield, Bradford, 1888–1909; Brighton, 1909–31. Chairman of the Congregational Union of England and Wales, 1929–30. Publications include *The Social Gospel* (1902) and *How I found My Faith* (1938). After R. J. Campbell, the leading expositor of the New Theology. Committed to independent Labour representation, but, on the advice of F. W. Jowett, never joined the ILP.

Index